REAL ESTATE INVESTORS

CLIENTS FOR LIFE

Opportunities abound in real estate. As a real estate professional, you can build a business through real estate sales, especially when it comes to working with investors. You can also build wealth by investing in your own industry. Or you could do both by creating a true Investor Business, making yourself your best client and by serving other investor clients. The choice is yours, but before you decide, this book is a must read! It will teach you the why's and how's and then you will see why you can have it all in service to yourself as well as others! Fred is walking proof and has profound knowledge and proven techniques that he gladly shares with you so you can make a positive impact on your own life. Catch his passion and change your life!

Theresa Barnabei
Best-Selling Author, Inspirational Speaker, Real Estate Educator

Fred's enthusiasm and knowledge of investing in single-family properties is unrivaled, and I applaud his willingness to share 40+ years of experience with others through this book and in the classroom. I routinely have Fred speak to our students about the subject… many respond accordingly by acquiring their first investment property before graduation.

David Beberwyk
Real Estate Program Director, University of Nebraska–Omaha

Fred has made many friends, admirers, and followers over his long and productive real estate career. He attracts people because he is very competent, honest, and works hard to help others succeed. Anyone who spends some serious time studying and applying the materials in this book will get to know Fred and like him, too. Plus, there is a rewarding professional life waiting for you to enjoy.

Dean Uhing
Associate Broker, Realtor, Builder, Adjunct Faculty with Metropolitan Community College in Omaha, Nebraska

I am a licensed real estate broker. My background for over a decade is in the management of commercial property. My real estate license allows me to buy, sell, lease, and manage property, and to help others do the same.

Even though I can buy my own investment property, I choose to work with Fred Tichauer on residential properties. I appreciate the depth of knowledge he has in this area. He helps me locate, purchase, and then sell residential properties. My education in real estate puts me at a point where I see the benefit of working with a professional in the specific area of buying and selling homes. I am looking for the best-fitting deal in the market. I do not just try to do it on my own because my license says I can. Working with Fred and his team gives me a good return on my investment.

John Krecek
Broker, Custom Realty

Fred Tichauer and I share many of the same traits: drive, determination, loyalty, responsibility, and a hardcore work ethic. He has changed my life in ways that otherwise would not have happened.

Fred sold me the home I live in, a foreclosure that my wife and I renovated and in which we are raising our family. He helped me acquire investment properties, and he motivated me to obtain my real estate license. He has imparted upon me his many years of real estate knowledge, which goes far beyond "Here is a great house to buy." It extends to "Here is the president of a bank" (a friend of Fred's), "Here is a contractor" (a friend of Fred's), "Here is an attorney" (a friend of Fred's), and the list goes on. This doesn't happen just by having a license or having some money to buy a house. It happens because Fred believes in himself and his capabilities, and his belief affects everyone around him.

Fred has taken a great step in writing this book and sharing some of his real estate knowledge. What he has to say will rival anything that has been said about real estate previously, but the most important aspect of this book is that Fred has given a piece of himself. The steps involved in buying a property or becoming financially secure are secondary. Having a friend like Fred who makes you believe in YOUR capabilities far outweighs information about what's on a purchase agreement.

Ultimately, Fred would say "First you must believe in yourself" before true success can be achieved. I'm fortunate to have Fred as my best friend. Now you have him through this book.

Shawn Prouse
Owner, Capture Pictures (Broadcast Media)
Investor and Realtor, Berkshire Hathaway Home Services
Ambassador Real Estate

Fred has been an agent here for a number of years. His wisdom, understanding, and experience of "How to help investors prepare for their future" is second to none. He facilitates a number of different classes for other agents so they can clearly understand how to communicate to their clients the value of buying investment properties. He has a gift. His presentations and ideas are brilliant! Fred's knowledge of the investment process and passion to help others is what makes him a special person. Rarely do you find an individual so willing to openly share what they have learned so they can help others. Fred's book is a must-read.

Vince Leisey
President/Broker
Berkshire Hathaway HomeServices Ambassador Real Estate

Meeting Fred has changed my life… I wish I would have met him in my 20's. His mentorship took me from an average agent to a successful Realtor who now has the tools to advise people on growing wealth. His passion for the business is infectious. Fred believes in you at all times, even when you doubt yourself. Because of his infinite wisdom, I now own and manage a portfolio of rental properties. Furthermore, I am able to customize strategies for my clients as well. He has played a huge role in my success and more importantly has become a good friend. My family and I can't thank you enough, Fred!

Rusty Johnson
Berkshire Hathaway HomeServices Ambassador Real Estate

As a single, self-employed woman I've spent much time worrying about how to feel more secure about my financial future. Being a real estate professional, I know that real estate is a great investment, but I've been unable to move forward because of the paralyzing fear of making the wrong investment decision. Fred Tichauer's book, *Clients for Life,* and his classes have given me the tools and the confidence I needed to pull the trigger. I now have two multi-family investment properties and enough equity to purchase a third with no money out of pocket. In two short years I've defined my retirement goals and moved them much closer to a reality instead of an uncertain hope and a prayer.

Julie Lauritsen
Real Estate Agent
Berkshire Hathaway Ambassador Real Estate

Fred truly is the expert in helping colleagues, clients, friends, and family with their wealth planning. His passion for sharing the success that he has had with investment properties with others is such an awesome gift. The knowledge, experience, and expertise that he has in this field is invaluable, and I am very thankful for his mentorship. You won't regret reading this book. It will change your life and the lives of those you love because real estate is a solid investment that you know you can count on when it comes time for you to retire, and Fred has mastered it. He is a one-of-a-kind gem, and both my father, Vaughn Wiebusch, and I are very thankful for him.

Anna Lemieux
Team Wiebusch
Re/Max Results

"I wish I had listened sooner! I wish I had done it sooner!" That's what my husband and I say all the time, referring, of course, to investing in real estate. It wasn't as if Fred did not tell me to do it every chance he could. I just thought, "I am not a real estate investor." Well, guess what: I am now! And so are a few of our soccer dad friends, our next-door neighbors, and our financial advisor. Investing in residential real estate is one of the best decisions we ever made for our future and for the future of our clients. If you are a real estate agent and you are not encouraging, educating, and leading your clients to start their own real estate investment business, you are missing a huge opportunity... and so are they. You invest a small amount of money into a home purchase and then you have other people move in and they pay off the mortgage for you. Tada! No, really, that's it. In 15 years you now have an asset all paid off. And then guess what: you and they do it again, and again, and again. Any chance you can. READ THIS BOOK. If you can't have Fred with you pestering you daily to do this, the book is the next best thing. It will teach you all you need to know to add this revenue stream to your real estate business. Your clients will thank you for sharing your knowledge and insight and opening their eyes to this additional path to wealth. And what do you get out of it—10, maybe 20 more sales per year? Win-Win. Love it when that happens. BUY THE BOOK!

Mamie Jackson
Berkshire Hathaway Ambassador Real Estate

REAL ESTATE INVESTORS

CLIENTS FOR LIFE

HOW TO FIND, KEEP, AND GROW WITH THEM
While Making More Income than You Thought was Possible

FRED TICHAUER

SECOND EDITION

FTCW

www.FredTichauer.com

Second Edition: May, 2019

Paperback: 978-0-9961382-4-6
Kindle: 978-0-9961382-5-3
EPUB: 978-0-9961382-6-0

LCCN: 2019938073

Printed in the United States of America.

10 9 8 7 6 5 4 3 2 1

This book is dedicated to the memory of my
parents, Walter and Helena Tichauer,
my children, Kelly, Randi, and Ryan,
and my grandchildren, Lauren, Emily, Jacob,
Baila, Avigayil, Esther, Yakov, and Quinn.

CONTENTS

FOREWORD

No matter whether you have an MBA, BA, two-year college degree, or high school diploma, don't ever let anyone tell you that you can't achieve financial freedom. As a matter of fact, it is much easier than you think. It depends on your willingness to pay the price to succeed. What value and expertise can you bring to the table?

If you have a mission, vision, passion, and a strong desire to succeed, you can make a very good living as an "investor-friendly" real estate agent while helping your clients achieve financial freedom. Best of all, you will leave a legacy that will make your family proud.

My mission: To help clients from all walks of life generate wealth so they are financially set up for their "golden years." To strive to always go above and beyond my clients' expectations by being a wealth advisor, coach, mentor, and the source of information for all of their investment needs.

My vision: To be the real estate agent of choice for those who want to become financially independent.

My values: To always be 100% honest and never put my own needs before the needs of my clients. I know that when they make money I will make money, so there's no need for me to worry about each commission check.

My legacy: To help real estate agents and clients by sharing my knowledge so that they can help others as well.

I am thrilled to say that since 2000 I've helped several of my clients achieve the status of millionaire real estate investors, and by following the same advice I give to others, I have attained that status as well.

Never underestimate the power and influence you can have as a real estate agent. I know you want your clients to feel confident they are in good hands with you, just as you would want to feel that same confidence in your own financial advisor. That's why you decided to read this book.

You gain strength, courage and confidence by every experience in which you really stop to look fear in the face... You must do the thing you think you cannot do.

—*Eleanor Roosevelt*

Introduction

If you are already working with real estate investors, congratulations! If not, you have been missing out on a tremendous opportunity.

If you're new to the real estate industry, the information in these pages will get you off to a great start. And if you already have some knowledge of the real estate investment market, this book will take you to the next level.

MY BACKGROUND IN REAL ESTATE INVESTMENT

I have a college degree, but it has nothing to do with real estate. I graduated from the University of Nebraska at Omaha in 1973 with a BS degree in recreation. I was able to graduate in four years, and nobody has ever asked me about my grade point average or my major.

I started investing in real estate at age 21 when I purchased a duplex, moved into one side, and rented out the other. I thought it was a cool concept to have somebody else covering most of my monthly mortgage payment. When I sold the duplex three years later, I made enough money to make a down payment on three properties.

At that point I decided that it might be a good idea to get a license, so in 1980 I enrolled in real estate classes. After failing the test twice, I finally passed on the third try. For more than two decades I used my license solely to find, buy, and sell my own investment properties while working full-time as an executive with the Boy Scouts of America.

After a successful 24-year career with the BSA, I decided to try the free enterprise system and expand my real estate holdings. In 1998 I began a new career as a full-time real estate agent, and I passed the test for a broker's license on my first try. The values I learned in the BSA, such as honor, trustworthiness, and integrity, have served as my guiding principles in this business.

Today I consider myself to be one of Omaha's most knowledgeable investment property experts. I am not claiming to be #1 or #100, but I do know that the expertise I have acquired as an investor has been invaluable.

I have bought and sold a lot of my own properties over the years and still control an extensive rental property portfolio. In other words, I walk the talk. I have flipped more than 150 properties over the years—many of these before the word "flipping" was even used. How times change.

I don't think of myself as a teacher, but I often conduct "Investing in Real Estate" seminars for the general public and for real estate agents. I have taught a course in real estate investment at a local real estate school, and today I am a provider of continuing education classes approved by the Nebraska Real Estate Commission.

I am also proud to say that I currently have clients who are also real estate agents and that several of my former clients have become real estate agents as well. I feel fortunate to be able to do something that I really love and have much passion for, and to make a very good living doing it.

I have found that investing in real estate is the fastest path to financial independence for anyone from the executive to the blue-collar worker. Building wealth and making a living from the workplace are totally different pursuits.

I hope this book will motivate you to reach out to your friends, to your current and potential clients, and to anyone else you can think of who has not yet discovered that investing in real estate is the ticket to wealth building.

WHY I WROTE THIS BOOK

When I was a novice investor in 1972, I knew absolutely nothing about real estate. Would I be in a different place today if Jerry Siciunas, my first real estate agent, hadn't taken me seriously?

I decided to write this book because I wanted to share my 40-plus years of knowledge and expertise with people like you, just as Jerry Siciunas did for me. If each of us had a mentor who took a little time to help us and if we took the time to become a mentor to someone else, the world would be a better place.

If you're an experienced agent, this book will give you the practical information, basic tools, and knowledge to become an "investor-friendly" real estate agent. You will find that getting into the investment market is the best way to jump start a career that perhaps is not producing the financial rewards you expected.

Have you ever wondered why some real estate agents are making six-figure incomes (as I have done since 1999) while others struggle to earn enough income to pay their bills and have little or no money set aside for the future?

According to the National Association of Realtors, there are 1,339,668 Realtors and the median gross income was $39,800 in 2017—a decrease from $42,500 in 2016.

Are you happy with your income? If you are looking to grow your business (income, volume, and transactions), then what are you going to do differently?

How many of you have achieved financial freedom and are still agents because you love this business? What if you could do both?

My advice to you, since this industry is changing by the day, is to invest in your own industry and also make this "niche" market a priority. You will stand out above other real estate agents and remain relevant. I can assure you that as you help people start a real estate investment business (as housing will always be a necessity to solve their financial and retirement concerns, as I will cover in later chapters), you will be irreplaceable.

Keep in mind that as you help investors, they will tell others. You will expand your network simply by referrals, and it won't be necessary to pay for leads.

I firmly believe that success comes down to believing in yourself and becoming a student of this business. You obviously believe in this industry, because otherwise you would never have become a real estate agent. Correct?

When you look at the facts, you will see that investing in real estate is one of the better options for anyone desiring to become independently wealthy. Your goal, my goal, and in fact the goal of most people is not to rely on anyone else for our financial future. What would happen if you got sick and couldn't work for a few months? Do you have another source of income to tide you over until you're able to go back to work?

A novice investor can become a millionaire by investing wisely. I have chosen to help clients and real estate agents like yourself to achieve financial success. There is no better feeling than knowing you have helped a client to become a millionaire real estate investor.

By the time you are done reading this book, you will have a better understanding of the most powerful facet of our industry: real estate investments. You will be able to bring value and expertise to a greater number of clients, and more and more people will seek you out.

When you earned your real estate license it gave you the opportunity to represent a buyer or a seller in a real estate transaction in exchange for a commission. It did not prepare you to work with investors in specialty areas such as single-family dwellings, multi-units, land development, commercial, industrial, manufacturing, hotel, motels, mobile home parks, shopping centers, and so on. Real estate agents who have taken these paths have had to acquire their knowledge through specialty training. In my opinion one of the major faults of our industry is that adequate training is not provided by broker/owners in the above areas of specialty. It is up to you to learn on your own or by enrolling in courses.

As agents we are constantly encouraged by our managers to prospect, generate leads, do open houses, and so on. However, if you decide to step out of your comfort zone and start working with one investor and then gradually extend your services to encompass many more, your income will skyrocket.

WHY REAL ESTATE INVESTORS ARE LIKELY TO BECOME YOUR CLIENTS FOR LIFE

Before you begin working with investors, it is imperative that you learn how to analyze a property and that you become knowledgeable about landlord issues and tenant-landlord laws, financing options, property evaluation, the goals of investors and the investment choices available to them. When one of your investor clients becomes successful, you will also be successful and will truly have a client for life. Why would they ever choose to work with anyone else?

And if you are going to provide guidance and expertise to others, would you not agree that it makes sense to become an investor yourself? When you are doing what you are trying to help others to do, people start to believe you. They start to think you are credible and that success is also possible for them. It generates instant credibility when you can offer practical knowledge rather than just theories.

As real estate agents, we are in an industry that is needed by everyone. We believe in it, yet we are not showing our belief if we don't become investors. Your credibility will grow as your clients reap the benefits of your experience.

So what is keeping you from jumping into this game? Follow my suggestions and you too will become an expert that people seek out. There are many people who need to invest in real estate to gain control of their financial future, even though they may not know it yet. It is up to you to make them aware of the potential. Help them, and in turn you will make more money than you thought was possible. This industry offers us a great opportunity to make a better living than most other sales-related jobs can provide. I wish you much success in whatever you decide to do.

ACKNOWLEDGMENTS

This book is dedicated to the memory of my parents because they were wonderful role models who laid a strong foundation for the person that I am today.

Early on I watched them work hard to provide for my brother and me. They taught me that in order to get ahead you have to make sacrifices, overcome obstacles, and have deep passion and enthusiasm for whatever you are doing. They inspired me to become a high achiever, not to be afraid to try new things even if I might fail, to be courageous and give of myself to others.

My parents moved from Europe to Montevideo, Uruguay in South America in the mid-1940s. From a young age I was aware that both of them worked extremely hard and had successful businesses. We had a very happy and normal life. They owned a nice home in a desirable neighborhood as well as a vacation home. Life was good for us, but they became concerned about the growing political unrest in Uruguay and decided to immigrate to the United States in 1963 when I was 12 years old. This was one of the most unselfish decisions they could have made, and to this day I continue to think "What if?" They came to this country because they wanted us to have the opportunity for a better life.

My parents instilled in me the drive to not let anything get in my way if I wanted something badly enough. I owe whatever financial success I have achieved to them. They taught me so many life lessons, yet it took me a long time to realize all that I learned.

They used to tell me, "You have to pay the price to succeed, because nothing in life comes easily." I am the product of the American dream—proof that anything is possible in this country if you work hard and are willing to pay the price.

Although I did not understand it at the time, subconsciously all along I was telling myself that I would never rely on anyone else for my financial future and someday I would become financially independent.

In addition to my parents, another individual who inspired me to achieve was a family member who predicted that I would probably end up in jail and not amount to much. I wasn't a juvenile delinquent; I just got into trouble at school fairly often. As a matter of fact, I had a chair reserved for me in the principal's and counselor's offices because I visited them regularly.

When I came to this country at 12 years old, I was scared to death and didn't speak English. I wanted attention, so I became the class clown. Finally when I was in eighth grade the principal told my mother that the next time I got into trouble I would be kicked out of school. That got my attention.

I was aware that this family member had told my parents that I would end up in jail and not amount to much, and her prediction ended up having a big impact on my life because I didn't want her to be able to tell my parents "I told you so."

I used this negative chapter in my life to challenge myself and focus. Even in my adult life I never thanked this individual for helping me. I wanted so badly to prove she was wrong about me that it inspired me to succeed. I turned a negative into a positive.

So many people have inspired me and had so much influence on my real estate career that it would be impossible to thank them all individually. One person who comes to mind immediately is Jerry Siciunas, the real estate agent who helped me buy my first duplex in 1972. Jerry ignited my lifelong passion for real estate investing.

Finally, I want to thank my children, Kelly, Randi, and Ryan, for their support, encouragement, and belief in me. I am especially grateful that my daughter Kelly has joined me as a partner in my real estate practice.

BEFORE YOU TURN THE PAGE
ASK YOURSELF 12 TOUGH QUESTIONS:

1. Do you have a mission, vision, and value statement?
2. What legacy do you want to leave behind? What do you want others to say about you?
3. Do you set annual goals for listings, buyers, income, and volume, and will you achieve the results you are anticipating in the next 12 months?
4. Have you approached your current data base regarding why they should be investing in real estate?
5. Have you discussed real estate investing with current and past clients that you have helped to either buy or sell their personal residence?
6. What training have you received so far in the real estate investment niche market?
7. Can you now compete with other agents for a potential listing or sale of an investment property?
8. Can you bring the value and expertise a client should expect from you?
9. What mistakes have you made (or are you making) at the expense of your clients?
10. Are your clients being properly served?
11. Do you have a business plan to accomplish your goals?
12. Are you happy with your career development to date?

The good news is that by the time you finish reading this book, you will be able to answer "yes" to these questions. You can; you will; you can't wait. The voice of the eagle is calling you to greater heights.

Working with Real Estate Investors, "Clients for Life"

As a real estate professional, if you are going to provide the guidance and expertise a client deserves from you, it is best if you are also an investor or become an investor as it will generate instant credibility.

Before you even think about working with investors, you should at least know and understand their short- and long-term objectives, the advantages and disadvantages of the real estate investment business, financing options, investment choices, property values, and how to analyze a property, just to name a few.

When they are successful, you will also be successful, and when they make money you will as well, so there's no need to worry about a commission check.

"The voice of the eagles is calling you to greater heights."

CHAPTER 1

COULD INVESTING IN REAL ESTATE BE THE BEST WAY TO BUILD WEALTH?

Do you know anyone who lost their entire investment in the stock market during the economic downturn of 2008–2011? How about somebody who lost all the money they invested in real estate?

No other investment option offers all of the benefits of investing in real estate, including appreciation, principal reduction, rental income, and tax benefits. (For the purposes of this book, a real estate investment is defined as a non-owner-occupied property. Throughout this book, "real estate investment business," "real estate investor," and "investor" will have the same meaning.) There is never a bad time to buy investment properties. During an economic downturn, real estate will continue to produce income. This may not be true for other types of investments.

With these facts in mind, I have always wondered why more people are not investing in real estate, and I came up with an answer that makes sense. We must do a better job and be the voice for this industry. If we are not knowledgeable enough to explain the many reasons why investing in real estate is one of the best ways to create wealth and retirement income, who else will explain it? How many people are looking for ways to put their money to work? But due to a lack of knowledge and a

sense of intimidation they steer clear of this type of investment
because they believe it's too risky.

Why do people view real estate as a risky investment? Maybe
they have a friend who lost money in real estate because they
were unprepared and didn't have a knowledgeable agent assisting
them. Maybe their friend bought a property they shouldn't have,
or paid too much for the property. Maybe they bought a property with very little cash flow in the hope that the value would
appreciate over time. With the right preparation and guidance,
none of these things would have happened. As I'll explain later
in this book, risk can be greatly minimized by buying undervalued properties that can be improved without spending huge
amounts of money on renovations.

How confident are you with your current investments? Are
you realizing the returns/dividends that make the investments
worthwhile?

Would more people invest in real estate if they knew the
benefits it provides for wealth building? As a savvy and knowledgeable real estate agent you can help people understand that
real estate doesn't have to be risky but instead can be one of the
better investment options available.

A large percentage of the world's richest individuals have
made their money from real estate investing, and most of the
top earners credit much of their wealth to investing in real estate
in one form or another.

According to Martin Thomas, investor and CEO of Opportunity–Investor.com, eight out of ten millionaires surveyed became
wealthy through real estate. That means an overwhelming proportion of the people we'd like to emulate earned their wealth
by trading in real estate.

A national survey of residential real estate investors conducted
in September 2012 found that this is a $9.2 billion industry with
over 28.1 million investors. It seems logical to me that people
would want to share in the wealth that is being created every

day by investors. Real estate investing makes so much sense. The real question is whether you are willing to become an investor (if you are not one already) and to help a client become one, too.

TEN WEALTHIEST REAL ESTATE INVESTORS IN THE UNITED STATES IN 2016

The combined wealth of the top ten real estate investors is a whopping $123 billion in net worth, according to Wealth-X, a global provider of information on the high-net-worth community. (Net worth and ranking data provided by Wealth-X.)

1. Donald Bren–Net Worth: $15.2B–Base of Operations: Southern California
2. Stephen Ross–Net Worth: $6.6B–Base of Operations: New York
3. Richard LeFrak–Net Worth: $6.1B–Base of Operations: New York
4. Ted Lerner–Net Worth: $5.4B–Base of Operations: Chevy Chase, MD
5. John A. Sobrato–Net Worth: $4.9B–Base of Operations: Atherton, CA
6. Sam Zell–Net Worth: $4.8B–Base of Operations: Chicago
7. Leonard Stern–Net Worth: $4.6B–Base of Operations: New York
8. Donald Trump–Net Worth: $4B–Base of Operations: New York
9. Jerry Speyer–Net Worth: $4.4B–Base of Operations: New York
10. Edward Roski Jr.–Net Worth: $3.9B Base of Operations: Los Angeles

While you may never have the opportunity to help someone become a billionaire, the greatest satisfaction of your career will be to play a significant role in helping clients from all walks of life to become "millionaire real estate investors."

WHO IS THE PERFECT PROSPECT TO INVEST IN A REAL ESTATE BUSINESS?

Anyone who is creditworthy—all the way from a young person just starting out to a high-net-worth individual who may be paying more than their fair share of taxes—is a perfect prospect for real estate investing. There are available properties at every price point, from the fixer-upper to move-in-ready. Each person has specific needs and objectives, and real estate can meet their needs. They should be among those who are most willing to consider the benefits of investing in real estate.

How many people do you know who consistently complain about the amount of taxes they are paying every year, yet do nothing about it? Has their accountant ever suggested that they explore the option of investing in real estate? It is up to you to help people understand the benefits of doing so. I am convinced that most people will thank you for caring enough about them to bring up this topic. Investing in real estate could be one of the most important options to consider for reducing taxes, minimizing the impact of inflation, and building wealth.

REDUCING THE IMPACT OF ECONOMIC DOWNTURNS

As a real estate agent, you know that purchasing a residence has always been a way for people to gain equity and generate wealth for the future. A downturn in the real estate market during the past ten years took a toll on home equity but did not wipe it out altogether. Those hit the hardest were people who had paid too much for their property. Today we are seeing an uptick in the market, and once again real estate is being recognized as a positive alternative for building wealth.

In communities throughout our country, investors have played a major role in stabilizing the residential market by purchasing foreclosed properties. Although the impact of the recession was unfortunate for those who lost their homes to foreclosure, the savvy investors who purchased these properties made huge profits and will continue to do so for years to come.

If you are not approaching or working with potential real estate investors—including your current clients, past clients, family members, and people you know well who like and trust you—then you are missing an opportunity of lifetime. They need your help in protecting their economic assets; they just don't know it yet. This client base could have a tremendously positive impact on your income stream. In other words, if you're not working with investors you are letting money go down the drain.

Building wealth by investing in real estate is certainly not easy. If it took no effort at all, everyone would be doing it. It takes hard work and sacrifice, but you don't have to be a genius to be successful. Genuine desire goes a long way.

Buying and holding income-producing properties represents the ticket to wealth building. People who choose this path can create a sizable portfolio that will generate residual income in the form of rent payments for many years to come.

How confident are you with the current economic outlook? My guess is that you are no different from many others who are uncertain about what the future will bring. If you assume that most people are deeply concerned about building wealth and retirement income, you will be correct, and you can be the ticket to renewed hope.

My guess is that more and more people would rather be in control of their financial future right now than ever before, because the system has failed them.

There has never been a better opportunity to seek out and work with investors.

While our economic future may be uncertain, more than 45 years of being a real estate investor has taught me that the opportunities are endless. When you invest in real estate, you can enjoy instant equity by buying undervalued properties that will make good rentals or by reconditioning them to "flip." Income-producing properties offer higher returns with lower risks than any other investment option. Keep in mind that with

real estate YOU are in control of your assets, not your stockbroker or financial advisor.

I am sure you personally know individuals who have created
a lot of wealth from owning their own business or from portfolio
profits or income from stocks, bonds, and annuities. But how
many ordinary, hard-working individuals do you know who view
the prospect of becoming wealthy and financially independent as
more of a dream than reality? You can pave the way by showing
them how to invest in real estate.

I want to encourage you to think of friends, current clients,
potential clients, people in the trades, and others in your sphere
of influence with whom you might be able to have a conversation
about real estate investment. What reasonable person would not
be interested in exploring how you can help them build wealth
so that someday they can be worry-free?

FOCUS ON LONG-TERM GAINS

Every type of investment including real estate goes through
cycles and may encounter setbacks along the way, just as we have
seen in the past few years with declining property values. But for
investors who purchased undervalued properties, or even those
who paid market price, all the benefits of real estate ownership
are still hard at work (cash flow, tax savings, appreciation, principal reduction). And how about the fact that their mortgage
is being reduced every month because of rental income? These
are some of the reasons why my personal wealth will continue
to be invested in real estate.

Wealth building through real estate is not a quick-fix solution. Instead one must look several years down the road to a
time when these properties will be paid in full. Think about
the residual income that will continue for the rest of your life.

Although the possibilities are endless, someone who has little
knowledge and lacks the assistance of an experienced real estate

agent could make a huge mistake. Very quickly their dream of achieving financial independence could become a nightmare.

You can become the investor-friendly real estate agent who has been the missing link for the novice or even the experienced investor. You have the power to help clients enjoy a prosperous future and a comfortable retirement. Real estate can be the ticket to financial security for them and for you.

RETIREMENT: FANTASY OR REALITY?

It used to be that you could work for a company for 30 years and expect to retire with a nice pension. Unfortunately, the workplace no longer offers that kind of job security. Retirement pensions have dwindled, and the value of many 401(K)s has greatly diminished. Today's employees will be lucky to get a gold watch when they retire.

I can recall my father working extremely hard in the 1960s and '70s at a job that paid the minimum wage. His employer did not offer a retirement plan, and I can't remember whether he had insurance coverage.

But fortunately my parents had enough wisdom to invest in three rental properties that provided $1,500 monthly residual income for many years until they sold them and had a little more security for their golden years.

The bottom line is that retirement prospects are not looking very good for many people, and economic uncertainty is greatly affecting the amount of money that is being saved. People are concerned that they might lose their job, some are underemployed, and others are unemployed and using the funds they set aside for retirement just to make ends meet.

Most of us have lost money in the stock market, 401(K) accounts, pension plans, and so on. Although the economy has rebounded in the last few years, the same pattern still applies. The market continues to go up and down, up and down.

Most people have no idea how the stock market works, or what their financial advisor does. Do you?

The picture is the opposite for investors who purchased undervalued properties during the past few years and gained instant equity by buying properties considered to be deals and began earning ongoing income from long-term rentals. These same properties made great flippers.

Property values and rents are on the upswing, and real estate is much easier to understand than the stock market. How many of you understand how the stock market works? How about how real estate works? You get my point. Why not be the voice for this industry and help others? Real estate investors will become your #1 best clients.

Many employees can no longer afford to contribute to their 401(K), so they are missing out on employer matching. If they had invested in a rental property, the benefits would have been tremendous: rental income, tax savings and perhaps even a fully paid property producing residual income in the form of rent.

What about the rising cost of medical care and health insurance, which has caused many to dip into their retirement funds to pay medical bills? How many of your close friends or family members would fall into this category?

The saddest news of all is that retirement statistics are very scary, as the net worth of most Americans has diminished dramatically. People now have more questions than answers. How can they regain what they have lost? As a real estate agent who works with investors, you can help them rebuild their wealth.

RETIREMENT STATISTICS

As you consider the retirement statistics on the next few pages, ask yourself how applicable they are to you. What about people that you may know or your current or past clients? Do you think you might be able to help people from all walks of life solve their financial concerns?

I am confident that by the time you finish reading this book, you will have the necessary knowledge to help people from all walks of life. A real estate investment business, in my opinion, is a winning proposition that will make a big difference in the lives of people. As you read the retirement statistics and concerns you will understand why.

Note: While the research findings and statistics may differ from source to source, the information should give an indication of the retirement and financial concerns facing Americans.

1. "Retirement Crisis Persists Despite Economic Recovery." Source: The National Institute on Retirement Income, September 2018

The report finds that the retirement savings levels of working-age Americans remain deeply inadequate despite the economic recovery. An analysis of U.S. Census Bureau data reveals that the median retirement account balance among all working individuals is $0. The data also indicate that 57% of working-age individuals (more than 100 million) do not own any retirement account assets in an employer-sponsored 401(k)-type plan, individual account, or pension.

The analysis finds that overall, four out of five working Americans have less than one year's income saved in retirement accounts. Also, 77% of Americans fall short of conservative retirement savings targets for their age based on working until age 67, even after counting an individual's entire net worth – a generous measure of retirement savings. Moreover, a large majority of working Americans cannot meet even a substantially reduced savings target.

Growing income inequality widens the gap in retirement account ownership. Workers in the top income quartile are five times more likely to have retirement accounts than workers in the lowest income quartile. And those Individuals with retirement accounts have, on average, more than three times the annual income of individuals who do not own retirement accounts.

Retirement is in peril for most working-class Americans. When all working individuals are considered—not just the minority with retirement accounts—the typical working American has zero, zilch, nothing saved for retirement.

What this report means is that the American dream of a modest retirement after a lifetime of work now is a middle-class nightmare. Even among workers who have accumulated savings in retirement accounts, the typical worker had a low account balance of $40,000. This is far below the savings levels Americans need if they hope to sustain their standard of living in retirement.

The retirement savings shortfall can be attributed to a multitude of factors, including a breakdown in the nation's retirement infrastructure. There is a massive gap in retirement plan coverage among American workers. Fewer workers have stable and secure pensions, 401(k)-style defined contribution (DC) individual accounts provide less savings and protection, and jumps in the Social Security retirement age translate into lower retirement income.

The catastrophic financial crisis of 2008 exposed the vulnerability of the DC-centered retirement system. Many Americans saw the value of their retirement plans plummet when the financial markets crashed and destroyed trillions of dollars of household wealth. Asset values in Americans' retirement accounts fell from $9.3 trillion at the end of 2007 to $7.2 trillion at the end of 2008.

The economic downturn also triggered a decline in total contributions to DC retirement accounts as many employers stopped matching employee contributions for a time, pushing total contributions below 2008 levels. Since then, the combined value of 401(k)-type accounts and IRAs had reached $16.9 trillion by the end of 2017. Unfortunately, this increase in total retirement account assets had not translated to improved retirement security for the majority of American workers and their families who had nothing saved.

In this uncertain environment, Americans face an ongoing quandary: How much income will they need to retire, and can they ever save enough? To maintain their current standard of living in retirement, the typical working American needs to replace roughly 85% of pre-retirement income. Social Security, under the current benefit formula, provides a replacement rate of roughly 35% for a typical worker. This leaves a retirement income gap equal to 50% of pre-retirement earnings that must be filled through other means.

The key findings of this report are as follows:

- **Account ownership rates are closely correlated with income and wealth.** More than 100 million working-age individuals (57%) do not own any retirement account assets, whether in an employer-sponsored 401(k)-type plan or an IRA, nor are they covered by defined benefit (DB) pensions. Individuals who do own retirement accounts have, on average, more than three times the annual income of individuals who do not own retirement accounts.

- **The typical working-age American has no retirement savings.** When all working individuals are included—not just individuals with retirement accounts—the median retirement account balance is $0 among all working individuals. Even among workers who have accumulated savings in retirement accounts, the typical worker had a modest account balance of $40,000. Furthermore, some 68% of individuals age 55 to 64 have retirement savings equal to less than one year of their annual income, which is far below what they will need to maintain their standard of living over their expected years of retirement.

- **About three-fourths (77%) of Americans fall short of conservative retirement savings targets for their age and income based on working until age 67, even after counting an individual's entire net worth**—a generous measure of retirement savings. Due to a long-term trend toward income and wealth inequality that only worsened during the recent economic recovery, a large majority of the bottom half of Americans cannot meet even a substantially reduced savings target.

- **Public policy can play a critical role in putting all Americans on a path toward a secure retirement by strengthening Social Security, expanding access to low-cost, high-quality retirement plans, and helping low-income workers and families save.** Social Security, the primary underpinning of retirement income security, could be strengthened to stabilize system financing and enhance benefits for vulnerable populations. States across the nation are taking key steps to expand access to workplace retirement savings, with enrollment in state-based programs in 2018 starting in Oregon, Washington, and Illinois. Other proposals to expand coverage are on the national agenda, but universal retirement plan coverage has not become a national priority. Finally, expanding the Saver's Credit and making it refundable could help boost the retirement savings of lower-income families.

To understand the challenges working-class individuals face in retirement, the report provides an analysis of the U.S. Census Bureau's Survey of Income and Program Participation (SIPP) data released in 2016 and 2017. The study analyzes workplace retirement plan coverage, retirement account ownership, and retirement savings as a percentage of income, and estimates the share of workers that meet the financial industry's recommended benchmarks for retirement savings.

Source: The National Institute on Retirement Security is a nonprofit organization established to contribute to informed policymaking by fostering a deep understanding of the value of retirement security to employees, employers, and the economy through national research and education programs.

Below are additional retirement statistics:

1. **One-third of Americans have nothing saved for retirement, and more than half of Americans have less than $10,000 saved for retirement.**

   A recent survey from GoBankingRates.com found that over half of Americans have no more than $10,000 saved for retirement, and one-third have nothing saved at all. The National Institute on Retirement Security estimates that the nation's retirement savings gap is between $6.8 and $14 trillion.

2. **Women are 27% more likely than men to have no retirement savings.** Women must save 18% of their income, while men need to save 10% to reach the same financial level in retirement.

   The gap between men's and women's retirement savings equates to as much as 27%. Nearly two-thirds of women have less than $10,000 in retirement savings, compared with 52% of men. It's harder for women to save in general, as they make 79 cents for every dollar men make in full-time positions.

3. The majority of baby boomers are not confident they've saved enough for retirement.

According to a survey conducted by the Insured Retirement Institute, 76% of baby boomers doubt their financial future. Of those lacking confidence, 68% wish they had saved more and 67% wish they had started saving earlier. More than half of baby boomers said they need Social Security to make it through retirement.

4. The number of seniors declaring bankruptcy has grown to 7%.

In 1991, only 2.1% of individuals filing for bankruptcy were 65 or older. That percentage increased to 7% by 2007, a scary number considering the limited options available to seniors who need to make money. The Employee Benefit Research Institute notes, "Without a job or income stream to convince lenders otherwise, you may have a hard time opening credit cards, securing transportation, or renting a home as a senior."

5. By 2033, Social Security will need to be cut by 23%.

Social Security is the most commonly cited source of income for retirees. Nobody knows what Social Security will look like in a few decades. Without reform, benefits will need to be cut by 23% in aggregate in 2033, according to the Social Security Administration. In other words, after the depletion of reserves, tax income will only be able to pay 77% of scheduled benefits in 2033. According to the Economic Policy Institute, Social Security currently keeps nearly 27 million Americans above the poverty threshold.

6. Nearly one-third of homeowners of retirement age still have mortgage debt.

Most financial planners recommend that their clients pay off the mortgage on their house before they retire. However, from 2001 to 2011, the percentage of homeowners of retirement age (62 and older) who still had mortgage debt increased from 22% to 30%. The percentage of homeowners age 75 and older with mortgage debt skyrocketed from 8.4% to 21.2% during the same time period.

7. More than half (55%) of retirees retired earlier than expected.

Poor health is the number 1 reason for retiring early, followed by job loss. Few people can continue working well into their eighties like Warren Buffett. Gallup finds the average retirement age is 62. This aligns with the Center for Retirement Research's findings: The average retirement age is 64 for men and 62 for women.

8. Many U.S. employees are not saving enough money to receive matching contributions from their employer.

According to Financial Engines, an independent investment advisor, one-quarter of employees are not saving enough money to receive their employer's 401(k) match. On average, those employees miss out on an extra $1,336 a year, or a little less than an extra $25 a week. This equals an estimated $24 billion nationwide in lost matching contributions.

9. Most baby boomers are not as knowledgeable about retirement as they think they are.

Eighty-seven percent of baby boomers who took a quiz on retirement strategies got a D grade or lower, even though 61% thought they had a high level of retirement knowledge and 75% expected to be financially secure in retirement.

10. Health care expenses can quickly demolish retirement savings.

Health equals wealth in retirement. Fidelity Investments estimates that the average 65-year-old couple retiring in 2016 will spend $260,000 to pay out-of-pocket health care costs in retirement, compared with $220,000 in 2014 and $190,000 in 2005. Longer life expectancy and anticipated annual increases for medical and prescription expenses are primary factors in these increased costs. In addition to paying for health care, about 70% of 65-year-olds will eventually need some form of long-term care.

When Nationwide Insurance surveyed women age 50 and older about potential health care and long-term care costs in retirement, 65% could not estimate their likely health care costs and 77% could not estimate their potential expenses for long-term care.

11. Many retirees fail to budget for entertainment expenses.

Factoring in entertainment expenses is crucial to a well-planned retirement. In fact, it's a good idea to plan for increased leisure-time expenses given the free time retirement allows. Sadly, nearly 60% of retirees don't budget for leisure-time pursuits as they save for retirement, according to a Merrill Lynch study.

12. Americans are worried about retirement.

According to Ramsey Solutions, about 56% of Americans lose sleep when they think about retirement, citing anxiety as the main feeling they associate with their financial future. If you have a solid financial plan for your future, you can rest easy.

13. Student loan debt may prevent younger people from setting aside money for retirement.

In 2015, the average student loan debt totaled $33,000, compared with $10,000 in 1990. The LIMRA Secure Retirement Institute found that millennials who start their careers with $30,000 in student loans could end up with $325,000 less in retirement savings than their debt-free peers. Debt can be a wise investment if it leads to increased earning potential. The trick is researching career options and understanding how to reduce the amount of money spent on a college degree.

14. Most adults lack basic financial knowledge.

About 3.5 billion adults worldwide don't understand basic financial concepts. Standard & Poor's interviewed over 150,000 adults in more than 140 countries to gauge global financial literacy. Only 33% of adults surveyed could correctly answer at least three out of four questions about financial concepts involving risk diversification, inflation, numeracy, and compound interest.

A lack of understanding creates an abundance of uncertainty and stress, which helps explain why 60% of employees report feeling somewhat or very stressed about their financial situation and why 62% of millennials want a financial advisor to walk them through every step of the retirement planning process.

15. Outliving your retirement savings is a legitimate concern.

Once you hit age 65 (roughly the average retirement age), your odds of living for another decade or two are quite high. Men age 65 have a 78% chance of living another 10 years, while women have an 85% chance, according to JPMorgan's research.

16. Debt in retirement has become a significant worry for many pre-retirees.

The average household owes $134,643 in debt including mortgages, according to Nerdwallet.com. The Employee Benefit Research Institute (EBRI) found that 63% of today's workers say that debt is a problem for them, and 37% of workers who have a major debt problem do not feel confident that they will have enough money for a financially secure retirement.

17. People are trying to deal with relatively low investment income on fixed-income investments such as savings accounts, CDs, and bonds.

In a Wells Fargo survey conducted in 2017, 37% of investors said higher interest rates would make them likely to transfer money out of the stock market and into safer investments, up from 23% two years earlier.

Many workers are confused and uncertain about what they should be doing for retirement, and only 16% in the EBRI survey felt confident that they knew how much to contribute to their retirement savings each month.

Capital One Investing reported a drop in the percentage of Americans who feel confident they are saving enough to retire comfortably—down from 72% in 2015 to 62% in 2017. Among the reasons cited were lack of knowledge and experience investing, and investing complexity. Just

23% of workers have spoken with a retirement planning professional, according to EBRI.

As you consider the above concerns, which ones are relevant to you? Which of these concerns may have meaning and application to others you may know?

Many people of all generations are looking for ways to improve their financial situation. I am hopeful that after reading this book you will become a real estate investor and encourage others to do so as well. Now is exactly the right time to invest in real estate. Are you up to the challenge?

A REALISTIC WAY TO BUILD WEALTH

As I previously mentioned, one of the few investment options available to the average, hard-working person is investing in real estate. How realistic is the stock market as a path to wealth for someone who has only $10,000 or $20,000 to invest? But anyone who is creditworthy can get a loan and use other people's money (OPM) and a down payment of 10 to 20% to amass a sizable real estate portfolio in a few short years.

Compared with the stock market, it is quite easy to invest in real estate if you have good credit, a solid financial statement, and collateral (such as equity on your personal residence or from other rental properties). Possibly you can get a line of credit or bridge loan. Offers can be written as cash, as long as the collateral is not tied to the subject property. The assumption is that the undervalued property needs some type of work to improve its value. Once the property has been improved, it can be refinanced and perhaps even pull out 100% of the money that was invested—the purchase price plus fix-up costs. In all likelihood when the improvements have been made, the property will be worth far more than its purchase price. Let's say the purchase price of a property is $60,000 and you spend

$20,000 improving it. Your total investment is $80,000. If the property appraises for $115,000, you can refinance the original investment amount ($80,000) and have $35,000 in equity to use as a down payment or even use as a college fund or for some other purpose.

> The secret is not how much money one makes but rather how much money one keeps and invests wisely. Far more people need to invest in real estate, although they may not know it yet. You are the key.

Buying and holding income-producing properties is the most realistic way for a majority of people to build wealth with minimum risk. In a later chapter we will discuss how to minimize risk by analyzing a property.

Changes in the value of real estate are much more predictable than those of other investments such as stocks. Furthermore, real estate offers control for the investor. With other forms of investments, you have to rely on someone else to handle your money.

I realize that money is being made in the stock market and also by gambling in the casinos or by buying a winning lottery ticket, but how realistic are those paths to wealth for the majority of us?

I am sure that many people would invest in real estate, but fear of the unknown has kept them on the sidelines. That is where you as a knowledgeable real estate agent can make a difference.

Yes, there will be challenges along the way, such as unexpected expenses, poor tenant selection resulting in damage to the property, vacant properties, and so on, but the advantages are well worth it. Most of us want to be in control of our future, and real estate offers just that.

If you are a savvy and knowledgeable real estate agent who can guide and assist clients along the way, you can alleviate a lot of their fear. When you help them find an undervalued property and they earn instant equity through minor renovation or updates, their fear will go away.

MY EIGHT KEYS TO BECOMING A MILLIONAIRE REAL ESTATE INVESTOR

1.   Dream the dream. Think about what it will feel like when you get there. (Think, buy using leverage, and then own a million free and clear.)
2.   Develop a business plan and evaluate your progress annually.
3.   Save, save, save. (Save enough for a down payment on a rental, then start over and buy another and another.)
4.   Live below your means. Ask yourself, "Do I really need this?" What you really need is real estate to support your lifestyle in retirement.
5.   Don't use credit cards. (If you must use credit cards, pay off balances monthly.)
6.   Let your money work hard for you; don't work hard for your money. Buy assets, not liabilities.
7.   Start your own real estate business. Take the first step and you will be glad you did.
8.   Be your own financial advisor. You know this business well.

You should be quite confident that most people of all generations are looking for ways to improve their financial situation.

If you are not already an investor, I hope that after reading this book you will be an investor and this "niche" market will be a big part of your overall business growth plan. You should reach out to people from all walks of life. They need your help, but unfortunately they don't know why. Are you up for the challenge?

In Chapter 13 you will find a series of questions (not in any specific order) that you can ask potential clients. If they answer these questions honestly, all you have to say to them is "If I can help you solve the concerns you mentioned, would you be interested in considering a real estate investment business?" The most important question they must answer pertains to their credit. If they have no credit issues, a solid financial statement, cash or access to money such as a line of credit, it opens up the opportunity of a lifetime and you can help them.

LET'S GET STARTED BY COMPARING A TRADITIONAL SMALL BUSINESS AND A REAL ESTATE INVESTMENT BUSINESS.

Ever wonder why some people start a business where the potential of succeeding is not very good? Don't get me wrong; I am absolutely 100% pro-entrepreneurship and I believe that if someone has the right business model, they should go for it. Unfortunately, the statistics are not in their favor.

Who would not be interested in living the American Dream and enjoying financial freedom to do whatever they want?

I am sure you know a friend or family member who thought they had the right business model and would succeed. They refinanced their personal residence or put down collateral to borrow money, only to have the business fail. They lost everything and had to file for bankruptcy.

As real estate agents, we are very fortunate to be in a career field that allows us to help people from all walks of life and make a living at it. Hopefully, you are also investing in your own industry.

When people work for someone they are making a living, but are they creating wealth? It's more likely that their employer is creating wealth. There is a big difference between making a good living and generating wealth. I understand why people would rather own a business than work for someone else and are willing to put everything on the line, but did they consider how their business model will differentiate itself from similar ones? This is one of the major reasons new businesses fail.

Here's something else to think about: do they really own that business or does the business own them?

I think you know where I am going with this, and I hope you agree with me that real estate is a much better option.

WHY DO SO MANY SMALL BUSINESSES FAIL?

Maybe you've heard that more than half of all businesses fail during their first year. According to the Small Business Administration (SBA), this isn't quite accurate. The SBA states that 30% of new businesses fail during their first two years, 50% during their first five years, and 66% during their first ten years.

According to Investopedia, the four most common reasons small businesses fail are (1) insufficient capital, (2) poor management, (3) inadequate business planning, and (4) spending too much on marketing. But there are many additional reasons many new businesses don't survive.

A CBInsights analysis provided the following information on business failures:

- 42% of small businesses fail because there's no market need for their services or products.

- 29% fail because they run out of cash.

- 23% fail because they don't have the right team running the business.

- 19% fail because customers prefer their competitors.

- 18% fail because of pricing and cost issues.

- 17% fail because of a poor product offering.

- 17% fail because they lack a business model.

- 14% fail because of poor marketing.

- 14% fail because they ignore their customers.

Clearly, there are many reasons small businesses fail, but a few keep coming up: capital access, cash flow, lack of demand, and poor management.

Just to make a point, I will use the example of pizza restaurants. According to the *2018 Pizza Power Report: A State-of-the-Industry Analysis,* a total of 4,992 new *pizzerias* opened their doors in 2018 and 5,291 closed. The Perry Group International and Restaurant Brokers have completed studies on the average lifespan of restaurants.

The Perry Group study concluded that most restaurants close during their first year of operation. Seventy percent of those that make it past the first year close their doors in the next three to five years. Ninety percent of the restaurants that are still operating past the five-year mark will stay in business for a minimum of 10 years.

The Restaurant Brokers study (the only one to make a distinction between chain and independent restaurants) found that up to 90% of independent establishments close during the first year and the remaining restaurants have an average five-year lifespan.

Here are the hard numbers associated with opening a restaurant:

- Median cost to open a restaurant: $275,000 (range: $125,000 to $555,000)

- Average cost (with a building): $425,000

I am guessing that when the doors closed and the equipment had to be sold, they were lucky to get 50 cents on the dollar.

What advice would you offer to someone who is thinking about starting a traditional business when you know their prospects of success are not very good?

Why not suggest that they consider a different business model with better odds? What are the prospects of success for people who invest in real estate?

LET'S CONSIDER WHY A REAL ESTATE INVESTMENT BUSINESS COULD FAIL:

1. Buying properties that or poorly maintained or located in high-crime areas.
2. Not taking the time to find an agent who is qualified to meet their specific needs and explain the advantages and disadvantages of various real estate options. A real estate agent who is also an investor understands the ins and outs of the investment business. Practical knowledge and expertise go a long way to help people with their biggest investment decision. Bottom line: You should have more knowledge than your client; otherwise they are only using you becuase they like and trust you.
3. Not having a good reason to invest in the first place. They can't answer the big "Why?" It should be to build wealth and retirement income, not just to obtain cash flow with no end goal in mind.
4. Failing to create and follow a business plan. A sample business plan can be found in Chapter 12. It is not just about cash flow or about buying properties for the sake of buying properties. It is about buying enough of the right properties to achieve cash flow, tax savings, appreciation and depreciation now, paying off the properties at some point, and having financial freedom in retirement. Properties in family-friendly neighborhoods will serve the end goal. If an emergency arises and the property

owner needs money, how easy will it be to sell properties that are undesirable or located in high-crime areas? Who would be the likely buyer?

5. Falling in love with the property rather than the deal and not taking the time to analyze a property under consideration. Basic formulas for analyzing potential investment properties are covered in Chapter 8.

6. Overleveraging properties by getting low down payment or no money down deals. A deal that seems to be too good to be true may not be a good investment. Why would anyone sell a property worth owning for no money down?

7. Buying "junk" properties instead of owning enough of the "right" properties.

8. Constantly refinancing properties instead of paying some off. I understand that building a portfolio is necessary, but paying them off at some point should be the goal. If you have insufficient equity, there's no protection if anything goes wrong. One's age should also be a consideration of how aggressive to be. Is it a good strategy to keep accumulating properties or is it more important to own enough of the right properties that are paid off? Why would anyone who is nearing retirement age want to be aggressive and overleverage?

9. Collecting rent and not making the mortgage payment. Believe it or not, some people actually do this.

10. Not maintaining the property. Why would anyone invest their hard-earned money only to let the property get run-down by not making repairs?

11. Poor tenant selection and failure to do proper due diligence. For example, it would not be wise to rent to someone who has the first month's rent and deposit and needs to move in today. How many potential tenants have a couple of thousand dollars in cash? I would be suspicious of their business model.

WHY IS A REAL ESTATE INVESTMENT BUSINESS A WINNER?

Anyone considering a new business venture today should think long and hard regarding the kind of business that is likely to succeed over the long term. Housing will always be a necessity. Take any city in our country and in all likelihood you will see the same types of small businesses (gift shops, independent clothing stores, restaurants, bars, gyms, thrift stores, auto parts stores, mechanic shops, and on and on). Do you know of any of these types of business that have gone broke? By contrast, how many people do you know who failed in their real estate business even though they followed good business principles?

Let's consider why a real estate investment business is likely to be successful for the long haul. The fact that housing will always be a necessity should be a good indicator that the demand will always be there.

Better yet, real estate can be done on a part-time basis with much less out-of-pocket investment, and the most powerful tool not used enough is leverage. (Why someone would want to pay cash for a property is beyond me.)

With a solid business plan and enough of the right properties, I am confident that anyone willing to make the sacrifices now will be rewarded later. Throughout this book, you will see examples after examples to prove my point.

HERE ARE A FEW REASONS WHY INVESTING IN REAL ESTATE IS A WINNER:

1. Housing (shelter) will always be a necessity. Real estate has met the test of time and will continue to be one of the most effective ways to create wealth and retirement income.

2. Even if a property has to be sold quickly, it is almost impossible
    to lose all the money you have invested in real estate. (Keep in
    mind that a savvy investor buys only undervalued properties
    that are likely to make money.)
3. Real estate investing can be done on a part-time basis.
4. Your real estate investment keeps working for you 24/7 because
    the tenant continues paying rent even if there are outside influ-
    ences such as bad weather. A traditional business that doesn't
    open its doors for any reason must still pay rent and other
    expenses despite receiving no income on the days when the
    business is closed.
5. Properties in desirable areas will always be in demand and
    will appreciate in value. Even if properties don't appreciate in
    value and are worth the same as the original purchase price, the
    investors are still better off than they would be if they hadn't
    purchased the properties. As an example, if someone purchased
    ten rental properties for $100,000 apiece ten years ago and
    has paid off all of them, the investor now has $1,000,000 free
    and clear that the tenant ultimately paid off. What a concept!
    A more likely scenario is that the properties will be worth a
    lot more ten years after they were purchased. Let's say each
    property is rented for $1,000 per month: $1,000 x 10 x 12 =
    $120,000 per year. If the taxes, insurance, and other expenses
    for each property total $250 per month, the yearly expenses
    equal $250 x 10 x 12 = $30,000. If you take $120,000 in rent
    and subtract $30,000 in expenses, you end up with $90,000
    annual income from your real estate business (cash flow before
    taxes). How many people do you know who make that kind
    of money annually from their small business or investments?
    With a traditional business, you have a lot more overhead, but
    there's really no overhead in this type of business. It works very
    hard for you 24/7.

6. To run most other businesses, you need office, retail, or man-
    ufacturing space. Phones, office equipment and other related
    overhead expenses make startup expensive. Real estate investing
    is ready to go as a business with stuff you already have: your
    kitchen table, smartphone, and computer. It's a zero-dollar
    startup.

7. You don't need to hire employees to help you run your real
    estate business. The people who repair or remodel your prop-
    erties are independent contractors. Others on the team could
    include an attorney, accountant, title company, pest control
    service, home inspector, and so on. These service providers
    are utilized as needed.

8. A real estate business is resistant to inflation. During period
    of inflation, property values and rent tend to go up.

9. When taxes, insurance, and expenses on your properties go
    up, these increases are passed down to the tenant in the form
    of higher rent.

10. In a worst-case scenario where the real estate market goes
    south, the savvy investor who purchased undervalued proper-
    ties is well protected. Ups and downs in the market don't matter
    because the properties are being used as long-term rentals and
    your tenants are making the mortgage payments.

11. A real estate business, in addition to the long-term rental model,
    can include wholesaling to other investors or "flipping" to own-
    er-occupied buyers.

12. The most powerful tool in your arsenal is the 1031 Tax Deferred
    Exchange that is only available to investors. It allows selling
    the property for a profit and deferring capital gains taxes in
    the year of the sale. This can be done over and over, and it is a
    terrific way to grow your portfolio.

I hope you can use this brief summary to explain to potential
clients why a real estate investment business is one of the best,
if not the very best, paths to building wealth.

What a concept! You purchase multiple properties, your tenants pay down your debt, and as the properties are paid off you eventually become a "millionaire investor." With a solid business plan, the right team in place, and especially with the knowledge you have acquired as a real estate agent, it is a winning proposition. The biggest roadblocks for most are analysis paralysis, never getting off the starting block, and trying to go at it alone.

Unfortunately for some, the American Dream is not alive because they don't realize that becoming a millionaire is within their reach. The opposite is true, because if I can do it so can you.

I am proof this is one of the most lucrative businesses to start today. Over the 45 years I have been doing this, it has been an amazing venture with very little drama. I have created more wealth than I ever dreamed was possible and also helped many a client achieve financial freedom. I have no doubt that real estate investing is the best business model to build wealth and retirement income over the long term, as long as properties are properly managed and maintained.

For me personally, starting my real estate business was the best decision I ever made. The results have been much better than I would have achieved by investing in the stock market. I didn't have to work 60 to 80 hours a week for little return; instead, I've probably spent an average of 15 to 20 hours a week on my business.

I like my business model much better than investing in the stock market as it easier to understand. My mode is simple: Buy the right property, rent it to a qualified tenant, collect rent, make the mortgage payment, and the money that is left over is the cash flow (I will call it dividends) that can be spent.

I am 100% certain that most people can understand this model and follow it, compared with not really understanding how the stock market works and not being in control of the outcome. With my business I am in control. I can touch, feel, drive by the property, make improvements, raise the rent, make the property more valuable, and so on. Changes in global economic conditions affect the stock market but have no bearing on my properties. Real estate is local.

Think about how powerful this information can be for you and others. How many people do you know who make just $200 per month in dividends from their current investments? It is very easy to make this much money from just one rental, which creates cash flow that you can actually spend. Do you know anyone who would benefit from receiving $5,000, $10,000, $20,000 or more on a monthly basis while the tenant pays down their debt? Real estate is a much easier way to create wealth than the stock market, and this is true for a majority of hard-working people, from an electrician to a CEO and everyone in between. I have personally witnessed many people become millionaires with this type of business.

Are you with me?

In the 45-plus years I have been an investor and for the past 20 years as a Realtor, I can't recall meeting anyone who had to close their rental business because of lack of demand. Think about it: if the tenant pays rent and the mortgage payment is being made, the property is well maintained and there is money left over every month (cash flow) to make repairs, spend, and so on, it is a winning business that more people should consider. By starting with one property and building along the way, you can accumulate a sizable portfolio worth several million dollars, generating a six-figure income. It's a pretty simple concept and a winning proposition.

A RECORD NUMBER OF AMERICANS ARE NOW MILLIONAIRES

Over the last two centuries, about 90% of the world's millionaires have been created by investing in real estate. I believe that for hardworking Americans, a real estate investment business is the best option to build significant wealth over time. Anyone can do it, assuming they are creditworthy and have access to money (line of credit, cash, etc.). People who are willing to work hard and make sacrifices now will be rewarded later.

There are more millionaires today than ever before in the United States. As of the end of 2016, there were a record 10.8 million millionaires nationwide—400,000 more than the previous year, according to Spectrem Group's Market Insights Report 2017.

The increase can be attributed to a recovery of the U.S. economy since the Great Recession in 2008 and the Wall Street rally that followed the election of Donald Trump, according to George Walper, Jr., President of Spectrem Group.

"The record levels of households reflect the significantly higher values of all asset classes, post-recession," Walper said in a press release accompanying the release of the report. "And the recent record level of the United States markets following the presidential election has added demonstrably to the asset level of most affluent investors.'"

In 2016, there were 9.4 million individuals with a net worth between $1 million and $5 million, 1.3 million individuals with a net worth between $5 million and $25 million, and 156,000 households with more than $25 million in net worth, the report says.

At the same time that there are a record number of millionaires in the United States, however, the middle class is shrinking. The percentage of American adults who are considered middle-income fell from 55% in 2000 to 52% in 2014, according to a 2016 report from the Pew Research Center.

Keep the following principle in mind as you continue reading this book: When you invest in real estate, you make your money when you buy (by purchasing properties that are considered to be undervalued or a deal). A rental property is not like day trading. Rather, it is a long-term investment. In 15 to 20 years the tenant ultimately pays off your mortgage and then residual income in the form of rent continues for years to come. What a wonderful concept!

Maybe you are fortunate enough to have worked with investors already, so you understand the impact of real estate investment on wealth building. I am one of those who have been greatly blessed by this industry. I have helped a lot of clients to attain financial freedom, and I did this by providing the expertise and knowledge they did not yet have.

Don't wait to buy real estate—Buy real estate and wait.

—*T. HARV EKER*

Over 90% of all millionaires became so through owning real estate.

—*ANDREW CARNEGIE*

Every person who invests in well selected real estate in a growing section of a prosperous community adopts the surest and safest method of becoming independent, for real estate is the basis for wealth.

—*THEODORE ROOSEVELT (1858–1919)*

Becoming a landlord is an excellent way for most hardworking people to become millionaires. Working for someone else is a way to make a living, and investing in real estate can be a terrific source of additional income and ultimately a path to financial independence.

Throughout this book I will make the case that there is no better opportunity than the present to begin working with investors. You will be amazed at how easily you can increase your income stream. If you are not an investor yourself, I will urge

you to become your best client for the reasons I have been sharing with you. Not only will you gain credibility with clients, but
you'll create a retirement fund for yourself.

How many relatives, friends, associates, and clients do you
know who would love to become a millionaire and retire early
but see it as only a dream rather than a reality? I can assure you
that the possibility is very real and within the reach of far more
people than you realize. Real estate is that avenue, no matter
what city they live in, their education, or their background. I
encourage you to take the next step and assist the hundreds of
potential clients who are at your fingertips.

While you are helping others, why not build your own
wealth? Over the next ten years you could purchase two properties yearly and ultimately control 20 properties that are fully
paid and worth millions, earning monthly residual income for
years to come.

What form of investment allows one to make money while
enjoying generous deductions in the form of tax benefits?
Stocks? No. Real estate? Yes. In a later chapter we will cover
the tax benefits in detail, including depreciation, maintenance, and so on. One of the most powerful methods the
IRS provides is the 1031 tax exchange, which allows you to
defer capital gains.

HOW BIG IS THE POPULATION
OF POTENTIAL INVESTORS?

The population is so big that the exact number really doesn't
matter. Everyone you know should be considered a prospect.
There are so many people in your community who need your
help that you will never run out of prospects. I can't think of
any reason why anyone should pay for qualified leads when
everyone who is creditworthy is a prospect.

Just to make my point, how do you think most people would
respond if you asked them the following questions?

1. Will you have enough money to maintain your current life-style in retirement, based on your current income and/or investments?
2. Are you prepared for life after work?
3. What would happen if you got sick and could no longer earn a living in your current occupation?
4. What is your current financial situation?
5. Are you comfortable with the amount of money you are able to set aside for future needs?
6. Do you have enough disposable income?
7. Are you more in debt than you would like?
8. Do you have a college savings plan for your children?
9. Are you satisfied with the return you are getting from your current investments?

You will find more questions like these in Chapter 13.

I can assure you that the majority of people will respond to these questions exactly as you expect they would. These are thought-provoking questions that many just don't want to deal with because they have no clue how to address their financial concerns. If you can help them, why would they be opposed to accepting your help? Why would they not be interested in hearing what you have to say? They need to think of you as more than just a real estate agent but rather as a consultant, coach, mentor, and wealth advisor. Keep in mind that if they were aware of the benefits of investing in real estate, they would already be investors.

According to data collected by the National Association of Realtors, ten million Americans own rental properties. Investors accounted for 15% of residential transactions in 2017. More people are renting now than at any other point in the past 50 years.

In 2016, 36.6% of household heads rented their homes, close to the 37% who rented their homes in 1965, according to a 2017 report by the Pew Research Center based on data from the Census Bureau. The total number of U.S. households grew by 7.6 million from 2006 to 2016, Pew reported. However, the proportion of households headed by property owners remained relatively flat, while households headed by renters grew by nearly 10% during the same time period. Rising home prices, lingering fears from the housing crash, and larger amounts of student debt are some of the reasons why many Americans see the appeal of renting. Millennials (adults age 35 and younger) are the most likely of all age groups to rent, Pew found. In 2016, 65% of households headed by young adults were renting, up 8 percentage points from 2006. Another reason for renting could be that young adults haven't had time to accumulate enough wealth for a down payment on a house Also, owning a home inhibits moving, and young adults are the most likely age group to move, so they may prefer not to own just yet.

These statistics suggest that rental properties will continue to be in demand for the foreseeable future, rents will continue to rise, and properties that are located in family-friendly neighborhoods or in niche market areas (such as in close proximity to colleges) will continue to appreciate in value.

The investment market will become more attractive as people seek to take charge of their own financial future due to the uncertainty of our economic picture. Historically, real estate has been a safe and solid investment option and more and more people are likely to become investors. Investing in real estate, unlike other forms of investing, is within reach of people from all walks of life. Real estate will continue to be one of the most consistently lucrative and favorable models for wealth building.

While there are many things to consider before making the decision to invest in real estate, new investors will benefit from the advice and expertise of a qualified and knowledgeable real estate agent like you.

So what does this mean for you? If you are planning to work with investors, you need to:

1. Believe that you are the source of investment information and the market expert for your community.
2. Understand the language of the investor. Terms like cash flow, net operating income, debt coverage ratio, and others are explained later in this book. You don't need to become a math whiz, but you do need to have enough knowledge to make the investor comfortable that you are the missing piece of their puzzle.
3. Belong to the local property owners' association and investors' group. These groups are excellent places for finding potential clients.
4. Know and understand the objectives of real estate investors. Keep in mind they think differently from homeowners. They are looking for deals, and they want to make a profit on their investments. Understand the preferred strategy of each client. Do they want to buy and flip, buy and hold, or wholesale for a quick profit? Know their long-term and short-term objectives. The more you know about them, the better you can help them achieve their objectives.
5. Know values and locations so you can find the best deals even before they are listed on the MLS.

Are you convinced that you can grow your business by working with investors and attain financial independence by becoming an investor yourself? If so, keep reading!

KEY POINTS TO REMEMBER:

- Investing in real estate is less risky than putting your money into the stock market, and it offers greater control for the investor.

- Risk can be minimized through careful planning and good advice.

- By becoming an investor yourself, you can build wealth while gaining credibility with your clients.

- Real estate continues to produce income even in economic downturns.

- The long-term prospects for receiving income from rental properties are excellent.

Chapter 2

The Many Benefits of Investing in Real Estate

When you think about it, why do you save or invest in the first place? Every time you earn a commission check, you probably put some of your money into a savings account, retirement account, or maybe bonds, stocks, or gold and hopefully real estate. I assume that you continue to be an agent because you love and believe in your industry, correct? Would you continue to do this if you achieved your own definition of financial freedom? Wouldn't it be great if you did, and you never had to worry about when you would receive your next commission check?

How often do you think about whether you will have enough money to enjoy your retirement? Do you feel confident that you'll be able to travel or do the things on your bucket list?

You are working hard right now so that someday your money will work hard for you. You are counting on your investment portfolio to provide the income to support your needs and lifestyle.

How many people do you know for whom the opposite is true? They make a decent income and perhaps earn more than $100,000 per year but have no real savings or retirement plan and are living day to day. Retirement is just a dream for them. This scenario probably applies to many of your neighbors, friends, and fellow real estate agents.

Although the economic crisis has raised awareness of the importance of retirement planning, millions of Americans still have a dismal outlook in regard to their ability to retire, as you read in Chapter 1.

What about people who dedicated 20 or 30 years of their lives to the workplace only to get laid off because of downsizing? Many of them are having trouble landing a new job with equivalent pay.

Luckily, there is a path out of financial insecurity. Investing in real estate puts you in control of your retirement income. And by helping other people learn how to invest in real estate, you can change their retirement outlook from dismal to optimistic.

Knowing how to provide the best service to clients becomes easier when you understand what is important to them. Here's a quick overview of how different generations view their financial priorities.

DIFFERENT GENERATIONS HAVE DIFFERENT FINANCIAL PRIORITIES

A survey of potential investors was conducted in March 2018 by LendEDU. Respondents were asked the following question:

If you were given $10,000 tax-free and had the ability to invest all of it in one of the following options, which would you choose?

Here are the results of the sample as a whole:

How to Invest $10K?	% of Respondents
Pay down debt	27.3%
Real estate	13.5%
Savings account or CDs	12.2%

How to Invest $10K?	% of Respondents
401(k) or Roth IRA	9.9%
Stock market	7.2%
Child's education	6.9%
Small business	6.2%
Virtual currency	5.1%
Education	3.2%
Other/Unsure	8.5%

Note: We've made slight adjustments to the original answers, combining one low-performing category (P2P loans) into the "Other" category

Paying down debt (27.3%) was by far the most popular response. It's also interesting to see that many people would opt to put the $10k towards their own small business, education, or even digital currencies like Bitcoin, Ethereum, or Litecoin.

Now, here's the same data grouped together by generations:

How to Invest $10K?	Millennials (<35)	Gen X (35–54)	Boomers (55+)
Pay down debt	22.4%	25.3%	33.1%
Real estate	15.1%	14.6%	11.2%
Education	9.9%	1.1%	0.3%
Virtual currency	9.2%	4.0%	3.1%
401(k) or Roth IRA	8.5%	9.4%	11.5%
Other/Unsure	8.1%	8.6%	8.7%
Savings account or CDs	7.7%	10.8%	17.1%
Stock market	6.6%	8.1%	6.7%
Child's education	6.3%	11.3%	2.8%

How to Invest $10K?	Millennials (<35)	Gen X (35–54)	Boomers (55+)
Small business	6.3%	6.7%	5.6%

Interestingly, certain answers had the same popularity for all generations.

All groups were equally interested in investing in their small businesses. The highest response here came from Gen X at 6.7%, but Millennials and Boomers weren't far behind at 6.3% and 5.6% respectively.

In addition, investing in the stock market was pretty consistent as well, with Millennials at 6.6%, Generation X at 8.1%, and Boomers at 6.7%. All these groups were mostly interested in doing this through a financial advisor, though Gen X gave robo-advisors a higher rate of consideration (20%) than other generations did (11% Millennials, 4% Boomers)

Some generational differences are predictable. For instance, barely any Baby Boomers (0.3%) wanted to put $10,000 towards their own education. This makes sense, since many are at or near retirement age already. On the other hand, 9.9% of Millennials opted to invest in their own education.

But here's a situation that might be a bit more peculiar. One would guess that with student debt being at $1.5 trillion in the United States, many Millennials would opt to pay down debt with their $10,000 check. Interestingly, fewer Millennials (22.4%) would have chosen to pay down debt than either Gen X (25.3%) or Boomers (33.1%).

By the same token, Millennials were more likely to choose either real estate (15.1%) or cryptocurrency (9.2%) as an investment. Among Boomers, 11.2% chose real estate and only 3.1% chose cryptocurrency.

Why is it important to understand generational differences in financial priorities? Because knowing how to approach potential clients can make us better agents overall. Since we deal with home buyers and sellers across the generations, we need to consider what they are looking for, not just immediately but over the long term. Clients in different age groups will have different reasons for purchasing real estate as their primary residence or as income-producing property.

Right now people from different generations are buying and selling real estate, and each generation takes a different approach

1. **Why Millennials (22- to 37-year-olds) are interested in investing in real estate**

    Americans have stashed the majority of their investment dollars in the stock market over the years, but there may be a new trend on the horizon. In 2007 nearly two-thirds of Americans were investing in the stock market, but ten years later just over half did. A new generation of investors may be turning to real estate instead.

    RealtyShares recently teamed up with Harris Interactive to publish the Real Estate Investing Report, surveying Americans on their investment preferences. According to the survey results, 55% of Millennials are interested in investing in real estate, the highest percentage among all demographics questioned. Research from Fannie Mae supports these findings, reporting that 85% of Millennials think real estate is a good investment. With such a strong preference for real estate, it is important to understand why Millennials are interested and how they may invest in the future.

    Why is it important to know this? In 2017 Millennials became the largest generation of Americans. According to a recent Pew report, there are 75.4 million Millennials compared with 74.9 million Boomers. As the largest age group in America, Millennials will have the greatest ability to shift the market as their net worth builds, making it crucial to take note of Millennials' views on real estate and investment opportunities overall.

In the RealtyShares survey results, 20% of Millennials
indicated they believe real estate has performed better
than other investment categories since 2000. In fact, Millennials were the age group with the largest percentage
holding that belief. The next highest group to believe real
estate has outperformed the stock market since 2000 is
comprised primarily of Generation X (ages 35–44), 16%
of whom chose real estate as the top performer.

Why are Millennials the generation most likely to value
real estate over the stock market? Many Millennials graduated from college and entered the job market during the
Great Recession. This major economic downturn made it
difficult for Millennials to find jobs. Simultaneously, they
watched the stock market undergo the worst crash since
the Great Depression. Although the burst of the housing
bubble contributed to the stocks' crashing, the stocks may
have lingered in people's minds longer than the housing
market did.

2. **How does Generation X (38- to 54-year-olds) view the
    real estate market?**

    Generation X is the generation that suffered the most
    from the 2009 housing crash and is making a comeback in
    real estate, yet this is also the generation no one is talking
    about. Generation X consists of people born between 1965
    and 1980, after the Boomers and before the Millennials.

    Generation X is sometimes overlooked because it is a
    smaller and usually less influential generation than Boom-
    ers and Millennials. During the 2009 housing crash, many
    people in this generation lost their homes. This is why
    until a few years ago, the majority of Gen Xers have stuck
    to renting homes. But if there's one thing they're proving,
    it's that they no longer want to solely rent property. With a
    stronger U.S. economy, an ever-growing job market, and
    increasing home values, times are changing for Gen Xers.

Why do we need to understand how Gen Xers view real estate investment? Simply put, because Gen Xers make the most money. They bank an average of $106,600 per year, higher than the average for Boomers ($93,800) and Millennials ($82,000). Because they're in their prime money-making years, they can afford to buy property and raise families. Many are trading their smaller homes for larger, more luxurious ones. As this trend continues to be prominent among Gen Xers, it's important to be able to identify other trends such as *where they're moving.*

Providing further support for the above data, a study conducted in 2017 by the National Association of Realtors showed that the number of Gen X home buyers had increased from 26% to 28% within the past year. As this percentage increases over time, we expect this generation's effect on real estate to become more substantial.

It's still important to note that while they make the most money, Gen Xers are not the largest segment of home buyers in the United States. Millennials take the title for that one.

Where and what are Gen Xers looking for in a property? Gen Xers are buying in urban areas, while Millennials are heading to the suburbs. Since they have the highest average income of any generation, the members of Gen X can afford to buy homes in urban areas.

Gen Xers usually look for homes that have several bedrooms, a home office, a living area, a dining area, a storage area, kitchen space, and even a yard. Gen Xers want to buy a property where they can settle in for the long term—a home that will meet most of their current and future needs. Additionally, Gen Xers are moving into areas with good school districts and higher quality-of-life standards to accommodate themselves and their families. After all, Gen Xers are the largest generation who still have kids living at home.

Understanding these trends will allow you to better
understand Gen X's effect on real estate. Do not expect
radical changes to the real estate game because of Gen X
trends, since their effect on real estate is not as substantial
as that of Millennials. But any force can bring changes in
the real estate industry, so it's important to understand
where Gen Xers are buying, the top cities they're moving
into, and their purchasing power, preferences, and overall
characteristics.

**3. Why Baby Boomers love to invest in real estate (age 55
and up)**

One of the key reasons many Boomers invest in property is to protect their assets from the negative impact
of inflation. History shows that property prices tend to
increase at a faster rate than inflation over the long term.
This issue of capital growth and inflation is very important for Boomers, with many of them now pulling their
money out of low-interest savings accounts and investing
it in real estate.

DEPPRO (an organization of depreciation professionals) has found that most Baby Boomer investors are
planning to retire within the next decade and therefore
need to ensure that their investment returns exceed the
inflation rate over this period. While many Boomers also
have savings, they believe their accumulated wealth is not
enough to give them a good quality of life in retirement.
With life expectancies increasing, many Boomers are also
concerned that their savings alone may not provide sufficient funds for a retirement years that could last more
than two decades.

Baby Boomer property investors tend to be well
informed about property investment opportunities and
confident in the future of the real estate market. Many

Boomers have been involved in the property market for many years by owning their own home and therefore understand the long-term capital growth rates that property ownership can deliver. An increasing number of Boomers now view property investment as a low-risk way of building wealth for their retirement in comparison with the stock market.

Many Boomers are attracted to buying investment properties because they can leverage the large amounts of equity they have in their owner-occupied homes to obtain home loans in excess of $1 million to purchase several investment properties.

DEPPRO has provided property depreciation reports for Boomers who own as many as seven or eight investment properties. Many of these investors are well informed about property investment opportunities and how they can fund their investment strategy through tax incentives such as negative gearing and property depreciation.

When you think about your current and past clients, how many fall into each of the generational categories described above? If you brought up the idea of investing in real estate with them, what was their response? Which generation is most likely to be interested in starting a real estate investment business, and how can you help them?

As mentioned in Chapter 1, "investment real estate" is defined as property that generates income or is otherwise intended for investment purposes rather than as a primary residence. It is common for investors to own multiple pieces of real estate, one of which serves as a primary residence while the others are used to generate rental income and profits through price appreciation.

The tax implications for investment real estate are often different from those for residential real estate.

Real estate is a commodity in which people invest their hard-earned money with the expectation that on a short-term or long-term basis they will receive profits. These profits can be achieved in many different ways, including rental income, principal reduction, appreciation, and "flipping" or reselling for a profit.

HOW DOES REAL ESTATE COMPARE WITH OTHER INVESTMENTS?

According to the RealtyShares 2017 Real Estate Investment Survey, from 2000 to 2016 real estate outperformed the stock market approximately 2 to 1, returning 10.71% annually compared with a 5.43% annual total return with the S&P 500 Index. The S&P has rebounded more recently, posting a 12.65% annual return compared with an 11.37% annual return for real estate. Residential real estate as an asset class is a $29 trillion market. The survey found that 40% of Americans weren't sure what type of investment had performed the best since 2000 among stocks, real estate, commodities, bonds, oil, gold, and others.

From my experience, people from all walks of life are interested in investing in real estate but they don't know how to do it or what type of property option is best. It is easy to understand why they think real estate is a winner. As you read this book, you will understand more and more why it is so powerful. What is important is that you need to be the voice for this industry. If you don't become the local expert in real estate investment, then who else will take that role? You have an awesome responsibility, but more importantly, the people you reach out to with this information will thank you for showing that you care.

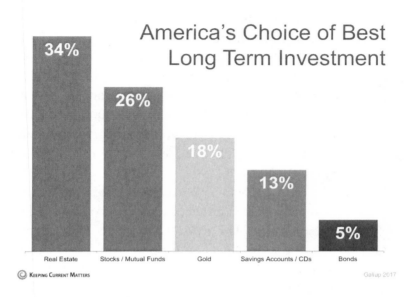

America's Choice of Best Long Term Investment

Real Estate	Stocks / Mutual Funds	Gold	Savings Accounts / CDs	Bonds
34%	26%	18%	13%	5%

KEEPING CURRENT MATTERS   Gallup 2017

Hopefully, you are or will soon become as passionate as I am in believing that real estate is a terrific option to build wealth.

Of all the investments that are within the reach of the average individual, no other investment offers the full range of benefits that are available to real estate investors. Investments such as stocks, bonds, savings accounts, mutual funds, and CDs have pros and cons when it comes to "risk versus return." For comparison purposes, let's look at a scenario that illustrates why investing in real estate is much better for most people than investing in stocks.

Let's assume that you have $50,000 to invest in either stocks or real estate. What would you do? You could use the entire amount to buy $50,000 worth of stocks or you could use the same amount of money for a 20% down payment to purchase real estate with a total value of $250,000. Depending on your area, you might be able to purchase anywhere from one to ten properties that would generate income. Keep in mind that investors generally buy properties that are considered to be good deals (priced 20% to 40% below what they sold for a few years ago). In that regard the initial $50,000 could be controlling much more than $250,000 because the properties are worth more than the purchase price.

If the value of your stocks or real estate went up by, say, 10%, then your stocks would be worth $55,000, giving you $5,000 profit. But your real estate would be worth $275,000, giving you $25,000 profit. That's a 50% return on your initial investment of $50,000.

How much control do you have over the future value of your $50,000 worth of stock? By contrast, could you do anything that might increase the value of your $250,000 worth of property?

Obviously, there is absolutely nothing you can do to increase the value of your stock. However, since your properties are undervalued they may need a little cosmetic work, such as paint, landscaping, new bathroom fixtures, or updated kitchen appliances. There are lots of things you could do to improve a property without spending a lot of money.

Offering	Real Estate	Stocks
Cash Flow (Dividends)	√	√
1031 Exchange	√	
Appreciation	√	√
Leverage	√	√*
Tangible Asset	√	
Owner Control	√	
Principle Reduction	√	
Liquidity	√**	√
Tax Benefits	√	

Now that the economy is on fire, all Americans should be rejoicing in their wealth, right? Wrong! Only 52% of Americans own any stocks, according to a recent Gallup poll.

According to the Federal Reserve, of the 10% of families with the highest income, 92% owned stocks as of 2013 (the latest year for their study), the same level of ownership as in 2007. But ownership slipped for people in the bottom half of the income distribution.

The wealthiest 10% of Americans owned an average of $969,000 in stocks. The next 40% owned $132,000 on average. For the bottom half of families, it was just under $54,000. With over a 200% rise in the S&P 500 since 2009, the wealth gap has clearly widened.

What is happening to the 48% of people that are not in the market? If you have clients who are investing in the stock market you can show them the above chart and they will see that real estate is a better opportunity to build wealth over the long term. When you consider the benefits of the stock market and real estate, and which one do you think is a better investment?

The vast majority of stocks and bonds in the United States are held by a small minority of the population, and most of the stocks are owned by the wealthiest 1%. If you have invested money in the stock market, is the amount significant enough to be able to maintain your current lifestyle in retirement? Would you be able to live off your investments right now if you could no longer make a living from what you are doing now?

Now let's assume your stock does well and the shares you purchased double in value. Your $50,000 in stock is now worth $100,000. What can you do with the equity? Just one thing: sell your stock. Of course, that will create capital gains tax liability and reduce the amount that is left to invest now or in the future.

By contrast, assume that your $250,000 property is now worth $500,000. What can you do to take advantage of the equity? Yes, you could sell the property, but that may not be the smartest option. Keep in mind the benefits your rental property is providing in the form of cash flow, appreciation, tax advantages, and principal reduction, to name a few. Why would anyone want to sell a property that is increasing in value and generating income at the same time? What's more, if you did sell it, you would have to pay capital gains tax on the profit.

A better option to take advantage of the equity would be to refinance the property or do a 1031 tax-deferred exchange (explained later in this chapter). The money would not be taxable and could be used to purchase other properties, such as a vacation home or additional investment properties.

Or how about this scenario: let's say you go back to your bank and ask for an 80% loan-to-value mortgage of $400,000. After paying off your original $200,000 loan, you would still have $200,000 that can be used as down payments to purchase more properties. That amount could give you $800,000 in purchasing power. The property you purchased initially is now worth $500,000 and you have acquired additional property worth $800,000 for a combined real estate portfolio of $1,300,000. What a great concept.

Can you now see the power of investing in real estate compared with buying stock? This is the power of leverage hard at work. To simplify this explanation the amount of principal reduction was not taken into consideration, but it would have made the scenario even better.

Clearly real estate is head and shoulders above any other investment. Imagine giving your stockbroker the following instructions:

"I would like to buy some stock, but I can only pay 20% down. I would like the stock to go up in value over time and also pay dividends. When the stock goes up, I may want to pull tax-free cash out of it and still keep the stock. At some point I may also want to sell it and pay no taxes and then buy other stocks with

the profit from the sale. Oh, and by the way, I would also like a tax deduction every year as long as I own this stock for the next 27½ years." (Note: A residential property can be depreciated for tax purposes for 27½ years and a commercial property for 39 years.)

What do you think your broker's reaction would be? He or she would probably laugh out loud, thinking you were making a joke.

Over the 40 years I have been investing in real estate, I have enjoyed having a high level of control over my investments. I can take steps to raise the value of my property and to increase the income it generates. By contrast, I lost most of the money I invested in the stock market because I did not understand it and had to rely on my broker for advice. I even had to pay a commission to sell the stuff. But with real estate my investment will always be worth something.

WHY SHOULD YOU INVEST IN REAL ESTATE?

You probably have figured out by now that I am a great believer in owning real estate. In fact, I can't think of any other investment that has so much potential to generate wealth. And I am not alone in this opinion.

When a potential client calls you and mentions that he or she is thinking about investing in real estate, what advice will you offer? If you own at least one rental property, you will create instant credibility and you can start telling them about the wonderful benefits of investing in real estate.

But maybe you don't own a rental property yet. Perhaps you are like hundreds of thousands of people who have thought about buying investment property but dismissed it as a fantasy. If so, the question you should be asking yourself right now is "Why not?"

Have you ever listed and sold a property for well below market value because it needed minor remodeling such as an updated kitchen, flooring, bathroom fixtures, and paint? What was your commission on the sale? Would your commission have been any different if you had been the purchaser? No.

As an agent, you know that real estate is an effective method of making money not only for yourself but for your clients, whether they are high-net-worth individuals, salaried employees, or hourly wage earners.

As a real estate agent you have a tremendous opportunity to help yourself and your clients generate wealth. If you are not yet an investor, you can begin mastering the art of real estate investment by buying your first rental property. Then watch your expertise grow to a whole new level as you gain first-hand experience as an investor.

REAL ESTATE NAMED AS TOP INVESTMENT BY MOST SUBGROUPS, ESPECIALLY WESTERNERS

Real estate is the top-ranking type of investment among most subgroups of Americans, across gender, age, and income categories—with a few notable exceptions. Young adults and residents of the East and Midwest are about equally likely to name stocks and real estate, and lower-income Americans' top choice is a tie between real estate and gold.

The selection of stocks as the best investment is fairly even by gender and age but differs by household income. The percentage who select stocks increases with income, from 19% among those earning less than $35,000 annually to 33% among those earning $75,000 or more

Perceptions of Best Long-Term Investment Among U.S. Subgroups:

Which of the following do you think is the best long-term investment: bonds, real estate, savings accounts or CDs, stocks or mutual funds, or gold?

	Real estate	Stocks	Gold	Savings accounts/ CDs	Bonds
	%	%	%	%	%
Gender					
Men	35	27	18	10	7
Women	33	25	15	19	6
Age					
18 to 34	29	28	11	21	9
35 to 54	37	25	18	15	4
55 and older	34	26	21	10	7
Income					
$75,000 and over	43	33	12	5	6
$35,000 to $74,999	33	23	17	18	6
Less than $35,000	25	19	24	20	8
Region					
East	36	34	11	14	4
Midwest	27	28	19	19	6
South	29	24	20	15	7
West	45	21	14	10	8

GALLUP, APRIL 2-11, 2018

SHORT-TERM PROFITS AND LONG-TERM EQUITY

Historically, real estate has shown consistent growth in value. This growth occurs even during periods when other investment choices are less desirable.

In the short term, real estate can be a wonderful investment because of the money that can be made by flipping. For example, you might pay $50,000 to purchase a home that needs work. Your total cost for rehabbing, holding cost, commissions, and so on is $25,000. Six months later, you sell the home for $100,000, earning a profit of $25,000 (less selling costs). How many people do you know who can make that kind of money in such a short time? Some people work for an entire year without earning $25,000.

Rental property, on the other hand, works well as a long-term purchase. When you buy rental property, your tenant ultimately is the one who reduces your mortgage balance. Building equity is the name of the game, and increased net worth is the outcome.

Real estate investors need to figure out whether they are looking for short-term profits so they can make a living or long-term equity so they can build wealth. Their answer will determine the type of property they buy.

Additionally, income-producing properties can serve different purposes for different investors. For example, a prudent way to supplement retirement income might be to start acquiring rental properties long before age 65 so that when the mortgages are paid off the investor can live off the residual income during retirement.

EQUITY BUILD UP

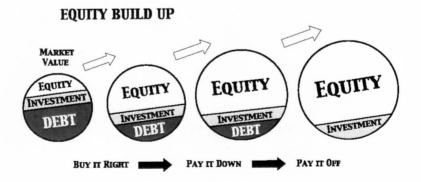

For a different investor, a more aggressive plan might be a better choice. This type of person might want to acquire a sizable portfolio of properties that generate enough cash flow that he or she will not have to rely on income from the workplace—the American dream of entrepreneurship in action.

BENEFITS OF INVESTING IN REAL ESTATE

When done carefully and intelligently, investing in real estate can yield substantial benefits that cannot be achieved through any other type of investment. Here are just a few reasons why real estate is one of the best investments around: leverage, positive cash flow, wealth building, hedge against inflation, appreciation, portfolio diversification, tax deductions, 1031 exchange, tax-free cash refinance, and being your own boss. Each of these benefits is described below.

Leverage

Leverage is the use of borrowed funds to finance and accumulate real estate. Leveraging lets the investor use other people's money (OPM) to acquire properties. This is one of the most powerful tools investors can utilize because it allows them to purchase and finance increasing numbers of properties. Through leverage, they can substantially increase their return on investment (ROI). Gaining access to OPM is easy if the investor has a solid financial statement and is creditworthy.

Few other investment options allow a person to make money on borrowed money. Based on a typical down payment of 10% to 20%, the potential profit on real estate is considerably greater than the profit for a non-leveraged investment such as stocks or mutual funds. You can't use leverage to buy stocks unless you have a significant cash reserve and a very strong financial statement. Margin is borrowing money from your broker to buy stock and using the stock as collateral.

Positive cash flow

Real estate should be a cash-generating investment over the long term. When you rent a property to a qualified tenant (having done due diligence in tenant selection to minimize risk), the rent payments can be applied to the mortgage, taxes, insurance, and maintenance. After these expenses are paid, the investment provides cash flow or residual income. When the property is paid in full, it can be an excellent source of retirement income.

Wealth building

Historically real estate has increased in value and should continue to do so over time. In later chapters we will cover what classifies a property as a good investment that will build wealth over time, how and where to find such properties, and how to fund investment property.

What defines a good investment property? A real estate investment can build wealth in the following ways:

- *Appreciation:* As property values rise, the difference between what is owed and what the property is worth will increase.

- *Cash flow:* When a property is rented for income, there should be more income coming in than expenses going out.

- *Tax benefits:* Deductions should offset the investor's tax liability for income from other sources (salary and other investments). Anyone contemplating the purchase of real estate should seek the services of a competent legal professional and tax advisor.

- *Principle reduction:* As you make payments on a mortgage, each month the amount owed decreases slightly until the last payment is made and the loan is paid in full.

A hedge against inflation

Real estate is one of the few assets that react proportionately to inflation. As inflation occurs, housing values increase and rents go up. Although some people see real estate as a risky investment, I believe real estate is one of the only safe investments left, given our ongoing financial crisis. Unlike the stock market, you can't lose all of the money you have invested in a rental property.

Appreciation

Real estate tends to go up and down in value, but the long-term trend is upward. Why? The answer involves supply and demand. As Mark Twain said, "Buy land—they're not making any more of it."

As long as the population of the United States continues to rise, good rental properties will always be in demand. And rents will tend to go up as well, especially if the property is well maintained and situated in a desirable area.

Diversification

We can agree that having a diversified portfolio is a good thing. To be well diversified, a financial portfolio should include different kinds of assets, which may include some or all of the following: stocks, bonds, real estate, cash, and other items of value (such as a coin collection, rare books, art, and so on). What seems to be missing in many portfolios is real estate. This absence offers an opportunity for real estate agents to build their client lists.

As a part of an investment portfolio, real estate allows the client to avoid putting all their eggs in one basket. Most investment professionals agree that diversification is a critical component of reaching long-range financial goals while minimizing risk. The key to successful diversification is to find a happy medium between risk and return.

Investments in each of the following asset categories do different things for you:

- Stocks help your portfolio grow.

- Bonds bring you income.

- Cash gives your portfolio security and stability.

- Real estate provides both a hedge against inflation and low "correlation" to stocks—in other words, the value of your real estate may rise during times when stock values fall.

Tax deductions

When your accountant prepared your income tax returns last year, how happy were you with the amount of taxes you paid? More than likely, you feel that you paid too much tax because you didn't have enough deductions. Most of your clients, friends, and associates probably feel the same way.

Don't get me wrong—I think paying taxes is a good thing because it means I am making money. But I believe in paying no more than my fair share of taxes. The amount of money we make is less important than how much we get to keep.

One of the best things about being a real estate investor is the many federal income tax advantages that become available to you. The Internal Revenue Service treats rental properties as a business venture, and therefore expenses involved in being a landlord are tax deductible. You may already be aware of some of the following deductions:

- Depreciation – After determining the cost or other tax basis for the rental property as a whole, you must allocate the basis amount among the various types of property you're renting. When we speak of types of property, we refer to certain components of your rental, such as the land, the building itself, and personal property such as the stove, refrigerator, and dishwasher you provide with the rental, and so on.

Why this effort to divide your tax basis between property types? Because they are each depreciated using different rules.

Below are the most common divisions of tax basis for a rental property, followed by explanations of the different methods of depreciation that generally apply:

Type of Property	Method of Depreciation	Useful Life in Years
Land	Not allowed	N/A
Residential rental real estate	Straight line	27.5
Commercial real estate	Straight line	39
Shrubbery, fences, driveways, etc.	150% declining balance	15
Appliances etc.	200% declining balance	5

In *straight-line* depreciation, the cost basis is spread evenly over the tax life of the property. For example, a residential rental building with a cost basis of $120,000 would generate depreciation of $4,363 per year ($120,000/27.5 years). (This does not include personal property, land improvement or land, only the actual property.)

In the year that the rental is first placed in service (rented), your deduction is prorated based on the number of months that the property is rented or held out for rent, with 1/2 month for the first month. If the building in the example above is placed in service in August, you can take a deduction for 4½ months' worth of depreciation, amounting to $1,636.12 (4.5 X $4,363/12).

Recovery percentages for five-year personal property: This kind of depreciation is calculated by multiplying the rate of the straight-line depreciation by the adjusted balance of the property at the start of each year over the remaining life of the property. To make matters somewhat easier, the IRS and others publish tables of percentages that can be applied to the original cost to determine yearly depreciation. For instance, below are annual depreciations for personal property with the 200% declining balance:

Year	Percentage
1	20.00
2	32.00
3	19.20
4	11.52
5	11.52
6	5.76
Total	100%

Examples: The 200% declining balance depreciation on $2,000 worth of appliances used in a rental would be $384 in Year 3 ($2,000 X .192).

Examples of personal property that can be depreciated over five years might include a snow blower, lawn mower, carpet, furniture, computer, and so on.

Examples of land improvements that can be depreciated over 15 years are sidewalks, fences, landscaping, and shrubbery.

Taxes and insurance on the property are deductible.

Expenses for repairs and upkeep are deductible.

Fees paid to a property management company and to your attorney and accountant are deductible. (By the way, you should find an accountant who is knowledgeable about tax laws related to real estate investment. My guess is that if you had your tax returns prepared by 100 accountants you would get 100 different tax returns.)

THE FOLLOWING ITEMS ALSO ARE DEDUCTIBLE:

- Home office – Anyone who works from home can take the home office deduction. This means that a portion of the expenses you pay for your primary residence, such as mortgage payments, tax and insurance, utility payments, and so on, can be deducted as home office expenses.

- Office supplies, cell phone for business, stationery, stamps, pencils, paper clips and so on. Just about anything purchased for the office may be deductible if it is used for your real estate business.

- Business expenses – You can deduct the cost of subscriptions, dues, and fees for membership in real estate organizations such as property owners' or investors' groups as well as expenses for attending real estate conventions.

- Mileage – You can deduct mileage if your personal vehicle is used for business purposes.

- Real estate professional – For tax purposes, anyone (not just a full-time real estate agent) can be considered a "real estate professional" if they spend at least 750 hours per year involved in real property trades and businesses and if more than half (at least 51%) of the personal services they perform during the year involve real property trades and businesses. One of the biggest benefits of investing in real estate is the ability to offset real estate paper losses (primarily caused by depreciation) against other income. If you meet the IRS criteria to qualify as a real estate professional, then 100% of your paper real estate losses may be used to offset your other income, reducing the amount you owe the government. This is a very powerful tool that should be emphasized with potential/current investors who may not be aware of it.

Even those investors who do not qualify as real estate professionals for IRS purposes can deduct up to $25,000 of their rental real estate losses from other income if they actively participate in their real estate business.

Keep in mind that tax rules involving real estate are complicated. For example, an investor who owns multiple rental properties will need to file a special form with the IRS if they want to treat all of their real estate interests as a single activity for tax purposes. If they don't do this, each rental property will count as a separate business. As I mentioned before, anyone who is thinking about investing in real estate should seek the advice of a qualified tax attorney or accountant.

Tax changes that will affect property owners

Disclaimer: The author has not verified the information pertaining to the 2018 tax changes and readers should rely solely on the expertise of their own tax advisor or attorney. It is important to keep up with tax changes that may impact investors from year to year.

In 2017 Congress approved sweeping tax cuts and tax reform that had not been tackled by the federal government in over 30 years (since the Tax Reform Act of 1986). The tax law formally referred to as "The Tax Cuts and Jobs Act" went into effect January 1, 2018. This section provides up-to-date information along with a summary of how the tax law provisions will affect homeowners and real estate investors who own all types of investment property. Although we will not delve into tax issues not associated with real estate, there are many new tax provisions that will be important for real estate investors to understand.

Investment property owners will continue to be able to defer capital gain taxes using 1031 tax-deferred exchanges that have been in the tax code since 1921. No new restrictions on 1031 exchanges of real property were made in the new tax law. However, the new tax law repeals 1031 exchanges for all other types of property that are not real property. This means 1031 exchanges of personal property, collectibles, aircraft, franchise rights, rental cars, trucks, heavy equipment, and machinery, etc. are no longer permitted.

Some investors and private equity firms will not have to reclassify "carried interest" compensation from the lower-taxed capital gains tax rate to the higher ordinary income tax rates. However, to qualify for the lower capital gains tax rate on "carried interest," investors will have to hold these assets for three (3) years instead of the former one (1) year holding period.

Some property owners such as farmers, ranchers, and other business owners will receive a new tax advantage with the ability to immediately write off the cost of new investments in personal property, a procedure that is commonly referred to as full or immediate expensing. This new provision will be part of the tax law for five (5) years and then will taper off. There are significant concerns that these business and property owners will face a "tax cliff" and higher taxes when the immediate expensing provision expires.

Investment property owners can continue to deduct net interest expense, but investment property owners must elect out of the new interest disallowance tax rules. The new interest limit is effective in 2018 and applies to existing debt. The interest limit and the real estate election applies at the entity level.

The new tax law continues the current depreciation rules for real estate. However, property owners opting to use the real estate exception to the interest limit must depreciate real property under slightly longer recovery periods of 40 years for a nonresidential property, 30 years for a residential rental property, and 20 years for qualified interior improvements. Longer depreciation schedules can have a negative impact on the return on investment (ROI), and property owners will need to take into account these longer depreciation schedules if they elect to use the new real estate exception to the interest limit.

The tax law creates a new tax deduction of 20% for pass-through businesses. For taxpayers with incomes above certain thresholds, the 20% deduction is limited to the greater of the following: (1) 50% of the W-2 wages paid by the business or (2) 25% of the W-2 wages paid by the business, plus 2.5% of the unadjusted basis, immediately after acquisition, of depreciable property (which includes structures, but not land). Estates and trusts are eligible for the pass-through benefit. The 20% pass-through deduction begins to phase out at $315,000 for married couples filing jointly.

The new tax law restricts taxpayers from deducting losses incurred in an active trade or business from wage income or portfolio income. This change applies to existing investment and became effective in 2018.

State and local taxes paid in respect to carrying on a trade or business, or in an activity related to the production of income, continue to remain deductible. Accordingly, a rental property owner can deduct property taxes associated with a business asset, such as any type of rental property.

The new tax law retains the 20% tax credit for the rehabilitation of historically certified structures, but taxpayers must claim the credit over a five-year time period.

Below are the federal income tax brackets for 2018 taxes, which are due in April 2019.

2018 Marginal Tax Rates
Taxable Income by Filing Status

Marginal Tax Rate	Single	Married Filing Jointly	Head of Household	Married Filing Separately
10%	$0–$9,525	$0–$19,050	$0–$13,600	$0–$9,525
12%	$9,526–$38,700	$19,051–$77,400	$13,601–$51,800	$9,526–$38,700
22%	$38,701–$82,500	$77,401–$165,000	$51,801–$82,500	$38,701–$82,500
24%	$82,501–$157,500	$165,001–$315,000	$82,501–$157,500	$82,501–$157,500
32%	$157,501–$200,000	$315,001–$400,000	$157,501–$200,000	$157,501–$200,000
35%	$200,001–$500,000	$400,001–$600,000	$200,001–$500,000	$200,001–$300,000
37%	$500,001 and over	$600,001 and over	$500,001 and over	$300,001 and over

1031 tax-deferred exchange

If a real estate investment is no longer meeting the investor's needs or the investor wants to increase leverage and free up equity, a 1031 tax-deferred exchange should be considered. In this type of arrangement, the investor exchanges the property for a more expensive one or for more than one property and defers payment of taxes on the capital gains. It is best to seek the advice of a tax attorney or accountant to determine whether this is the best course of action for your situation.

Refinancing

As rents and property values continue to go up, refinancing can be used to purchase additional properties if the appraisal will substantiate the value. For example, let's say a property appraises for $100,000 and has a mortgage balance of $40,000. With a loan-to-value (LTV) ratio of 80%, the amount that you can pull out by refinancing your mortgage is $40,000 less refinance expenses.

Is it better to pay off the loan or to refinance? The answer depends on the investor's age, acquisition objectives, and other factors.

Being your own boss

One of the most powerful advantages of owning real estate is the fact that you become your own boss. As a real estate investor you get to choose which properties you will invest in, which tenants you will rent to, how much rent you will charge, and how you will manage and maintain the property. This is very different from working at a job where you have to do what your supervisor wants you to do. And when you work hard at a job you are making the owner of the company wealthy, not you.

Lots of people buy stocks in companies or shares in mutual funds without understanding why the value of their investment goes up or down. Who knows what the CEO or other people in the company are doing with your money? But as a real estate investor you are in control, and the entire responsibility for the success or failure of your investment rests with you.

Real estate is a tangible asset. You can see it, drive by it, and improve it. You get to decide what to do or not do with it, and you will reap the benefits of your decisions.

A GREAT TRACK RECORD FOR REAL ESTATE

About 90% of those who are considered millionaires made their money through real estate. On February 27, 2012, Warren Buffett (the "Oracle of Omaha") described single-family homes as a very attractive investment. He said he would buy up "a couple hundred thousand" single-family homes if it were practical to do so. If houses are purchased at low rates and held for a long time, Buffett explained, they are even better than stocks.

Once you fully understand the major advantages of investing in real estate, it is easy to conclude that few other investment options can compete with it. Think about the power of owning just five duplexes that are paid off and worth $100,000 each, earning a total of $10,000 a month ($1,000 per unit) in gross rent. Keep in mind that ultimately the tenants paid off the debt on those properties and you now own half a million dollars' worth of real estate. What a concept!

Note: I am aware that real estate prices in your community may be much higher than they are in Omaha, but the concepts described throughout this book still apply. I think it is a huge mistake to purchase real estate with the only goal being appreciation. Many investors have lost everything they had when they applied this strategy. Keep in mind that appreciation is a goal along with cash flow, principal reduction, and tax benefits. All four are important.

Perhaps clients in your community who would like to invest with your help should look at communities where the property values are more desirable. Why not network with agents that you may know and at least get a referral?

If you are asked whether this is a good time to buy real estate, how will you respond? Think about how property values and rent have gone up since 2008. If you had owned one house and collected rent on three other properties over the past ten years, would you be better off today? Think about if you owned 10 properties how amazing it would have been.

After reading this chapter, are you convinced that you can generate wealth for yourself by becoming an investor (if you are not one already) and for your clients as well? Are you excited about the opportunity to grow your business and increase your income stream? If you choose to specialize and work only with investors, you can make a very good living as an "investor-friendly" real estate agent. But if you also work with homeowners, you have a wonderful opportunity to introduce them to the world of real estate investment.

KEY POINTS TO REMEMBER:

- The main reason people save or invest part of their earnings is to maintain their current lifestyle during retirement.

- Understanding how different generations approach buying and selling real estate can help you work with them more effectively.

- As an investment, real estate offers more profit, greater control, and lower risk than stocks.

- Improving undervalued properties and selling them can bring substantial short-term profits, while holding income-producing property for decades builds wealth over the long term.

- Owners of rental property can control their retirement income or become less dependent on making a living from the workplace.

- Real estate investments can provide benefits that include leverage, positive cash flow, wealth building, hedge against inflation, appreciation, portfolio diversification, tax deductions, 1031 exchange or tax-free cash refinance, and being your own boss.

CHAPTER 3

YOUR ROLE AS AN AGENT— HOW TO BRING VALUE AN INVESTOR EXPECTS

When someone asks you what you do for a living, what do you say? Most likely you tell them, "I'm a real estate agent" or "I help people buy and sell houses."

Would that type of answer be helpful to someone who wants to invest in real estate? Probably not, because you haven't mentioned anything that sets you apart from most of the other real estate agents in your area.

If you are looking to start a real estate investment business, are you the best agent to represent yourself?

How about describing yourself in a way that will make an impact and attract investors? You could say that you are a real estate consultant (or coach, mentor, wealth advisor) and you help clients generate wealth. You work with clients who invest in real estate. You provide information, analysis, and recommendations of real estate options. All of these responses would get the attention of a potential investor because you have presented yourself as a specialist instead of a generalist.

My idea of an investor-friendly real estate agent is one who sees things others don't see... one who has an eye for an opportunity – for spotting "the deal."

Here's another way to put it. Real estate agents have different credentials, just as doctors do. If you have a problem with your heart, would you make an appointment with an oncologist, gynecologist, or cardiologist? Would you want to find out about your doctor's training and credentials?

WHAT DO INVESTORS EXPECT FROM THEIR AGENT?

If someone wants to invest in real estate, will their expectations differ from those of someone who wants to buy or sell a personal residence? Of course they will. A potential investor will expect you to understand different types of investments, be able to help them analyze whether a property will be a good investment, and so on.

You can do the following things to ensure that you will bring added value to clients who want to invest in real estate (thereby separating yourself from other real estate agents):

- You are an investor and know more about this topic than they do.

- You have knowledge and experience that other Realtors do not possess.

- You have credibility and practice what you preach (you can offer life experiences).

- You see yourself as a mentor, coach, consultant, or wealth advisor.

- You see opportunities others don't see, having that "eagle eye."

- You are the fastest path to help them accomplish their wealth-building objectives.

- You can suggest ways to improve property values.

- You understand the tax benefits of owning real estate.

- You know how to analyze a property.

- You know the real estate investment options available to clients.

- You understand 1031 Exchanges and IRAs.

- You know areas, values, and comps.

- You know how to search MLS for deals.

- You can help them make lots of money.

- You have established relationships with banks/lenders, attorneys, accountants, contractors, and others who deal with investors.

- You know your state's landlord-tenant laws (www. thelpa.com/lpalllaw.html).

- You know the real estate investment options available to them.

- You meet annually with clients to review their real estate portfolio.

- You help them stay on course for the long term.

Bottom line: To be taken seriously as a real estate consultant or wealth advisor, you will need to provide services that other real estate agents do not offer.

Would you be comfortable working with investors if you acquired the knowledge mentioned above? Would your skill set separate you from other real estate agents who lack this knowledge? If you are willing to go the extra mile to develop this skill set, you can become the missing piece of the puzzle who helps your clients build wealth by investing in real estate.

The greater your willingness to go beyond your comfort zone, the sooner your success will materialize. You can start by thinking of yourself as a real estate wealth advisor rather than as a real estate agent.

Your real estate license gave you the opportunity to represent buyers and sellers in a real estate transaction in exchange for a commission. By itself, however, it did not give you the expertise investors are expecting from their real estate agent. If you lack this knowledge but some of your clients are using you anyway to help them buy investment properties, they are doing it because they like you, trust you, and have a relationship with you, not because they value your knowledge.

Think about how much better you could help these same clients after acquiring specialized knowledge. You would become irreplaceable. Would they buy more properties? You can count on it.

TIME FOR A MIND SHIFT

Unless you took an investment class, your real estate training did not prepare you to work with investors. Most real estate agents lack this knowledge, and maybe that is why so few of us understand that real estate is one of the best investment options to generate wealth.

Does your broker offer any training in working with investors? Probably not.

Does the top producer in your office work with investors or own any investment properties? If not, why not?

You may be an extremely talented real estate agent who has built a sizable client base and sold a lot of properties. Of the properties you sold, how many were not owner occupied? If the answer is "none" or "just a few," why aren't you taking full advantage of what this industry has to offer?

How many of your associates make a terrific living from commissions but are paying more than their fair share of taxes because they don't have enough tax deductions? With all of the benefits that real estate offers, I was surprised to read in an industry publication recently that less than 3% of real estate agents own at least one investment property.

After reading Chapter 2, you should be familiar with the benefits of investing in real estate. Here's a brief review:

1. Buy properties at huge discounts (instant equity)
2. Principle reduction through monthly rent payments
3. Appreciation of property values
4. Rehab and fix-up profits (flipping)
5. Cash flow or residual income
6. Numerous tax deductions
7. Ability to pyramid gains through 1031 tax-free exchanges
8. Ability to grow net worth and pay no tax until you sell
9. Availability of leverage to make purchases if you are creditworthy, have a solid financial statement, and own some type of collateral

BECOME AN ADVOCATE FOR YOUR INDUSTRY

Unless a financial advisor owns investment properties, they are unlikely to be bullish on real estate. What is their compensation for recommending real estate?

Are there better ways to make money while minimizing risk? I agree that it makes sense to be diversified, but I haven't found a better option than real estate investing.

We can make a living by helping clients buy and sell their personal residences, but we can generate wealth by investing in real estate. Here's the bottom line: When you don't own real estate, it is extremely difficult to accumulate net worth.

If you are not an investor, it's time to invest in yourself. Instead of working so hard for your money, why not let your money work hard for you?

Think of real estate as a retirement tool and accumulate as much real estate as you can. Set a goal to accumulate at least $1 million in real estate.

Decide that it is not a bad thing to work with investors and then watch your business volume and income grow to levels you never imagined. When you help your clients generate wealth, they will thank you.

WORKING WITH INVESTORS IS LIKE CULTIVATING A GARDEN AND WATCHING IT GROW

Since I got my license in 1998, I have sold a lot of properties for my clients and bought and sold a fair amount of my own properties. I continue to do a fair amount of business, yet I don't consider myself to be any better than other agents.

My business hasn't grown as a result of doing phone duty or through luck but rather because I am an investor with the credentials to help clients generate wealth. I have the mindset of an investor instead of a real estate agent. It is much easier to gain credibility with investors when you can proudly say you are an investor.

If you are not an investor, the first and most important sale is the one you make to yourself— When you subscribe to what you recommend to others, you become more believable.

If someone asks you whether you own any rentals or have flipped a property, wouldn't it be better to be able to enthusiastically say "Yes" instead of "No"?

Perhaps you have worked with one or more investors in the past but you didn't enjoy the experience. Do you prefer to work with customers who are likely to buy an expensive home rather than with traditional investors who are primarily looking for a deal? Keep in mind that even if the commissions are smaller when you work with investors, repeat business is the norm.

There are many agents in every real estate company who work hard and are knowledgeable and experienced but are struggling to make a living. They don't do a lot of business and are always looking for more customers. Why are they missing out on potential income by overlooking clients who are investors?

If you are an agent who for some reason is not working with investors, you are not alone. The old 80/20 rule applies here, just as it does in so many other aspects of life. I have even heard some people say it is more like 90/10. A few of us are making most of the income by working with investors while the vast majority of agents are earning less.

The company I am associated with recently merged and now has more than 800 agents, and only a handful of them work mainly as a residential investment specialist. How many investor-friendly agents are in your company? Why not become the go-to agent and make your mark in this "niche" market? You will always be relevant, as this industry is changing rapidly.

You can have tremendous influence in helping investors make profitable decisions. I believe a knowledgeable agent is the most important member of an investor's team. (The roles of other members of the team will be discussed in later chapters.)

If your client base consists mainly of buyers and sellers of owner-occupied properties, why not expand your knowledge and upgrade your skills so you can work with investors? Here are some points to keep in mind:

1. Investors expect their real estate agent to be knowledgeable. It helps if you are also an investor (even on a small scale) because it means you have gone through the process.

2. Investors expect their real estate agent to be comfortable writing multiple offers. You must be willing to write a low-ball offer even if you think it is a waste of time. At some point, if they don't listen to you, you must decide if you want to work with them or not.

3. Investors expect their real estate agent to have some experience helping investors. They gain comfort from knowing they are in good hands. Keep in mind that this is not playtime. Some of your clients will be making their biggest financial investment ever.

4. Investors expect their real estate agent to have a good reputation in this area of the market. Success breeds success. When you do a good job for one client, referrals become the norm. Most of my clients have come to me through referrals.

5. Investors expect their real estate agent to be honest with them. I would rather lose a deal than not tell the truth. You must be able to put yourself in the client's shoes when you are evaluating a potential deal. Ask yourself whether it make sense financially. Will it accomplish their objective if they intend to flip the property? Will their spread be enough to make it worthwhile?

6. Investors want their agent to behave with integrity. They expect you to do the right thing.

7. Investors expect you to find deals that meet their needs and objectives, and they value your guidance and expertise. For example, cash flow is more important to some buyers than to others. You will need to listen carefully so you understand what they're looking for.

WHY SHOULD YOU WORK WITH INVESTORS?

First and foremost, investors have great potential for repeat business. How much repeat business have you seen from buyers or sellers of owner-occupied property? Did they remember your name when it was time to list their home? A buyer of owner-occupied property may utilize your services every five to seven years if you are lucky, while investors will use you over and over if you can bring them deals that make sense. When you are working with investors, repeat business is the norm.

One of the most rewarding referrals I ever received has been my client since 2005. That same client has purchased more than 100 properties in the past nine years. One year he made $300,000 by flipping properties. If your clients consider you valuable, you can expect repeat business and one referral after another.

Investors are not as emotional as home buyers. Many times they will write an offer right on the spot. A 10-minute showing can result in an accepted offer.

Investors are not as concerned about minor cosmetic details as home buyers are. Their focus is on the financial numbers and whether they can make money from their investment by flipping it or holding it as a long-term rental.

Not only will you earn a commission when an investor buys a property that they intend to flip, but also when they sell it. If they buy a property for $100,000 and sell it for $200,000, you end up with $300,000 volume. Ten clients that flip as in this example would bring you $3,000,000 in additional volume.

It's not necessary to work with a lot of investors. You just need to work with the right ones who have the financial means to continue investing. In comparison with homeowners who buy one property at a time, your investor clients will keep you very busy writing a lot of offers. You won't have to spend time waiting for the phone to ring or doing open houses.

Working with investors is not only financially rewarding but also deeply satisfying. When you have earned their trust, they will listen to your advice and be grateful to you because you are helping them make a good living and build wealth. Often you are bringing them more value than their financial planner or stockbroker. You won't have to negotiate your commission because they know that you have helped them make money.

Investors are expecting you to find great deals for them on the MLS or through other sources even before the properties are listed. When they want you to write a low-ball offer, you may have to advise them that the seller will probably receive multiple offers including some that are higher than the asking price, so their offer will probably be rejected. But the outcome may surprise you, as it has surprised me on several occasions.

If you find yourself working with an investor who is unreasonable, you will have to make a decision about whether or not to continue working with that person. If you allow them to gain control, they will eat a lot of your time by having you write offers that do not materialize. Providing good comparables is imperative.

BECOME IRREPLACEABLE TO YOUR CLIENTS

Your goal should be to become invaluable. Your clients need to know that the fastest way to accomplish their objectives is through you. You should be seen as their mentor, coach, or wealth builder.

How many lives will you touch along the way as you help your clients achieve financial freedom?

You know the neighborhoods and are familiar with property values. You know where to find an undervalued property. Your problem should be which client you will call first when you find out about a great deal.

Here are a few ways you can make yourself irreplaceable to your investor clients:

1. Suggest sources of financing. Recommend banks that are friendly and are willing to issue loans on investment properties. In my experience, local banks are much easier to work with than nationwide banks such as US Bank, Bank of the West, or Wells Fargo.

2. Provide information that will help your client decide whether an undervalued property is a good deal. Estimate the potential rent for the property. In Omaha, Nebraska, rents have gone up by at least $150 to $200 since 2014, as I'm sure they have in your community. In 2019 a 2-bedroom property rents for $750 to $900 or more and a 3-bedroom for $1050 to $1300 or more. When rental properties are close to a university, medical school, or law school, the rents can be extraordinary. I own a 4-bedroom, 2-bath property close to a medical school that rents for $1,400. The purchase price was $32,000 with improvements of an additional $30,000. I consider that a pretty good return on my investment.

3. Recommend lawyers who specialize in real estate, accountants, contractors, and property managers.

4. Be prepared to handle a multitude of details after the offer has been accepted (such as contractor inspections, home inspections, termite inspections, and surveys).

5. Provide information about what is going on in your market area, including neighborhoods that may be improving or declining.

6. Suggest simple cosmetic things your client can do to increase the value of their property, such as the following.

Interior:

- ☐ Replace wall-to-wall carpeting
- ☐ Refinish wood floors
- ☐ Repair doors and doorknobs
- ☐ Replace window blinds
- ☐ Update light fixtures
- ☐ Replace light switches and outlets
- ☐ Replace registers
- ☐ Paint/refinish/replace cabinets and install new hardware
- ☐ Replace countertops
- ☐ Install new sink or faucet
- ☐ Replace ceramic tile/backsplash

Exterior:

- ☐ Mulch flower beds, plant bushes, etc.
- ☐ Fix driveway and sidewalks
- ☐ Repair/paint front door
- ☐ Repair/paint/replace gutters
- ☐ Paint house
- ☐ Add shutters

I'm sure you can think of others.

As the investor-friendly real estate agent in your company or community, you will become a trusted partner and the missing piece of the puzzle for your clients. Once they understand how you operate and you have had time to become familiar with their needs, desires, short-term and long-term objectives, you can expect to have a long and meaningful relationship.

In advising your client, always keep their best interests in mind. If you are too excited, aggressive, or desperate you could push your clients to make bad decisions. If you are too conservative, your clients could miss an opportunity. Remember that you are talking about your client's money and not yours, so try to use the word "you" rather than "we" when discussing a potential deal.

If you have been hesitant to invest in real estate or to work with investors in the past, now is the time to let go of your hesitation and move forward. Think about what you will gain from taking this step: growth, success, self-confidence, additional opportunities, more money, and most of all—financial freedom.

KEY POINTS TO REMEMBER:

- People who are thinking about investing in real estate want to work with an agent who has special knowledge in this area.

- You will need to develop additional skills in order to work effectively with investors.

- Investors are more likely than home buyers to become repeat customers and to recommend you to others.

- When you become an investor-friendly real estate agent, you will be irreplaceable to your clients.

Chapter 4

Who Is a Real Estate Investor?

A real estate investor is someone who buys real estate for investment purposes rather than for their primary residence. A home buyer, by contrast, is someone who buys real estate with the intention of living there. Most real estate investors are also home buyers (because we all need to live someplace), but not all home buyers are real estate investors.

Real estate investors purchase various kinds of real estate, ranging from single-family homes, duplexes, and apartments to commercial properties, land, and industrial parks. Upwards of 90% of my own clients are real estate investors who prefer to purchase single-family homes, duplexes, small apartments, and some commercial properties.

REAL ESTATE INVESTORS HELP THE ECONOMY

As a real estate agent you know that you must make sacrifices to be successful, and you also have encountered agents who are less disciplined than you are and not as willing to work hard to reach their goals. The same is true of real estate investors.

Most successful investors started out making sacrifices. They did much of the work on their properties with the goal of someday having a portfolio worth owning.

In my experience, few investors are interested in buying run-down properties in undesirable areas. Instead, they gravitate to family-friendly neighborhoods with properties that can be reconditioned to rent or flip. They take tremendous pride in the portfolio they own.

Real estate investors have a positive impact on local economies when they purchase properties with the intention of fixing them up. They hire contractors, electricians, plumbers, and others to do some of the work.

Although the housing crisis of 2008 had a devastating effect on people who lost their homes to foreclosure, the investors who purchased more than 4 million foreclosed properties helped to bring about an economic turnaround. They recognized a once-in-a-lifetime opportunity to buy multiple undervalued properties to rent or flip. From coast to coast, investors played a key role in stabilizing the residential real estate market.

Today, however, far fewer foreclosed properties are available and multiple offers are common. It is common to pay more than the asking price for a foreclosed property, and low-ball offers usually are rejected.

WHAT IS THE DIFFERENCE BETWEEN ACTIVE AND PASSIVE INVESTORS?

Investors may actively or passively invest in real estate. Active investors are those that may make their own repairs or hire contractors. In other words, they are involved in this business on a regular basis.

By contrast, a passive investor is someone who does not want the day-to-day involvement and instead pays a property management company to handle maintenance, repairs, rent collection, and so on.

When I talk to people about the benefits of investing in real estate, some of them tell me "I am too busy" or "I don't have time to do that." It is true that being an active investor takes time and effort, but the rewards are well worth the sacrifices. For those who have the financial wherewithal to purchase property but not the time and energy to handle the day-to-day responsibilities of property ownership, being a passive investor is a good alternative.

SUCCESSFUL VERSUS UNSUCCESSFUL INVESTORS

In my 45-plus years as a real estate investor I have encountered hundreds of investors. My investment clients range from contractors to doctors and everyone in between. I work with investors at every level of experience, from beginners to veterans. I even have a few clients who are real estate agents.

I've paid attention to the reasons why some of my fellow investors are successful while others are not. By "successful" I don't mean that they necessarily own a lot of properties but that they take a sensible approach to investing in real estate.

Based on my experience, here are the top ten characteristics of successful real estate investors:

1. They are not emotional in their buying decisions. Unlike home buyers, they will not buy a property simply because they fell in love with it. Rather, they always have a logical reason for buying a property. They might intend to purchase it as a long-term rental, to flip it (fix up and sell), or (if the deal is good enough) to wholesale the property "as is" to another investor and make a quick profit.

2. They minimize their exposure to risk by making calculated decisions and utilizing analytical tools to determine whether an investment is a good deal.

3. Their primary objective is to benefit from the long-term wealth-building opportunities that real estate offers, not to get rich quickly.

4. They utilize strategies that reflect their objectives and their risk tolerance.

5. They make the necessary sacrifices to accomplish their objectives, and they are 100% dedicated to reaching their investment goals.

6. They will not overpay for a property, and they often write multiple offers.

7. They have a system in place and they stick to it even if they encounter disappointments such as losing money on a property they purchased to flip.

8. They know what they will buy and what they will walk away from.

9. They don't waste a lot of time analyzing a property before it is under contract.

10. They don't leave things to chance; instead, they treat each investment as a business venture.

By contrast, I have met several individuals who thought of themselves as investors but had portfolios that didn't make sense. They either paid too much for their properties or purchased properties with inadequate cash flow. Most of the blame for these errors belongs to the real estate agents who helped them, because the basic principles of real estate investment were not followed. It would be interesting to find out what goals these individuals had for their properties and how they selected the real estate agents who assisted them.

AN AMAZING OPPORTUNITY AWAITS YOU

- Since 2000, real estate has outperformed the stock market approximately 2-to-1, returning 10.71% annually compared with a 5.43% annual total return with the S&P 500 Index (from Dec. 31, 2000 to Dec. 30, 2016).

- Residential real estate as an asset class is a $29 trillion market, and the commercial sector adds another $10 trillion.

- Only 15% of Americans are currently investing in real estate other than their primary residence.

- Most Americans (two-thirds) believe in investing in real estate, whether for a flip or buy-and-hold.

- Many Americans are unaware that real estate requires much less initial capital than traditional investment opportunities.

- Younger generations are more interested than ever in real estate.

- They are not making land anymore, and there is money to be made in this alternative asset.

- For the average investor, real estate offers the best way to develop significant wealth and retirement income and, ultimately, financial freedom.

- People from all walks of life would be interested in real estate investment, but they do not realize that it is such a powerful way to build wealth. Are you working this "niche market"? Are you looking to grow your business this year? Of your total income, what percentage of volume and transactions from the last couple of years is a result of working with investors?

I highly recommend that you take the time to prospect for investor clients. I can't understand why more real estate agents don't take the time to work this market. If you take the step, you can watch your income volume and transactions grow to levels beyond what you thought was possible.

If you put time and effort into learning what it takes to represent investors, you will have many clients who will do repeat business with you.

I cannot think of anything I would rather do than work with investors. It has been a rewarding experience not only financially but also socially because I have made so many lifelong friends. I can proudly say that I helped a number of my clients become millionaires.

Never be confused by appearances. How a person dresses, the car they drive, and where they live has nothing to do with how much wealth they have. Fancy clothes, fancy cars, and a big house do not prove that someone is better off. Looks could be deceiving. Take everyone seriously, and who knows? You may find your next client for life.

WHAT DO INVESTORS CARE ABOUT MOST?

Purchase price

Many real estate agents struggle with the fact that investors like to write low-ball offers—maybe as low as 30% to 40% below asking price, depending on the condition of the property. They don't want to compete with home buyers. They would prefer to buy a property that is not suitable for home buyers because of the amount of work that will be required to fix it up.

Financing terms

Most of the investors I work with purchase properties by paying cash for foreclosures, estate properties, and REOs (properties that have been reclaimed by a bank or government agency after the foreclosed property has failed to sell at a real estate auction). They prefer to purchase properties for which there are no financial contingencies and little hassle (no appraisals required). Of course the traditional, conventional loans with a 20% to 25% down payment are sometimes used, but cash seems to be the preferred method.

THE BENEFITS OF REPEAT BUSINESS

A major reason you should be excited to work with investors is that you can expect repeat business from this group.

How much time do you currently spend prospecting for buyers of owner-occupied properties? And how many of those buyers call you when they are ready to sell their house a few years later? Most of us are fortunate if they even remember our name. On average, home buyers purchase a property every five to seven years.

The opposite is true for investors who are really "in the game." They buy regularly. One of my clients has purchased more than 300 properties from 2005 to the present. Many of those were purchased as "flippers." Not only did I earn a commission when each property was purchased but also when it was flipped. (No, I did not give the client a discount on my commission.)

Some of us are spending way too much of our time showing properties to home buyers with no guarantee that they are going to buy anything. If you decide to work with an investor, they are almost certain to buy if they are presented with a good deal.

Doesn't it make more sense to work with one investor who is capable of buying five properties than with five different home buyers who may buy one property apiece and hold onto it for several years? When you work with an investor, you can build a lasting relationship that will pay long-term dividends.

LOYALTY GOES BOTH WAYS

Some investors may work with multiple real estate agents. If you find yourself in such a situation, I would encourage you to have a meeting of the minds with your investor. I have a policy that if an investor is not 100% loyal to me, I will not do business with them.

Loyalty is a two-way street. If you are actively involved in this niche market, which clients will you notify when you find a special deal? Your loyal clients or the ones who use multiple agents? Your loyal clients should get the first opportunity to say yes or no.

When you bring the value and expertise that real estate investors are expecting, they will start to use you exclusively. Additionally, investors who have been working with less knowledgeable real estate agents will seek you out. If you do a good job for them, the opportunities are endless. They will continue to buy properties and more importantly will tell their friends about the great job you are doing for them. You can count on more referrals than you ever thought would be possible.

Working with investors is not cyclical. Regardless of economic conditions, a successful investor will always be "in the game" and will buy and buy and buy if you continue to find them the deals.

Investors expect their real estate agent to know more than they do. As a real estate agent who takes the time to learn about their needs, you will become a huge asset to them. As you are well aware, not all real estate agents are alike. It makes sense to set yourself apart by making sure you are irreplaceable.

Ultimately, you can continue to grow your business and work with traditional home buyers, but why not also start working with investors? They will help to grow your business, and you will get more referrals from them if you do a good job. You will ultimately become a better and more well-rounded real estate agent, and new clients will seek you out.

Real estate agents who have built meaningful and trusting relationships with their clients can be huge assets to them. However, the opposite is also true—a real estate agent can become a liability if he or she does not take the time to understand the client's objectives.

HOW TO MAINTAIN CONTROL OF THE AGENT-CLIENT RELATIONSHIP

If you intend to bring value and expertise to your clients, you need to be in control when you are meeting with prospective clients. Although they may think that they are interviewing you, the opposite is true. You need to gather enough information to decide whether you want to do business with them, because not every prospect will be a good client. There are some investors that you may not want to do business with.

How can you decide whether to work with a prospective client? Getting answers to the following questions should help you determine whether a prospect is a viable candidate for your services. And be sure to listen to your instincts—do they appear to have commitment and integrity? Do they seem trustworthy? Trust your hunches about people.

What is their experience level?

Find out as much information as possible about each prospect's investment history. Do they currently own any rentals? What kinds of properties do they own (houses, duplexes, apartments, land, strip malls)? Do they have a background in business, real estate, or finance? Why do they think they may want to invest? Did they attend a hype-filled free seminar where the speaker made a lot of promises but provided little substance?

Keep in mind that all of us have to start somewhere. I am grateful that my first real estate agent took me under his wing way back in the 1970s. Where would I be today if he hadn't taken a chance on me?

What are their short-term and long-term objectives?

The sooner this subject is brought up, the better. Many times a potential investor does not have a clear enough road map to know what kind of investment opportunities may be best for them. If someone is in their thirties or forties, they will have different goals from someone who is in their late forties or fifties and expects to retire in 10 to 15 years. What may work for one client may not work for another. When you understand what a client wants to accomplish, you will be in a much better position to offer suggestions that will meet their goals and objectives.

How do they intend to purchase their investment?

Do they plan to fund their purchase with cash, financing, a line of credit, 1031 exchange, or an IRA?

What kind of business plan do they have in mind?

Are they interested in flipping, buy-and-hold, or wholesaling?

What kinds of properties are they interested in purchasing?

Do they want to buy single-family homes, multi-units, or commercial properties? In what areas, neighborhoods, and communities are they thinking of investing?

How much capital do they have available?

They should be able to tell you how much money they intend to invest.

Are they credit worthy?

Ask what their credit score is. Do they have access to cash? Do they have a working relationship with a bank or lender?

Are they looking for a deal for themselves or for someone else?

A "bird dog" is someone who scouts properties for potential investors and gets paid a referral fee if the investor buys the property. To me, dealing with a bird dog is a waste of time because the bird dog is not the decision maker. I want to deal with the decision maker.

Do they appear to have commitment and integrity?

Do you feel you can trust them?

YOUR PROSPECTS MAY WANT TO ASK YOU A FEW QUESTIONS AS WELL

Investors want to work with real estate agents who have knowledge and experience in this area. That's why you should be prepared to answer the following questions from a prospective client:

1. How many investment properties have you sold in the past? What types of properties have you sold?
2. Are you working with any investors now?
3. Do you own any investment properties?
4. What types of multi-units have you sold?
5. Do you have any knowledge of the commercial real estate market?
6. Do you know any bankers or lenders who are familiar with investment properties?
7. Do you have a list of contractors that you could recommend?

SUCCESSFUL INVESTORS HAVE DEVELOPED GOOD HABITS

My story may not be any different from yours. Becoming a successful investor required me to make sacrifices. When I had a full-time job working 50 to 60 hours a week as an executive with the Boy Scouts of America, I handled my investment properties on the weekends. I did just about everything except for major electrical work, plumbing, and roof replacement.

When I became a successful real estate agent with a busy practice, however, I decided that my time would be better spent if I hired a property management company to take care of my rentals so I could free up more time to work with investors.

I consider myself to be an ordinary person. However, working hard has never been a problem for me. I believe there is no replacement for hard work and paying the price to achieve success.

I didn't have any wealthy role models in the real estate business, yet I knew quite a few friends and acquaintances who had wealth. Some were lucky enough to have a family business, while others were CEOs and so on.

Subconsciously I probably thought about what these individuals had that I didn't. Were they smarter than I was? Did they work any harder than I did? Did they have more drive or ambition than I had? Everything about me indicated that I was a high achiever and a hard worker, so I began to believe that I too could someday become financially independent

In the process, I developed some habits that have served me well as an investor. First of all, I learned to set achievable goals. I think that everything that is worthwhile should have measurable goals. Creating a business plan will provide you with a way to measure your success.

My goal was to become a millionaire real estate investor. On paper I achieved that goal a number of years ago.

If you are working with investors, a good goal might be to control a million dollars' worth of real estate. Depending on the area where you live, that could include different combinations of properties. In my community, it could be in the form of twenty $50,000 properties or ten $100,000 properties. If your properties are well maintained and continuously occupied, within 20 years these properties will be paid in full.

As an example, let's say these ten $100,000 properties average $800 each in monthly income. You would be earning $8,000 per month or $96,000 annually less operating expenses (taxes, insurance, maintenance, and so on).

There are many ways to become a millionaire real estate investor, and that is why real estate is such a powerful opportunity for the average hard-working individual. It's next to impossible to become a millionaire by working for someone else.

Becoming a millionaire real estate investor seemed like a distant dream to me at the beginning of my career, but that lofty goal gave me the drive and determination to make steady progress toward my objective.

As I look back over the past 15 years, the success of many of my clients has been based on having an action plan. I also have seen the mistakes made by people who didn't treat real estate as a business.

If you want to have a worthwhile portfolio, your real estate investments must be treated the same as running any other business. Positive and measurable goals ensure accountability.

Many years ago I heard about a survey that found 90% of all millionaires in the United States had made their fortunes in real estate. My guess is that the majority of these millionaires are a lot like one of my clients whom I'll call Joe. In 1980 he bought a couple of rental properties, and over the next three decades he kept buying more and more until he had acquired a sizable portfolio worth a few million dollars. Joe is just one of several of my clients who now control real estate portfolios worth several million dollars. I still find it amazing that you can buy these properties using other people's money (OPM) and your tenants will pay down your debt.

Few business ventures can provide the wealth that a hard-working individual can build by investing in real estate. This is one reason why more and more people are jumping into the investment game. The question you need to ask yourself is this: Are you going to be the next real estate millionaire, and are you going to help your clients become millionaire real estate investors? Real estate agents who are not prospecting for potential investors are missing out on the opportunity to generate sizable income.

In my humble opinion, real estate remains the single greatest vehicle for the average person to achieve financial freedom. That's why I am still actively investing in real estate and see this as my pension plan.

The following investment formula has served me well over the years:

INVESTOR LOYALTY + REAL ESTATE AGENT LOYALTY = WIN-WIN AND SUCCESS

Our profession has just as much responsibility as any other profession that deals with people's finances. It is not uncommon for real estate agents who are fully engaged in this niche market to work with clients who spend hundreds of thousands of dollars on properties annually. Talk about responsibility. You have more power than you realize to help people generate WEALTH. Are you up to the challenge?

According to NAR, as of July 2018 there were 1,334,668 Realtors in the United States. Of course there are many more real estate agents who are not members of the NAR. I am very confident in speculating that the number of us who work this "niche" market is very insignificant, yet this industry is changing rapidly. Will you be relevant in the future? What if you could bring added value and expertise that others don't have? If you can help people solve their financial concerns, not only will you be relevant but more and more clients will want to use you. When you help them solve their problems, they will tell others about you. What separates you from the other agents in your office? Why should people use your services? How many of your fellow agents are working with investors?

Believe me when I tell you that if you follow my suggestions you will become the go-to agent in your office or community. Even people from other states who are looking to invest in your community will seek you out.

In conclusion, investing in real estate is a much more effective way for most hard-working people to build wealth than speculating in the stock market. When you invest in the stock market you have no control over your investments, and very few people understand what makes the market go up or down. By comparison, real estate is much easier to understand.

KEY POINTS TO REMEMBER:

- A real estate investor is someone who buys real estate for investment purposes rather than for their primary residence.

- Real estate investors help the economy in two ways: by employing people to help them fix up their properties and by purchasing foreclosed homes and stabilizing the residential real estate market.

- A real estate investor can be an active investor (doing hands-on work on his or her properties or hiring contractors) or a passive investor (hiring a property management company to handle the day-to-day work involved in maintaining their investment properties).

- Unlike home buyers, real estate investors are not emotional in their buying decisions. They also are more willing to write multiple offers.

- Seven out of eight adult Americans are not real estate investors yet, which represents a significant opportunity for you to introduce people to the benefits of this type of investment.

- Real estate agents need to maintain control of their relationship with investor clients by asking questions to determine whom they will work with. Agents should also be prepared to answer questions from prospective clients.

- As an investor, you should set challenging yet realistic goals about how much property you intend to acquire.

CHAPTER 5

WORKING WITH INVESTORS— HOW TO FIND, KEEP, AND GROW WITH THEM

One of the most rewarding experiences of my career has been helping some of my clients to become millionaire real estate investors. It's a great feeling to have such a positive impact on someone's life. As an investor-friendly real estate agent, you will be able to enjoy the same sense of fulfillment.

Unfortunately, not everyone has the best interests of the investor in mind. There are lots of companies that try to make a quick buck (or a few thousand bucks) by taking advantage of folks who are eager to get into the investment game but have no idea where to begin.

A few years ago I attended a real estate seminar in Omaha that made me sick to my stomach. The information I heard at the seminar was far from the truth. The speakers made it seem so easy to buy real estate, and they gave out tidbits of information along with a lot of hype. Not much substance, just empty promises. They pretended to know a lot about the metro Omaha area, yet it was clear to me that they had no clue. The first thing I noticed was that the so-called guru was not even in attendance.

The meeting room was filled with at least 200 people who basically heard nothing they could use in our community. All they received were generalities and lots of hype on why real estate investing is the best path to becoming financially wealthy. You already know that I agree with that statement because real estate has served me so well over the 40 years that I have been an investor.

One of the speakers began his presentation by asking the audience, "How many people in this room are happy with their income or feel like they are making enough money?" Of course no one raised their hand. After this lead-in question, he proceeded to tell everybody that they could make a lot of money by following his company's tried-and-true methods.

The underlying purpose of this "free" seminar was to sell a mentorship program for thousands of dollars. Have you ever attended one of these seminars? I hope you weren't one of the people who got sucked in. After spending a couple of hours listening to the speaker, I heard nothing that was new. After the seminar concluded and the majority of attendees were heading for the exit, a handful of poor souls lined up to purchase this company's "bullet-proof" course materials. The seminar had accomplished its purpose: a few people were spending money to attend a three-day "boot camp." And that was just the beginning; there was more to come.

Investing in real estate is not rocket science, and there are no "secrets" worth paying for. Much of the information that this type of program provides is not totally accurate, and the rest of it is readily available to the public.

In my opinion, enrolling in these mentoring programs is a horrible waste of money. There are people who make money from real estate investing, and there are people who make money from selling get-rich-quick schemes. Don't confuse the two.

Anyone who is interested in becoming a real estate investor would be better off working with a reputable, knowledgeable real estate agent who has experience in the local community. Instead of spending thousands of dollars on boot camps and course materials, why not use the money for a down payment or for remodeling expenses?

I firmly believe that anyone who wants to invest in real estate should educate themselves, but I don't think it makes sense to spend thousands of dollars on course materials that in all like- lihood will end up collecting dust on a bookshelf. It is much better to find a local mentor who knows and understands the market. Are you ready to step into that role?

If you are not comfortable responding with an enthusiastic "Yes," think about what you will need to do in order to reach that point. Until you get there, you are letting a lot of money go down the drain by not working with investors.

This is an ideal time to get into the "investment game," because in today's real estate market there are more and more people who would like to become the next millionaire real estate investor. They may not feel ready to jump in with both feet, and that is where you as a mentor can come in.

BECOME KNOWLEDGEABLE SO YOU CAN EDUCATE YOUR POTENTIAL CLIENTS

There's a reason why 20% of real estate agents sell 80% of the investment properties. (I have even heard that it is now 10% who sell 90%.) Are you part of this select group?

I have been investing in real estate since 1972, and my practi- cal knowledge has been invaluable to my clients. I have developed a very lucrative and enjoyable niche for myself, and I am sur- prised that so few real estate agents focus their business on the investor. I blame a lot of this on real estate agencies that are not providing adequate training. I personally have attended network-wide conventions where the subject of real estate invest- ment wasn't even offered as a seminar topic.

WHY WORK WITH INVESTORS?

I enjoy working with investors because they are so much more focused than home buyers. They will not hesitate to buy a property that meets their investment criteria or to walk away from one that doesn't.

I have written hundreds of contracts on the spot for investor clients. In my opinion, this is a much better use of my time than having to show properties for a second or sometimes even a third time to a potential home buyer who ultimately decides they are not interested. Does that scenario sound familiar to you?

Unlike home buyers who purchase a property and then forget to call you a few years later when they are ready to sell it, investors will buy multiple properties each year. If you do a good job for them, you can expect a loyal client who ultimately becomes an endless income stream. And a savvy investor will continue to buy in good times and bad. You can bring value by finding the deals before anyone else does.

A majority of investors pay cash, which makes it easier to get offers accepted. Would a seller rather receive a cash offer or an offer subject to approval of a loan?

As a knowledgeable real estate agent you can educate investors about the local market and the reasons they should invest in real estate. If you have decided to work with investors, now is the time to become an expert in this field.

BECOME A PROVIDER OF INFORMATION

As a real estate agent, you can provide your clients with a wealth of knowledge about your industry. You should be able to explain with your eyes closed the advantages and disadvantages of investing in real estate.

As a mentor, you can become the local real estate investment "guru." You can quickly become the source of answers to your clients' real estate investment questions, and you should also be able to advise them on how to best maximize their profits. Should they buy a property to improve and flip, or would they be better off owning a rental property? Should they purchase single-family dwellings, multi-units, or apartment buildings? When you understand their short- and long-term objectives, you can help them develop a workable business plan.

If you become a well-informed real estate agent who has expertise that other agents lack, you will be extremely influential in helping clients get their business off the ground or grow their portfolio. In your role as a consultant you will have more power and influence than you realize, and therefore you will be well worth your commission. You should be able to guide new investors through all the steps from finding and evaluating properties to negotiating the deal and closing. They will think of you as the real estate agent who is the one-stop source for all their needs.

HOW TO ATTRACT INVESTORS

Before people will do business with you, they need to know, like, and trust you. Why are your current clients working with you? Because you have established a meaningful relationship with them, they like you, and they trust you. If they have used you to purchase an investment property even though you had no previous experience with investment, more power to you. But did you bring anything to the table, or did you just write the offer?

If you were not in the real estate business but you were interested in buying or selling property, would you hire an agent who had the same qualifications that you possess right now? Buying or selling an investment property may be the largest financial transaction a client makes, and they should be able to count on you to bring the value and expertise that will help them accomplish their goals and objectives.

WHAT IF YOU DON'T HAVE EXPERIENCE WITH A SPECIFIC TYPE OF PROPERTY?

What categories of investment properties are you likely to deal with? Strip malls, 100-unit apartment buildings, or land? Probably not, because these listings don't come around often. You will have far more opportunities to work with investors who purchase single-family dwellings and multi-units because these are the types of properties most investors will be interested in purchasing.

What would you do if you received a call from a friend who asked you to list his 48-unit apartment complex? Would you be comfortable listing it? If not, then you might want to team up and co-list the property with an agent who has experience with apartment buildings.

You can bring value to your investor clients by finding a way to take care of their needs. When they know you are willing to go the extra mile for them and that you will respond to their calls on a timely basis, you can expect a loyal client.

HOW TO FIND PROSPECTIVE INVESTORS

In the last 30 days, how many people did you come into contact with? That group is your circle of influence, and it's probably a lot bigger than you realize. Many of those people are either potential clients or referral sources.

When you think about it, your circle of influence has three levels: inner, middle, and outer. Your inner circle includes current clients, past clients, friends, family members, and neighbors. Your middle circle includes people you associate with on a regular basis, such as attorneys, accountants, and appraisers, along with members of your religious institution, health club, service club, and other organizations. Your outer circle includes tradespeople such as plumbers, handymen, electricians, and roofers.

The last time you talked with someone from your circle of influence, did you bring up the subject of real estate investing? If you did, congratulations! If not, why not? Unless you have a conversation with them, they will never realize how much you know about this topic.

The individuals in your circle could be your best source of free advertising. Are you asking them for referrals? They have friends, and their friends have friends. All of them know someone who could become your client. Can you see the mushrooming effect this can have for you? It could be jackpot time, but unless you have a conversation with them they will never know how much value you can bring to the table. You have knowledge that they will be very interested to know about.

Your friends and close confidants are people who already like you, trust you, and want you to succeed. Your expertise and knowledge will be a big hit if you aren't afraid to share it with them. You are the key to wealth building and the missing piece of the puzzle.

Did it make you mad when you found out that one of your friends or clients purchased an investment property from another agent because they didn't know you worked this market? Your challenge and opportunity is to position yourself with them so they will think of you first when they consider buying an investment property.

POTENTIAL CLIENTS

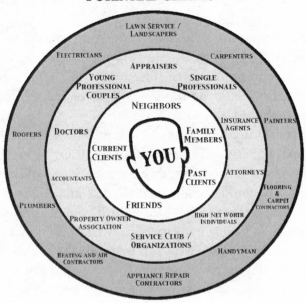

☐ **INNER CIRCLE**
☐ **MIDDLE CIRCLE**   ☐ **OUTER CIRCLE**

MIDDLE CIRCLE

-DOCTORS

-ATTORNEYS

-ACCOUNTANTS

-APPRAISERS

-PROPERTY OWNERS'
ASSOCIATION

-HIGH-NET-WORTH
INDIVIDUALS

-INSURANCE AGENTS

-PROFESSIONAL COUPLES

-SINGLE PROFESSIONALS

-SERVICE CLUBS/
ORGANIZATIONS

OUTER CIRCLE

-ROOFERS

-ELECTRICIANS

-HANDYMEN

-APPLIANCE REPAIR CONTRACTORS

-LAWN SERVICE /
LANDSCAPERS

-FLOORING & CARPET
CONTRACTORS

-HEATING & AIR CONTRACTORS

-PAINTERS

-CARPENTERS

-PLUMBERS

Educate your friends and family members about the investment market. You want them to take you seriously for your knowledge so they begin seeing you as a wealth advisor, coach, and mentor and not just as their friend or family member, or as an ordinary real estate agent. You are extraordinary. People in your circle must feel comfortable that if they refer you to someone, it will not backfire. They will be more likely to put their neck on the line when you convince them that you know your stuff.

Your challenge is for the people in your circle of influence to begin seeing you as the go-to person for anyone who is thinking of investing in real estate.

When you are working your "circle," the effort you put forth will determine your success. Don't be bashful. They need you even if they don't know it yet. Here are some suggestions to help you get started:

1. If you have helped high-net-worth clients buy or sell their personal residence in the past, do you know if they have any investment properties? Maybe they do own properties but have no idea that you are interested in working with investors. If you care about your clients, it makes sense to talk with them about investing.

2. Bring up the topic of real estate investment when you're talking with acquaintances and friends. If you want to get their attention, ask them if they are pleased with the amount of taxes they paid last year. My guess is that the answer will be "No, I paid too much." A response like "Have you ever considered investing in real estate?" will at least trigger a conversation on this topic.

3. Do you belong to a service club, religious institution, or neighborhood association? You may know plenty of people who would welcome a conversation about real estate investing.

4. Join a property owners' association or investment club that meets monthly and get acquainted with the other members.

5. My guess is that if you sit down for 15 minutes you can easily come up with a list of 100 people you can talk with about the benefits of investing in real estate. How about people that you personally do business with, such as your insurance agent, roofer, plumber, painter, electrician, lawn service person, appliance repairman, attorney, or CPA? The people you come into contact with on a daily basis could be excellent clients and sources for lead generation. If you don't ask, you will never know.

6. Check out your local newspaper's real estate section under "Properties for Rent" and look up names on the assessor's website. You may be surprised to find out that many will own multiple properties

7. Reach out to prospective clients in emerging markets, particularly Hispanic Americans and single women.

Hispanic Americans: According to a residential real estate brokerage firm called New Western Acquisitions, the fastest-growing segment of the U.S. population is Hispanic Americans. In 2014 the Hispanic population in the United States reached 53 million, and this demographic is growing so quickly that it could reach 120 million by 2050. Today, one in every four children in the United States is Hispanic, and a whopping 20% of millennials (people born between 1982 and 2004) are of Hispanic descent. Hispanic Americans formed 320,000 new households in 2014, which represented about 40% of all new households nationwide.

I personally have sold many rental properties to Hispanic clients, as have my Hispanic colleagues at other real estate companies in metro Omaha. If there is a sizeable Hispanic population in your community, this group could be an excellent source of potential clients.

Owning a home is a starting point for wealth creation and a stabilizing force for working families. Hispanic real estate investors who flip houses or become landlords can have a highly positive impact within their communities.

Single women: More than 60% of U.S. real estate agents are female, so it seems logical that women would be equally represented among the ranks of real estate investors. However, only 30% of real estate investors are women.

Single women are more likely than single men to purchase a home. Single women accounted for 18% of all home purchases in 2016, compared with just 7% by single men, according to survey data from the National Association of Realtors. This makes single women the second-largest segment in the home-purchase marketplace, behind married couples.

Citing data from the most recent U.S. Census Current Population Survey, which covered 60,000 households, Ralph McLaughlin, chief economist for consulting firm Veritas Urbis Economics, found that the share of home purchases by single women in 2017—including never-married individuals, widows, and divorcées—hit 22.8%, the highest on record. The gap between single women and single men was not as dramatic as it was in the Realtor study, however.

Many single women would be interested in real estate investment if an agent told them how effective it is in building long-term wealth. Also, they may not know how to get started. You can fill this gap.

If you are looking to grow your business, don't overlook these two groups.

1.   Maintain a Facebook page for your business and write a blog on the investment market in your area.

2.   Help clients build a worthwhile portfolio based on their short- and long-term objectives (see the sample business plans in Chapter 12 and in the Resources section near the end of this book).

3.   Your best prospects will be your current and former clients. They already believe in you, trust you, and probably have given you a number of referrals, but they might not realize that you could help them build wealth in this way.

4.   Even if you are still learning about real estate investment, you probably already have credentials and knowledge that will bring value to your clients. Owning rental properties is the best way to ensure that you will be taken seriously.

HOW TO KEEP CLIENTS AND GROW WITH THEM

1.   Remember that your top priority is to help your clients make money, money, money. That is why they are in the investment "game."

2.   Your clients should like you, believe in you, trust you, and most of all respect you for the knowledge you possess.

3.   Remember that investors have a different mindset from owner-occupied buyers, so you must always keep in mind their short-term and long-term objectives.

4.   Keep your clients' best interests in mind and bring them deals that are difficult to pass up.

5.   Provide extraordinary service, knowledge, and the value so your clients will have no reason to use another agent.

6. Be 100% honest. Sometimes that means stating facts they may not want to hear, such as the fact that writing ridiculously low-ball offers in today's market will not get the prize. Tell them not to waste time analyzing a property until it is under contract. If it appears that a property will meet the criteria, move to the next step of writing the offer with contingencies. Don't exaggerate what a property will be worth once repairs are done.

7. Act quickly because the deals will not last. When you find out about a good deal, make that call quickly to your loyal clients. What a great problem to have–deciding which client to call first!

8. Know what is important to each client. Most investors will write offers with the same terms each time, such as cash, close in a short time, contractor/inspector contingency. Will the property you have in mind be a better flip than a rental?

9. Don't waste their time by sending them properties that don't meet their criteria.

10. Make yourself visible. Invite them to attend your local investors' or property owners' association meetings.

11. Meet with your current investors at least annually to find out whether their properties are still meeting their needs.

12. Stay in touch with them. Send them articles of interest. Be their ongoing source for all their real estate investment needs.

HOW TO BUILD A WORTHWHILE REAL ESTATE PORTFOLIO

Investors who make a lot of money in real estate and have a sizable net worth follow a plan. They don't leave things to chance. Below is a step-by-step guide for building a worthwhile real estate portfolio.

Step 1: Develop a business plan. Real estate investment is a business whether you have one property or 100. A sample business plan is provided in Chapter 12.

Step 2: Make good, practical decisions right from the start. Become a student of this "game" and learn as much as possible before you make your first deal. Develop a working relationship with a real estate agent who has expertise and also is an investor.

Step 3: Look for properties in family-friendly neighborhoods. The right property attracts the right tenants or buyers. Try to find the worst property on the best block, since you can make many changes to a property but you can never change its location.

Step 4: Develop a relationship with a local bank.

Step 5: Decide how much financial risk you are willing to take on. Real estate requires money, and a majority of the time the funds will be borrowed from a bank. Get comfortable with the financial numbers and concentrate on increasing your property values.

Step 6: If you do not yet own any investment properties, a good way to begin is to purchase a single-family home or duplex.

Step 7: Fix up your property. This may include exterior paint, updating the kitchen and baths, landscaping, and so on. Try to hire a contractor who can do most of the work. Nicely updated properties will merit a much higher rent and a better tenant. Find out if remodeling will require a permit.

Step 8: Keep your personal expenses low. Reinvest any profits to grow your holdings.

Step 9: Continue purchasing properties as you become more and more comfortable with the process and have the financial resources to do so.

Step 10: Diversify your holdings. For example, you might want to acquire a mix of properties such as houses, duplexes, fourplexes, and so on.

Step 11: Rent only to tenants who meet your criteria (credit report, criminal check, landlord verification, employment history).

OVERALL TIPS AND WARNINGS TO GIVE NEW INVESTORS

When you are getting started as an investor, it's a good idea to interview several local banks to determine which one will give you the best terms. As I mentioned in Chapter 3, your best option will often be a locally owned bank rather than a nationwide bank. Getting a loan with a favorable interest rate is only one aspect to consider. Can you establish a line of credit? If so, this will allow you to pay cash for properties upfront. It is important that you buy undervalued properties so you can raise the value by remodeling and then term them out (obtain a permanent loan for the property).

As I mentioned at the beginning of this chapter, the real estate industry is filled with "get-rich-quick" programs that sell empty promises at exorbitant prices. Their best strategy as a new investor is to work with a reputable real estate agent who has firsthand experience and familiarity with the local real estate market. They can guide you step-by-step and offer practical advice instead of theoretical ideas.

Whatever you do, take the first step. If you don't get off the starting block, you will never be on the road to generating wealth. Buy today so you can profit tomorrow.

KEY POINTS TO REMEMBER:

- Real estate investing is not complicated, and there are no secrets involved. Instead of paying thousands of dollars to enroll in a mentoring program, use the money to make a down payment or pay for property improvements.

- Investor clients are easier to work with than home buyers in many ways and are much more likely to generate repeat business.

- You can help your clients become successful investors by providing answers to their questions and being the first to notify them about good deals.

- Some of your home buyer clients may already be investors or may be interested in talking with you about becoming investors.

- One of the best ways to develop credibility as an investment expert is to build your own real estate portfolio.

- Success in real estate investment requires a step-by-step plan.

Chapter 6

Financing Investment Properties

When one of your clients is interested in writing an offer on an investment property, one of the first questions you should ask is how they intend to purchase the property. Their decision to finance or pay cash will determine their return on investment, so finding the best financing option is critical.

As previously mentioned, you should focus on working with clients who are creditworthy, have a solid financial statement, are employed or self-employed, and have some cash reserves. These prospects have an amazing opportunity in today's market to acquire a sizable portfolio and generate wealth.

Although some real estate "gurus" have proclaimed that people can buy property with no credit, poor credit, or no job, there is no such thing as free real estate. Would you sell a property that is worth owning to someone who has no credit? If a seller has a property they can't sell any other way, however, this may be the only option.

As a real estate agent you expect to be compensated for your efforts. Can you imagine a seller being willing to sell a property with no money down yet pay a commission out of pocket? I have never met anyone who bought a property that was worth owning with no money down. Does it happen? It probably happens on rare occasions, but the message that anyone can buy property with no money down is highly exaggerated.

In some instances I have paid cash for a property and used a line of credit to cover fix-up costs. Once the work was completed, the bank appraised the property and I was able to refinance for the exact amount of money I had invested. In effect, this was a "no money down" proposition that was available to me because I was credit worthy.

The key is that I bought an undervalued property and even after the fix-up cost the loan-to-value ratio was 60% of the appraised value—not a very risky proposition for the bank. This type of scenario is still possible, but if one is not creditworthy or does not have a solid financial statement to back it up, in all likelihood it will not work.

One of the most important ways you can assist your clients is to establish meaningful relationships with banks, lenders, and other financing sources. Keep in mind that banks are in the business of loaning money, so this is a win-win situation for you and for them. Ideally, you want to pick lenders who understand the real estate investment market, but if they lack this knowledge you can educate them.

As mentioned in Chapter 3, I have found that local institutions including community banks are much easier to deal with than nationwide banks, especially for lines of credit and commercial-type loans.

As you already know, investors prefer to use OPM (other people's money) as much as possible, so establishing good relationships with bankers will be to your benefit.

I have introduced a lot of my clients to the same lenders I use. These lenders know me and realize that I am knowledgeable and successful, making it much easier for my clients (as long as they are in good financial standing) to secure credit lines or loans.

To provide the greatest amount of help to your clients, you should become familiar with the most common financial options that are available to real estate investors.

OPTIONS TO PURCHASE PROPERTIES

1. Cash – Most of the investors I work with pay cash for their
    purchases (a line of credit works the same as cash). They
    use cash to purchase properties that they intend to flip
    rather than properties they will use as long-term rentals.
    As previously mentioned, it doesn't make sense to use cash
    to purchase a rental. It is much better to use the cash for
    down payments on a few properties, thereby leveraging your
    purchasing power.
2. Conventional mortgage – What else can I say about conven-
    tional financing that you don't already know? You may not
    be aware that some lenders require more than the usual 20%
    down. In fact, the required down payment can be as high as
    30% to 35%. It is best to check with several lenders, as some
    may offer special down payment programs for investors.
3. FHA loans – FHA loans are accessible to buyers who may not
    have enough money for a down payment on a conventional
    mortgage, because the minimum down payment on an FHA
    loan is 3.5%. An FHA loan can be used to purchase an invest-
    ment property up to four units as long as the purchaser plans
    to live in one of the units. This is an excellent strategy to use
    with a younger client who is ambitious but may not have a lot
    of money besides the down payment.
4. FHA 203k loans – This type of loan can be used to purchase
    a property that is in need of rehabbing. The buyer can use the
    money to finance repairs and other improvements. The 203k
    loan is available to an investor who is planning to occupy at
    least one of the units.
5. Seller financing – In some instances it may be advantageous
    for a seller to partially finance the property, especially if it is
    owned free and clear (because the seller will receive tax ben-
    efits from issuing the loan). Although I haven't seen much
    seller financing, this would be a great option for a short-term

loan, perhaps amortized over 15 years with a 5-year balloon. It is common for a seller who has a free and clear property to record the deed of trust. However, you need to make sure the property truly is owned free and clear. If there is a loan against the property, the note can be called by the lender immediately through a "Due on Sale" clause.

6. Hard money lenders – If traditional financing is not obtainable, hard money lenders may offer a temporary solution. Any private individual can be a hard money lender. This type of loan is based on property value. The term of the loan is usually three to six months, and the interest rate is very high: 10% to 20%. Hard money lenders charge high fees for loans. In addition to paying the high cost of these loans, a borrower who is unable to meet the deadline for repayment may face foreclosure or have to pay additional fees to renew the loan.

7. Line of credit or bridge loan – This is the most popular way to purchase properties other than an outright cash offer. For anyone who has equity in their personal residence or other collateral and a solid financial statement, this type of financing is very easy to obtain. Investors who flip properties can use a line of credit to cover the purchase price, remodeling, and other expenses. Once the property sells, the line is paid back and the investor moves on to the next project.

8. Family, friends, and other individuals – This form of financing is unique because of the relationship between the lender and borrower. Family members may pool their financial resources to invest as a "family activity." As another example, a family member may have discretionary funds such as $100,000 in the bank earning very little interest but could do much better by loaning the money for a set period of time and receiving a 5% to 7% return.

9. Partnership – Partnerships come in all forms. I have two partners in my real estate business. All three of us are equal partners who share in profits and expenses. You might know someone who is willing to take an ownership position but may not want to have direct involvement in the project. Partners receive tax benefits based on their percentage of their investment (cash flow, appreciation, depreciation, and so on) as well as profits when the property is sold.

10. Commercial loans – These types of loans are typically used for large projects such as apartments, office buildings, and everything else above four units. Underwriting in the commercial market focuses more on the property than on the income of the borrower. If one of your clients is interested in purchasing a $5,000,000 apartment building, the lender will want to make sure that the income it produces will support the mortgage payment if anything goes wrong. The lender will still want to ensure that the buyer is creditworthy, and this type of loan is not likely to be issued to a first-time investor.

Although most investors will continue to rely on traditional financing methods such as conventional or FHA loans, bridge loans, or lines of credit, the other options discussed above may be helpful to clients who are not in a position to finance their purchase in a traditional way. Investors also might want to consider using funds from a Roth IRA to finance real estate purchases (see Chapter 12 for a discussion of this topic).

Always think of ways you can facilitate the investment process and open doors for clients. Know the options and share lender contacts with your clients. When your clients have their finances in order, you will be well on your way to achieving success in this business. Understanding the different financing options available will make you truly invaluable, and clients from all walks of life will seek you out.

KEY POINTS TO REMEMBER:

- Deciding whether to pay cash or to use other people's money is critically important because the type of financing will affect the return on investment.

- In addition to traditional loans, investors may qualify for FHA loans, loans on foreclosed properties, or other kinds of financing.

- Some investors may be able to form partnerships or borrow money from friends and family members.

- An invaluable way to help your clients is to form good relationships with local bankers who understand real estate investing and to share lenders' contact information with your clients.

CHAPTER 7

THE F-A-B-F-S/R SYSTEM: FIND, ANALYZE, BUY, FIX, SELL/RENT

Would you agree that fear of the unknown is a big roadblock that keeps people from investing and possibly keeps you from working with investors? (Money is found on the other side of fear.)

I am hopeful that the information in this book will make it a little easier for you to get past that roadblock so you can help your clients generate wealth while also growing your client base and income.

Hundreds of books have been written on the subject of investing in real estate and I have read some of them; however, most of my knowledge comes from practical experience. Like many others, I made a lot of mistakes early on in my venture. I learned by trial and error, buying the wrong properties in areas I shouldn't have, paying too much for properties, spending too much on remodeling, and so on. Fortunately, real estate is very forgiving and I learned from my mistakes.

GET OFF THE STARTING BLOCK

If you don't take the next step, nothing will be lost and nothing will be gained. If you get in the "game," however, the opposite will be true. It will open up a new and exciting chapter in your real estate career and a new opportunity to help one, two, or ten clients to become millionaire investors. Along the way, you and your clients will enjoy all the benefits that real estate offers, including tax deductions and additional income.

In this chapter I will take you step by step through the system I have used in my own real estate business and shared with my clients for many years. This system will give you and your clients a solid foundation for building wealth by investing in real estate.

By following my model you can avoid the trial-and-error stage and produce measurable and worthwhile results that can be repeated with one client after another. The difference you can make for your clients will be powerful.

THE SYSTEM

According to Business Dictionary.com, a system is "a set of detailed methods, procedures and routines created to carry out a specific activity, perform a duty, or solve a problem."

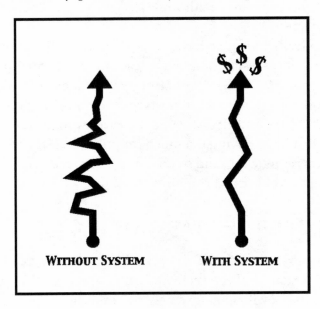

WITHOUT SYSTEM   WITH SYSTEM

To use my system effectively, you will need to develop clear criteria for identifying the properties you will consider, the properties you will buy, and the properties you will walk away from.

The types of properties that will generally offer the best opportunity for immediate equity are foreclosures, REOs, estate sales, properties that have been neglected and need cosmetic improvements, and properties that have been tagged by the city for violations.

Keep in mind that location, location, location should always be considered when deciding whether to make an offer. Buying real estate in various locations is a lot like buying blue chip versus penny stock. As a savvy real estate agent, you should be aware of the emerging areas in your communities and be able to identify available properties that your clients would likely have an interest in.

The goal is to purchase undervalued properties that have a big enough spread to achieve the desired profit.

Since investors come from all walks of life and have different reasons for investing, a one-size-fits-all strategy will not work. Factors to consider may include how much money you want to invest, your age, your needs, whether you are looking for short-term profit or long-term income, how much risk you are comfortable with, and so on. With your help, your clients will need to develop their own set of criteria for choosing properties.

When it is all said and done, if:

1. The investor has the correct mindset,

2. You help them find deals,

3. You help them analyze the property,

4. You help them negotiate the deal, and

5. The property gets to the closing table, then you can expect to have a loyal client for many years to come. As an investor-friendly real estate agent in your community, you will be able to make lots of offers for your clients (and more importantly, sales) by following my five-step system, F-A-B-F-S/R, summarized below. Each step will be described in detail later in this chapter.

Step 1. FIND

Select a property that has investment potential. If the property is truly a great deal, you must act quickly or it will be gone. Keep in mind that you are competing with other investors for limited properties that are available. Does the property initially meet your objective of maximizing the profit given the risks? If yes, move to the next step.

Step 2. ANALYZE

Depending on the type of property, this step may be very easy to accomplish. If it is a single-family dwelling, comparable properties are the best indicator of the value after fix-up costs. If it's a multi-unit, more information is required to run the numbers. (This topic is discussed in Chapter 8.) If the property passes the analysis, move on to writing an offer.

Step 3. BUY

Write the offer while paying attention to the bottom line. If your offer is accepted, follow through with the purchase and go to the next step.

Step 4. FIX

Make repairs and/or updates to get optimum rents or profits. Staying on budget is key.

Step 5. SELL / RENT

Flip quickly or rent the property after repairs have been made within the desired time frame and budget.
The system in detail:
Find, Analyze, Buy, Fix, Sell/Rent
(F, A, B, F, S/R)

In the rest of this chapter we will take a closer look at each of the five steps.

STEP 1: FIND A PROPERTY

A key factor in finding an investment property is to base the decision on numbers, not emotion. Keep in mind that this is a business venture, not playtime. An investor should buy a property because it is a good deal, based solely on the numbers. Will the property meet the investor's financial objectives? Simply put, that means looking at cash flow, tax benefits for a rental, and profit potential for a flipper. To evaluate a potential flipper, answer the following questions:

1. What can the property sell for, based on prices of comparable properties in the same neighborhood?

2. How much will it cost to make the needed repairs and updates?

3. How much profit do you (or your client) want to make?

If an investor pays too much for a property or spends considerably more than the budgeted amount for the rehab, the desired profit may not become a reality.

How can an investor recognize a good deal? This is where you come in as a real estate agent who understands the local housing market. Your knowledge will bring tremendous value to your clients. Experienced real estate agents who are also investors bring a wealth of knowledge based on experience, research, and education.

Different ways to find a good deal

Although those who haven't been in the investment game may have missed out on some excellent buying opportunities, it doesn't mean there are no deals available. Deals can still be found even though they are not as readily available as they were a few years ago. Investors should utilize your services because you know how to spot the good deals that exist.

Multiple Listing Service (MLS)

- There are many ways to find properties for investment purposes, but my primary choice is the MLS. Although the competition is quite fierce for properties with investment potential, on any given day you can find properties that will meet most investors' criteria. Sometimes searching the MLS four or five times a day instead of once a day make a difference between finding properties or not.

  » Look for expired listings, properties that have been listed for 90 days and more, and properties that have been reduced in price. Use search terms like *foreclosures, REOs, cosmetics, motivated, must sell, as is, handyman, TLC,* and *cash only.* Keep in mind that what may be a good property for one investor may not be good for another. When you work with a lot of investors, the chances are very good that a specific property will meet someone's criteria.

Network with other real estate agents who work with investors (not just agents at your own company)

- When you are engaged in this niche market, you get to know other agents that do the same thing. This is not about competition but about helping sellers sell their property in the shortest amount of time.

- How many real estate agents in your own community specialize in investments? Fortunately for you there will be very few compared with the masses of real estate agents who compete fiercely for residential listings and sales. Get to know agents who list foreclosures or short sales. Help each other because you never know when you may have a buyer for their listings or vice versa.

Use word of mouth

- Let other agents know that you have buyers who are always looking for properties in need of repairs (cosmetic or major work). These properties make great flipping candidates or rentals. With agents who are not working with investors, this can be a very effective strategy because they might not have a potential buyer for this type of property.

Advertise

- Advertise in your local newspaper's real estate section that you have buyers who are looking for properties in any condition. Get a one-party listing or even a listing for a week. Avoid gimmicks like saying "I buy houses in any condition."

Visit the county assessor's website

- This is an easy way to find out who owns multiple properties. Contact them. They are truly investors if they own multiple properties. You may be able to get a listing/sale.

Auctions

- An innovative way to buy real estate is through a public sale of properties, also known as a real estate auction. You should still be able to receive a commission if you register your client in advance.

Craigslist

- This free website has a Real Estate tab for property owners and real estate agents. This can be a good place to spot opportunities.

Costar Group

- Costar is the number one provider of commercial real estate information. Visit this site to connect with the world's leading commercial real estate professionals.

Loop Net

- is the most heavily trafficked commercial real estate marketplace online with more than 8 million registered members and 5 million unique monthly visitors.

Why should you focus on finding good deals?

There is no reason for an investor to pay retail price for a property in the hope of appreciation. In real estate you make your money when you buy, so why not purchase an undervalued property and gain instant appreciation?

As a real estate agent with expertise and experience, you understand why it is so important for your clients to purchase properties that are good deals. There is no reason for them to chase properties that do not meet their criteria. There will be a property tomorrow that will be better suited.

Do you know anyone who overpaid for a property? No amount of wishing or praying is going to make that investment worthwhile or profitable.

What about someone who bought with the idea of yearly appreciation? The market may take a downturn and they end up losing money. An investor should buy a property based on how much it is worth right away (after fix-up has taken place), not what they hope it will be worth in the future.

Now that you understand that investors want you to help them find great or good deals, not just okay deals, how can you find properties that meet their selection criteria?

Investors are not created equal, and therefore they will have different needs, objectives, and criteria. For example, some only care about cash flow, while others care more about the tax benefits.

Their defined criteria will keep you focused on finding properties that meet their objectives rather than wasting time showing properties that don't meet their needs. They are likely to pull the trigger and write an offer or multiple offers on the spot when you find the types of deals they are looking for.

When your clients specify their criteria, your search will become more manageable. Can you imagine how difficult it would be for you if they just told you they were looking for a "deal"? What does that mean? What area, how many bedrooms and baths, garages? To you a good deal may be a $20,000 house, but to others it may be a $150,000 fourplex. Make sure you have specifics to guide your search.

Criteria may include any or all of the following: price range, financial terms (such as owner financing), location, schools, amenities/features, property condition, construction (brick or frame), number of bedrooms and bathrooms, with or without garages, close to a college or medical school, style of home or property, a property that needs minimal work and is virtually ready to rent, a property that needs updating to flip, and so on. But ultimately the property can be considered a good deal if it makes sense financially.

Based on the above, you now have enough information to establish a plan of attack. It's like digging for gold to find the types of properties your clients are likely to purchase.

Classifying properties as A, B, C, D

As you and your client evaluate properties it is important to use a consistent system. For our purposes we will classify properties as A, B, C, or D.

These letter grades are assigned to properties and areas based on characteristics such as age, property condition, growing or declining areas, appreciation potential, amenities, and potential rental rates, to name a few characteristics.

It's important for you to understand various property classes and areas so you are able to explain to your clients why a similar property in area D costs much less than one in area B.

It is important to recognize the values of similar properties in different areas and how these differences can affect your investments so that you can meet and exceed your investment goals. When you have this understanding, you will also be able to communicate effectively with industry insiders concerning what you are looking for.

Characteristics of properties

Although assigning letter grades to properties can sometimes be more of an art than a science, the property classes will typically be characterized by the following characteristics:

"A" properties

These types of properties are like blue-chip stock. They tend to be newer properties built within the last five to fifteen years with the most up-to-date amenities, and will typically demand the highest rents. There is no deferred maintenance. Older properties in excellent condition that are located in extremely desirable areas also can fall into this category, as can properties located near universities.

"B" properties

These types of properties may be a notch or two below an A property. They may not have all the amenities. They tend to be a bit older and will not command as much rent. They may have some deferred maintenance. They usually have appreciation potential. The savvy investor can quickly raise the property's value by making minor improvements.

"C" properties

These types of properties are typically older properties built 30+ years ago with far fewer amenities. They may be a notch or two below a B. They may be located in up-and-coming neighborhoods. Rents are lower than for B properties. They usually have more deferred maintenance. The savvy investor can very quickly transform a C into a B by making minor improvements.

"D" properties

These types of properties are located in undesirable areas such as high-crime neighborhoods. The neighborhood is a bigger problem than the condition of the property, because properties can be improved but little can be done about the neighborhood.

D properties may have a lot of deferred maintenance. Rents are low, and the quality of the tenant may not be great. Unless the neighborhood turns around there will probably be little to no appreciation. They require intense management. These types of properties are not recommended for the brand-new investor.

A lot of money is being made in these types of areas, and although they are cash flow machines they require a lot of attention and repairs. These properties can be compared to penny stock.

Characteristics of neighborhoods

As a real estate agent you should be knowledgeable about areas that are improving as well as areas that are declining. Depending on the neighborhood, what may be a D property today could become a B property in a few years and vice versa.

When you evaluate areas, you can use a similar A, B, C, D classification system:

A – Newer growth areas
B – Older, stable areas
C – Older, declining, or stable areas
D – Older, declining, or potentially rapidly declining areas

These guidelines will help you and your clients to determine the property types and locations they are looking for. The key is to identify properties that will accomplish their investment goals.

In choosing a property, investors should focus on properties in areas that are equal to or better than the class of the property itself (for example, a B property in a B or A area) and avoid properties in areas that are lower that the property class (for example, an A property in a C area). The area class they invest in will have a great deal of influence on the stability of their portfolio over time and will determine whether it appreciates or declines in value during times of economic fluctuation. An A property is going to have a much harder time performing like an A property if it is located in a C area, but a C property might perform better over time if it is in an A area.

If your clients are looking for investments with the highest appreciation potential and the best initial cash flow, they will want to look for A and B properties located in A and B areas or in the path of progress. They will want to avoid C properties in C areas. If they are not as interested in appreciation but are looking for investments with strong cash flow, then B and C properties in B and C areas would be the best fit.

Now that you're more familiar with the ABCs of property and location classifications and how they can affect the value of an investment, you will be able to more effectively guide your clients in selecting properties that can meet and exceed their investment goals.

STEP 2: ANALYZE A PROPERTY

The most important criterion for choosing a property is the financial component, and every offer made by a potential buyer should be based on careful analysis to maximize profits given the risks.

Depending on the type of property that is being evaluated, the analysis can be very easy to do. If it is a single-family dwelling, the selling prices of comparable properties are the best indicator of value after fix-up costs. Multi-unit properties are evaluated differently.

A house is very simple to analyze. How much rent can you expect compared to the PITI (Principle, Interest, Taxes, and Insurance)? If a three-bedroom property rents for $900 and the PITI is $600, the cash flow is $300 a month before expenses. Is this a worthwhile investment or not? The simple answer is yes. You also should consider the financial impact of repairs, vacancies, and possibly property management.

What if your client is interested in buying a duplex or a four-plex? How would determine whether it's a good deal or not? Running the numbers will tell you whether the subject property is a poor or good investment opportunity.

To recognize whether a property is likely to be a good investment, consider cash flow, leverage, equity, appreciation, and risk.

1. Cash Flow

- Will this property produce the desired cash flow?
- What is the current rental market like?
- What is the vacancy history for this property?
- How much is the down payment (10%, 20%, 30% or more)?
- What is the interest rate?
- Will this property provide income for the investor?
- How important is income to the investor?
- Does the investor have other income?
- Does the investor need more income now, or is future equity more important?
- How will this property's cash flow compare with that of other potential properties?
- Is the subject property a single-family unit, duplex, fourplex, or something else?

You should take all of these factors into consideration when you are evaluating a property. For example, if you are analyzing several properties in the same neighborhood, ask yourself whether a $50,000 house that rents for $750 a month would be a better deal than a $100,000 duplex that rents for $1,050 per month or a $150,000 fourplex that brings in $2,000 per month. Instead of buying a duplex for $100,000, would it make more sense to purchase two $50,000 houses that will produce a combined rental income of $1,500 per month? Would the two houses cost more to maintain than the duplex would cost? If so, how much more? Which of these potential purchases would be a better investment for you or your client?

There are no right answers to these questions, but cash flow should always be considered when you are looking at a potential purchase.

2. Leverage

The less cash the investor uses as a down payment on each property, the more buying power they will have and the greater their opportunity will be to expand their portfolio.

Example of leverage:

- Investor A purchases a property for $200,000 cash. The property appreciates 5% in the first year ($10,000), so the return on the investment is 5%.

- Investor B purchases a property for $200,000 with a $20,000 down payment and a mortgage of $180,000. The property appreciates 5% in the first year ($10,000). Based on the initial $20,000 investment, the return on the investment is 50%. Investor B benefits greatly from the power of leverage.

3. Equity

Is the property offered at a huge discount? Investors should only buy home runs, because a great deal will have instant equity.

Equity can take a number of forms, depending on the situation. All of the following types of properties could be great deals:

- A property that is undervalued

- A potential fixer-upper

- A rezoning opportunity

- A poorly managed property

- A foreclosure

- A short sale

There are many ways to create equity, but the easiest way is to buy a property that is a great deal.

4. Appreciation

If a property is a great deal, appreciation and equity will happen instantaneously. Buying in the right neighborhoods should minimize the risk if a good decision is made. In today's market, an investor should be able to purchase a property at 20% to 40% below or above the price that the same property sold for just a few years ago.

5. Risk

- How much risk is the investor willing to take?

- What happens if their assumptions are not correct?

- Can they continue making the mortgage payment if they have a vacancy?

If an investor is comfortable with the level of risk involved in a potential purchase, they are well on their way toward building wealth or making a living from their investments.

Cosmetic versus structural problems

It may seem like an easy task to determine whether an issue with a property is a minor or major problem, but it depends on the viewpoint of the person who is doing the evaluating.

From a seller's perspective, all the issues with their property are minor problems. For many real estate agents many problems are minor because they are common to a specific type of property of a given age and price range.

From a buyer's perspective some problems are major, some are minor, and many are in between the two. As you are aware, buyers look to home inspectors to provide them with input as to what are minor or major problems. Some investors may not use a home inspector and prefer to use a contractor instead.

Opportunities to purchase properties with minor or major issues can be found quite readily on the MLS. For the savvy investor, dollar signs are written all over them.

---

*Spotting an Attractive Potential
Rental or Fixer-Upper*

Look for these signs that a residential property is likely to be a good investment:

☐ Located in a desirable area

☐ The ugly duckling of the neighborhood

☐ Vacant and may be tagged by the city

☐ Good bones but needs updating

☐ Absentee owner

- ☐ Available through an estate, distressed sale, or foreclosure

- ☐ Desirable floor plan with character and charm

- ☐ May have hardwood floors under the carpet

- ☐ Spacious kitchen that may need updating

- ☐ Three bedrooms, including a good-sized master bedroom

- ☐ Finished basement with enough room to add another bedroom by putting up a wall and adding an egress window

Bottom line: If minor improvements will increase the property value, the decision to buy is a no-brainer.

I've had clients who were able to purchase properties for pennies on the dollar because they required some foundation work, while other clients didn't want to touch these properties. Everything depends on the investor's mindset. Are they a first-time investor or someone who has flipped numerous properties and owns several income-producing properties? There can be opportunities galore for an investor who is receptive.

The lists that follow should make it easier to distinguish between cosmetic issues and major problems.

Cosmetic issues

- Interior/exterior paint

- Replace carpet

- Refinish wood floors

- Replace light fixtures

- Replace damaged kitchen cabinets

- Replace ceramic/vinyl floor

- Remove junk and debris from a property sold "as is"

- Landscape an overgrown lawn

- Property tagged by code inspector (the violation may be major or minor)

- Repair or replace siding

- Replace old appliances

- Update old bathrooms/kitchen

- Upgrade outdated electrical service

- Repair broken windows

- Any other "quick-fix" things

Structural /major issues

For the beginner, any of these issues with a property may be a deal breaker, but for the savvy investor they may signal a great opportunity. Regardless, one should proceed with caution.

- Foundation or walls

- Plumbing issues including galvanized pipe

- Leaning chimney

- Floors that slope

- Asbestos siding

- Lead in the property

- Rotting wood in the frame

- Lead paint

- Roof replacement: A roof may be serviceable but have two or three layers. If so, what will be the cost to replace the shingles?

- Buried underground oil tanks

- Old furnace and central air (HVAC) problems

- Mold

I'm sure you can think of other examples of major issues, but you get the point. The key is to understand that for some clients a minor cosmetic issue may be a problem, while to others a major structural issue may not be a deal-breaker. A client who is a contractor and understands construction probably will not walk away from structural issues and may choose to buy a property that no one else wants.

How to gather property information

Before you make an offer, it is important to know what factors contribute to the value of a property.

Accurate information is critical. The minimum information that would contribute to making an informed decision to either buy or pass on a property may include property details, financing, income generation, and expenses.

Property details. How old is the house or building (new, old, or run-down)? How many units does it have? Does the owner pay for the utilities or are the units separately metered? How much does the property cost? What are the expected costs for any repairs or updates?

Financing details. What is the loan amount, down payment, closing cost, loan terms (10, 20, 25, 30 years), and interest rate?

Potential income. How much income does the property generate (rent, laundry, vending machines, and so on)?

Expenses. What is the annual cost to operate the property? Include such things as taxes, insurance, maintenance, lawn care, snow removal, advertising, supplies, and so on. Also consider setting aside funds to cover the cost of deferred maintenance. A good property inspector can point out major repairs or expenses that the property is likely to incur in the future (for example, replacing the roof, furnace, central air units, and so on).

The income minus expenses determines the net operating income (NOI). NOI is one of the most important measures because it is used to determine a property's income stream. Concepts such as NOI, Cap Rate, debt coverage ratio, and others will be explained in detail in Chapter 8.

All of the information you are working with must be accurate in order to determine whether a property is a great deal, an okay deal, or a horrible deal. The value of the property is directly related to how much income/profit the property produces for the investor.

It is not uncommon for a seller to provide numbers that are inaccurate. For example, they may inflate how much rent the property produces, not include any vacancies, and overlook certain maintenance expenses. In other words, by overestimating income and underestimating expenses, they make the property seem to be more valuable.

Your job as an agent will be critically important here. You can help your client make a good decision or leave things up to chance. Make sure you have the best available information, all or most of which can be verified. (You may ask for tax returns for the past two years, for example.)

If the seller uses a property management company, they would be an excellent source of information and should be able to give you accurate information.

As a real estate agent, you probably are familiar with the difference between *pro forma* information and actual information.

Pro forma means "estimated," and that is the information that is generally found on the MLS listing. You can analyze a property using pro forma but it is better to base your analysis on actual information. Ideally, the pro forma will match the actual information.

Another piece of information to consider is the assessed value of the property. Are the taxes going up or down? It makes a difference on the bottom line if the income goes up and the expenses go down or vice versa.

It may not be a good idea to spend a lot of time on analysis before a property is under contract should be considered. Depending on the level of the investor's experience and the complexity of the property, a detailed analysis can also be done in at the next stage.

Keep in mind that after it is all said and done, an investment property must produce enough income to cover the debt service to the bank as well as other measures listed below. These concepts will be discussed in detail in Chapter 8. In other words, the numbers matter.

Financial measures for evaluating an investment property include the following:

- Annual Debt Service (ADS)

- Break Even Ratio (BER)

- Capitalization Rate (Cap Rate)

- Cash Flow Before Taxes (CFBT)

- Cash Flow After Taxes (CFAT)

- Cash on Cash Return (COC)

- Debt Coverage Ratio (DCR)

- Gross Operating Income (GOI)

- Gross Rent Multiplier (GRM)

- Gross Scheduled Income (GSI)

- Loan to Value (LTV)

- Net Operating Income (NOI)

- Operating Expense (OE)

- Operating Expense Ratio (OER)

- Return on Investment with Appreciation

- Return on Investment without Appreciation

- Vacancy and Credit Loss

STEP 3: BUY THE RIGHT PROPERTY, BASED ON THE INVESTOR'S NEEDS AND OBJECTIVES

Everything that needs to happen from purchase agreement to closing happens at this stage. It is also important to do whatever due diligence is desired: inspections by contractor(s) and so on to determine whether the expected remodeling costs are satisfactory to the buyer. Of course, "satisfactory" will have a different meaning for each investor.

Is your client comfortable with all the findings? Did the property pass the test if the client intends to use it as a rental or "flipper"?

What if the property is a multi-unit? The same due diligence may apply, but the decision to buy is also subject to insurance quote or inspection of all units, review and approval of leases, tax returns, rent rolls, and so on. The greater the amount of due diligence that can be accomplished at the analysis stage (step 2), the better. However, sellers are sometimes reluctant to provide the information until the property is under contract.

Assuming that the property meets the criteria, the offer is either written or not written at this stage. If a property will be used as a rental, the investor may be able to pay more than if it is intended as a "flipper."

For a rental, the bottom line is how much income the property will produce. Over the long term, paying $5,000 to $10,000 more for a property may not make much of a difference in the payment (PITI). An additional $5,000 at 5% interest with 20% down amortized over 20 years will be an additional $33 a month in the payment. Sometimes buyers lose sight of the big picture and fail to realize that it might make sense to pay a little more for a property that will generate more income.

For a property that is being purchased to flip, a higher price makes a big difference and may not work. A price that is $5,000 to $10,000 higher than the investor's desired price may interfere with the ability to pay for a big chunk of the remodeling expenses. More information on flipping will be covered in Chapter 9.

How will the offer be written?

Will the offer be written as cash or conventional financing? Keep in mind that the preferred method of acquiring these types of properties is cash. This does not mean that an offer subject to a loan cannot compete with one from a cash buyer, but there is a good chance that even if the cash offer is lower it will get the nod. Sellers prefer cash offers because there is no need for appraisals to meet underwriting guidelines.

Other options for making cash offers include a line of credit or bridge loan as long as the subject property is not used as collateral.

The collateral may be tied the buyer's personal residence, securities, or other assets. The buyer may be able to use this method to purchase and fix a property and then have it reappraised and perhaps pull all their money back in. The experience level of the investor, their credit worthiness, their financial statement, and so on will affect the feasibility of this approach.

A little-known fact is that investors can use their self-directed/Roth IRAs to purchase properties. A self-directed IRA requires account owners to make active investments on behalf of the plan. To open this type of account, an owner must hire a trustee or custodian to hold the IRA assets and be responsible for administering the account and filing required documents with the IRS.

Lately, many real estate agents and investors have been getting frustrated because they can't find "deals." The common complaint is that when a property that is priced right hits the market, there are multiple offers that lead to a bidding war and the resulting price is drastically higher. This is totally different from the real estate market a few years ago, when investors enjoyed the best opportunities in over 40 years.

I am not saying that good deals are not available. It is all relative. You may pay more for a property, but rents are going up and so are the selling prices of flipped properties. The bottom line is that "lowball" offers are more likely than ever before to be a waste of time.

After the investor has purchased the property, the next step is to improve it.

STEP 4: FIX THE PROPERTY

At this stage, the investor makes repairs and/or updates to get optimum rents or profits. Staying on budget with the remodeling project is crucial.

How does one know whether certain repairs should be made or not? To illustrate how to make this decision, let's use an example of a $60,000 property that requires $15,000 in repairs for a total investment of $75,000.

Scenario 1

Let's say that comparable properties in the same neighborhood sell in the $110,000 range and the investor bought the property with the intention of flipping it. Carrying costs and selling expenses are $12,000 for a total expense of $87,000. The spread is a potential profit of $23,000 less tax consequences. Not a bad return in just a few short months. The credit line is paid back, and the investor moves on to the next deal.

Scenario 2

If the property is going to be used as a rental, it must be nice enough to attract tenants who will meet the investor's criteria.

Rental properties are intended to be work horses and not race horses. In that regard they should be upgraded to a level that sets the tone for how the tenant should treat the property. First impressions are important, and that means the property should be clean and the appliances should be in working order. Tenants should be just as picky about the property as the investor should be about the tenant. I believe that when tenants know what is expected, they will meet those expectations.

The more time that the owner spends upfront fixing up the property, the more pride on the part of the investor and tenant. When tenants see the owner taking interest in the property, they will be more inclined to take care of it. A property that is in disrepair sends a strong message that the landlord only cares about collecting the rent.

If a property is in poor condition, the tenants are not likely to be "blue ribbon." On the opposite side, well-maintained properties attract tenants are likely to do their part to maintain the property.

Here are a few easy and inexpensive ways to improve a property:

- Clean the house thoroughly, including the appliances.

- Paint the interior a nice neutral color.

- Replace linoleum with ceramic tile, and replace carpet that is old (you can only clean it so many times).

- Replace kitchen knobs if necessary, as well as faucets that are old.

- Rake the yard, trim bushes, cut the grass, and plant some flowers to ensure that the property is presentable and has nice curb appeal.

Although there will always be opportunities to purchase properties that are considered to be good deals, it would be unrealistic for investors to expect to compete successfully with home buyers for properties that require little to no repairs. Buyers of owner-occupied properties will pay more than investors, perhaps even above the seller's asking price.

In my experience, owner-occupied buyers are likely to walk away from properties that need work and are considered to have structural or major defects. These types of properties offer the best opportunity for good to great deals for real estate investors.

Some of my clients who are investors have walked away from certain properties that involved major remodeling tasks or structural issues, but there are investors for every type of property. Some may consider a new roof, furnace, bathroom, or foundation repairs to be a major project while others will think nothing of it.

Will a new or inexperienced investor with no real construction knowledge make an offer on a property that is considered to have major issues or a major project? Even if they wanted to buy it I would probably advise them against doing so. I operate under the philosophy that I am looking for clients for the long term, so why not look at the big picture? A costly and unsuccessful experience is likely to be the end of a relationship. Even if you earned your commission, you have lost a client and the opportunity for repeat business and referrals. There are properties available for investors at all experience levels, and one that is better suited for this particular client will show up. Some people believe that real estate agents only care about the commission check. What a powerful statement you can make with your clients when you provide advice that is in their best interests even when it means missing out on a sale.

Instead of showing a property with major issues to a first-time investor, I would show the same property to a more experienced investor who has flipped a few. It may be great property that meets their criteria. The outcome of making the needed repairs most likely will be higher rents or increased profit (if the property is flipped). Kitchens and bathrooms are two major remodeling jobs that are regarded as nice updates.

On the other hand, taking things to the next level makes sense only if the property is a good deal. There is no need to buy the property if by the time all the remodeling is done the cost is no different from paying retail price.

STEP 5: SELL/RENT

If you have a client who wants to know how much effort and money they should put into fixing up a rental property, here are a couple of good questions they can ask themselves:

CASH FLOW GROWTH

BUY IT RIGHT ➡ PAY IT DOWN ➡ PAY IT OFF

Would they let one of their relatives live in the property?

Would they be proud enough to show the property to one of their best friends? If the answer is yes, they are a proud property owner. Good for them.

Renting a property quickly is key. The longer it takes to get the property rented, the lower the income for the investor.

What are some good ways to advertise a rental property?

For property owners, vacant rental properties represent a significant cash drain. Accordingly, an all-important job for any owner or property manager is to fill all rental units. To that end, below is a list of 24 websites where you can market your units when you have a vacancy. You should provide photos and detailed information of your rental property as well as your contact information so prospects can easily get in touch with you.

1. **Craigslist.** People turn to Craigslist to find almost everything, including housing in a specific metropolitan area. Craigslist is inexpensive, and it allows you to write in your own way and with your own photos. However, you will get many inquiries, and many of them will be from people who are not serious about your rental.

2. **Oodle.** Like Craigslist, Oodle is a classified listing service that includes rental housing. It's not just property-focused, but it's good for attracting renters who are local and may stumble on your listing as they browse for other items.

3. **Zillow.** With its photo listings, interactive map, and ability to easily sort by features such as bedrooms, bathrooms, and rental price, Zillow is a popular rental property listing site. It also allows prospective tenants to compare two listings side by side.

4. Hotpads. Looking for a website that allows you to list your unit in a multi-family building? Try Hotpads. This site also caters to pet owners with pet information upfront, and like Zillow, it's based on an interactive map.

5. RentalHouses.com. Although the website itself is a little bit dated, RentalHouses.com lets property owners and managers post their rentals to the nationwide database in a few clicks.

6. Realtor.com. This website manages both rentals and real estate sales. It only accepts listings from property managers and owners. The interface is a little less straightforward and attractive than sites like Zillow, but it provides a simple search function for price and location.

7. Padmapper. A fun, interactive map allows prospective renters to set a price, set a number of bedrooms, and look at cities across North America that suit that price range. Renters won't see your actual listing until after the initial search when they dig a little deeper.

8. Trulia. This attractive and simple property listing site allows renters to set parameters to see a group of photo listings with vital statistics about a property. Make sure you have a single great photo for adding your property to this site.

9. Lovely. This site has a simple, graphic format with an interactive map. The latest listings show up in red on the map so renters can see what's fresh on the market. It's also easy for tenants to see whether a property is pet-friendly, and there's a bullet list of amenities that you'll need to fill out.

10. **Rentals.com.** Tenants can search for exactly the type of home they want, with searches compiled into condos, lofts, duplexes, and more. It requires less information about amenities, and it has your contact information and the availability flagged to encourage people to call.

11. **Rentdigs.** This site features free photo listings. Prospective tenants can not only find rentals, but they can also find rent-to-own homes and moving company quotes. Rentdigs features a single photo and some simple information on the listing, so make sure your photo is a good one.

12. **Rent.com.** At first glance, Rent.com is largely geared towards apartment rentals but it also provides information on a significant number of rental houses. It's also one of the higher-traffic sites on the list, so it's definitely worth looking into.

13. **Zumper.** This value-added site includes neighborhood information and city guides for your prospective tenants. Its initial listings feature minimal information and a single photo, but its detailed listings offer you the opportunity to add a paragraph about your property.

14. **Social media.** If you have a listing on a site or on your website, you can advertise it to your community online by posting a link on social media. If you're having difficulty renting a property, create an infographic with property details. While Facebook, Twitter, and Instagram may not be property-focused, they allow you to reach out to your communities and turn the search for tenants into a more sociable experience.

15. **Airbnb.** This home rental site connects homeowners directly to customers seeking short-term rentals. Airbnb is a dominant player in the home rental sharing economy or peer-to-peer (P2P) activity of providing or sharing access to goods and services.

16. **Apartments.com.** Apartments.com (as well as Apartmentfinder.com) provide a free popular tool for long-term rentals of apartments and condos. Apartments.com offers deals and can provide upfront savings for users if they end up renting through the site.

17. **Vacation Rentals By Owner (VRBO).** VRBO is a top-ranked site that specializes in vacation rentals homes, apartments, condos, B&B cabins, beach houses, villas, etc.

18. **Nextdoor.com.** This is a private social networking site for local neighborhoods, with 80% of neighborhoods across the US relying on the information and services it provides to its members. It's a popular site for realtors to brand their services and for landlords to list rentals.

19. **Facebook Groups.** With over 500 million users, these discussion groups are like forums with many varied topics of interest. Rental groups can be found here by a highly customizable location search function. It's a great way to get the word out to your Facebook contacts about a rental property.

20. **HomeAway.** This site guides registered users to its inventory of short-term rentals. It differs from Airbnb in that it offers rentals of entire properties as opposed to rooms, hostels, or even beds.

21. **Walk Score.** As its name suggests Walk Score is another niche site whose stated mission is to promote walkable neighborhoods for those residing in apartments. This site appeals to renters concerned with transportation costs, commute times, access to public transportation or a property's proximity to activities, businesses, schools, etc.

22. **Sublet.com.** This site is not just about sublets—every type of rental can be listed here: short term, long term, vacation, furnished and unfurnished as well as private and room rentals. Landlords can post a Standard listing for free, but a Premium listing can receive up to 500 times more leads, and tenant screening, employment, and criminal background check services are provided for a sliding scale fee based on the market you're listing in.

23. **Move.com.** This site is geared toward experienced renters or buyers who know exactly where they want to live and want they want in a home or apartment. It also caters to seniors who may require assisted living, continuing care, or independent living. This company has a database of listings that is viewed by a customer base of 40 million people and provides many helpful tips and links for topics like owning pets, rent vs buy, painting, decorating, and moving.

24. **People With Pets.** This site is essentially a national directory of pet-friendly homes, apartments, and hotels. For renters, this site is free to use; for property managers this site will charge $299 a year for advertising your pet-friendly property to the approximately 72% of renters who own pets.

In addition to online advertising, offline methods can work well. A yard sign is a very inexpensive way to advertise, and word of mouth is both effective and free. Of course advertising in the newspaper real estate section works also, but it will cost $30 to $50 each time an ad is published.

How should you screen prospective tenants?

Tenant selection is probably the most important step that will greatly improve your chances of succeeding in this business. The question you need to ask yourself is what type of tenant you want. I prefer a blue-ribbon tenant commensurate with the quality and condition of the property.

It is a huge mistake to rent to anyone without doing the necessary due diligence. There are several tenant screening services to help you determine whether someone is qualified to rent a property.

Credit checks, criminal checks, landlord verifications from two previous landlords, and employment verifications are all important.

Probably the least important screening tool is the credit check. Keep in mind that if everyone had good credit there would not be a rental business. Your gut instincts can also tell you a lot about a potential tenant.

Renting to anyone without verifying information will backfire. Careful tenant selection minimizes the risk that a property will be trashed.

A good tenant will leave the property in just about rentable condition. The opposite will occur with a poor tenant that no other landlord would rent to. Careful tenant selection determines whether this business will lead to success or failure.

Most of the horror stories one hears about poor tenants come down to inadequate screening. If you take any shortcuts you will regret it later. Take your time with each applicant and make sure you follow the same procedures with each applicant who you don't run into any discrimination problems. You should also become very familiar with the landlord-tenant laws in your state.

Be aware that not all tenants are completely honest about their backgrounds or past issues, so the due diligence is critical. The fact that they drive a nice car or wear nice clothes is not a good reason to overlook anything. If they have cash for the first month's rent and deposit, a red flag should go up. It is also important to verify the person they put down as their previous landlord. You can do this by going to your county assessor's office and looking up who the owner of record is for the property. I caught a few lying as they put the name of a relative as their landlord. Of course, their relative gave a stellar review, yet they were evicted.

A word of advice: You don't have to be a friend to your tenant, but it is your responsibility to be friendly and respectful.

Sampling of Tenant Screening Services

- Turbotenant.com All-in-one platform where you can screen tenants and also post rental listings. Quick and easy tenant screening, including criminal, credit, and eviction reports. Manage property easily. Market like a pro. Free for landlords. Rental estimate reports. Free landlord software. Landlord rental forms. Customizable applications.

- Mysmartmove.com Free to sign up, no membership fees. Pass the cost of screening on to your tenants. Create your online account; get screening reports delivered in a matter of minutes, online and secure.

- Myrental.com An innovative suite of tenant screening services including renter eviction.

- Applyconnect.com Online screening services and tenant credit checks to help separate the good renters from the bad.

- Experian.com Industry-leading provider of tenant verification and tenant background check solutions.

- Zumper.com Easiest way to screen prospective tenants. Services include landlord credit checks, evictions, and criminal checks.

- Cozyco.com 100% free for landlords. Screening tools make finding the perfect tenant simple. Online rent collection. Credit checks. Services: tenant screening, collect rent online, property listings, expense tracking, etc.

- Leaserunner.com Advance applicant record matching. 36 million eviction records. Easy-to-read screening reports. Screen directly from a listing ad or website.

- Rentalhistoryreports.com/small-landlords/ tenant-screening Try the leading small landlord tenant screening service... we've pretty much seen it all and know how to help you fill your properties with the best tenants.

- AAAscreening.com You get instant credit reports and tenant scorecards for making fast tenant approval decisions.

- Tenantsreports.com Our mission is to provide a tenant screening solution with the most accurate tenant reports, fastest results, supported by the best customer service.

- Tenantbackgroundchecks.com Tenant screening services for landlords and property managers.

- Rentprep.com Community-driven tenant screening service. Ideal for landlords who want certified live screeners who can verify key information.

- Nationaltenant.com Focuses on a single goal: to help property owners and managers make the best leasing decisions possible.

Note: The author does not promote one tenant screening service over the others. Readers of this book should make their own determination as to which service will best meet their needs.

Is it important to require tenants to sign a lease?

A lease is the contract between a landlord and a tenant. The lease sets forth the rights and responsibilities of both the landlord and the tenant.

The lease allows the tenant to occupy and use the property for a specific period of time. In return, the tenant generally pays rent.

The lease may set forth other duties and responsibilities of the landlord and tenant. Once both parties have signed the lease, both are bound by its terms.

What should a lease include?

1. Names of the tenant, the landlord or the landlord's agent, and the person or company authorized to manage the property.

2. Address of the property and what appliances, if any, are included.

3. The amount of rent required, date when the monthly payment is due, any grace period, and any late charges or nonsufficient funds fees.

4. How the rent should be paid (check, money order, or cash).

5. Methods for terminating the agreement prior to the expiration date and what, if any, charges will be imposed.

6. The amount of the security deposit.

7. Whether the tenant or landlord pays for utilities.

8. Rules and regulations such as pet rules (pet deposit), pest control, and many others.

9. Methods of resolving maintenance issues.

A sample lease is provided in the Resources section near the end of this book.

The result of following the F-A-B-F-S/R system

The end result of following this five-step system is rental property that generates monthly cash flow and builds wealth, or a property that if flipped for a profit. The same five action steps can be done over and over. When you teach this system to your clients, risks are minimized and you have a happy client who will tell others how good you are.

Selling the property

You helped your client find a good deal, and in all likelihood your commission wasn't huge. When it is time for them to sell the property, you want them to come back to you. You can do this by making your expectations clear early in your relationship with each client. I have two rules:

1. I help them find deals, but when it is time to sell, I am the listing agent. The first time my rule is not followed, I will no longer work with that client.

2. I do not reduce my commission.

When your clients are successful, you are successful and you can expect a client for the long term.

KEY POINTS TO REMEMBER:

- Success in real estate investment is more likely when you follow a system and teach it to your clients.

- You and your clients can follow the same five steps over and over: Find, Analyze, Buy, Fix, Sell/Rent.

- Following the F-A-B-F-S/R system is likely to produce a satisfied client who will recommend you to others.

- Proper screening of tenants is paramount.

CHAPTER 8

DEFINING FINANCIAL TERMS— THE NUMBERS MATTER

Success in real estate investment requires you as the real estate agent to become familiar with a number of financial measures or formulas. Even if you are not a "numbers person," you will need to acquire this knowledge in order to bring the value and expertise clients are expecting from you.

You are playing a role in some of the most important financial decisions that your clients are likely to make. They may spend more money on real estate than they do on the stock market.

If you don't know how to evaluate a property, how can you advise a client about whether it is likely to be a good investment? Remember that real estate investors make their decision based on money, not emotion.

Taking time to run the numbers will make a difference. I'm sure there are far more investors who don't take the time to evaluate an investment and fly by the seat of their pants, but to me that is the quickest route to disaster.

Why not take the time to evaluate an investment opportunity correctly? If you "wing it," a lot of money may go down the tubes.

The information in this chapter is essential for you to absorb. This knowledge will separate you from other real estate agents who have no idea how to evaluate a property.

I realize that there are more complicated formulas that I don't even understand, but the basic ones offered in this chapter (such as net operating income, capitalization rate, debt coverage ratio, cash on cash return, vacancy and credit loss, just to name a few) will go a long way in bringing the value, knowledge, and expertise your clients are expecting from you.

As an investor-friendly real estate agent, my business model has always been geared toward investors who buy and sell houses, duplexes, and small multi-unit apartments (I call them "Ma and Pa" types of investments). I also do a fair amount of business with owner-occupied buyers and sellers, many of whom have decided to become investors.

While I don't feel bad that this has been my path, there are far more knowledgeable and sophisticated real estate agents who know a heck of a lot more than I do and deal in other investment areas such as land, commercial, industrial, hotels, motels, golf courses, and so on.

My personal investment choices led me to work this segment of the market (people who invest in houses, duplexes, small multi-units, and so on). That is my comfort zone; therefore, it also has been the area of emphasis for my business.

It is important to realize that some investors think they know a lot more than you do and may decide not to use your services. If they choose to fly solo, I believe they are making a huge mistake. Your services could help them accomplish their long-term objectives, especially if you get a handle on the financial analysis.

If you are already highly respected as an investor-friendly real estate agent, congratulations. When you have the skills to help your clients run the numbers or analyze property you are invaluable and will always be in demand. Expect your business to grow more than you thought was possible.

What is your own experience as an investor? Do your prospective clients know more than you do?

If so, I am confident that this situation will change if you make an effort to acquire the necessary expertise. You can become an expert in a short period of time.

If you don't know how to run the numbers, how will you go about recognizing whether a property is an okay deal, a good deal, or a great deal? Do you have a gut feeling that tells you whether a property is a good deal or not? To an investor, a real estate agent who deals with facts will make a better impression than an agent who goes by gut feelings or intuition.

Have you ever had one of your associates come to you and mention a property that they just listed for 100K that would make a great rental? Do they know specifically why they think this is so? What is the upside potential? Will it be a $175,000 property after repairs? How much will the repairs cost? There is a lot of information to consider before you can decide whether a property is a good deal or not.

When agents have no idea how to run the numbers, how can they know whether a property would be a great deal for a rental or possible flip? Are they basing their assumption on facts or simply because they deal in the high-end market and any property priced far below what they are accustomed to listing or selling seems like a good deal?

Wouldn't it be more convincing if they mentioned the capitalization rate for a rental property, or the NOI or ROI, cash on cash return, debt coverage ratio, or gross rent multiplier? You may be impressed or feel that they are talking in a foreign language if you have no clue what these terms signify.

GETTING DOWN TO BUSINESS

If a client asked for your opinion about whether property A, B, or C is likely to be the best investment, what would you tell them? Your response should be "It depends, but I can let you know after I analyze the numbers." You might have time to do some calculations on the spot, but this is not likely.

The bottom line is that a series of calculations will have to be performed to determine if the investment is likely to be a good one. When you run the numbers you will be able to say "According to my analysis, this property is (or is not) likely to be a good investment."

Analyzing a single-family dwelling is very easy. Does the property cash flow after paying the taxes, insurance, mortgage, and so on? After making these payments, the amount that is left over from the rent payment is cash flow. How much cash flow on a monthly basis will be acceptable: $50, $100, $200, or $300? Probably $50 or $100 will not be enough, but $200 should work. What do you think?

The most common way to determine the value of a single-family dwelling is to look at market comparables. For example, if a property can be purchased for $70,000 while others in the same subdivision are selling for $110,000, it may be a good deal. Let's say it will require $15,000 worth of repairs, bringing the total investment to $85,000. Still sounds like a good deal to me. What do you think? Would it be a good investment if you would get $25,000 equity just by buying the undervalued property? This would be an example of making your money when you buy.

However, a multi-unit property (two units and up) is valued differently from a single-family dwelling. Its value is directly related to the property's income and expenses.

Would it be possible for a multi-unit to increase in value in the same general area as the example above while houses are declining in value? Yes, because multi-units are valued by the income and expenses, overall condition, and so on. A financial analysis is critically important to make the determination.

What if two identical multi-unit properties are for sale one block apart from each other? Property A has deferred maintenance and rents that are well below market, and Property B is in very good condition and rents that are close to market rents. The client is considering writing an offer and asks you to determine how much they should offer and which property would be a better investment. They are seriously thinking of writing offers on both. You can figure out the answers to your client's questions by running the numbers.

Commercial-type properties such as large apartment buildings, industrial properties, and strip shopping centers require much more information before for a financial analysis. If you are given an opportunity to list such properties, I suggest that you find someone who has knowledge and experience with commercial real estate and either co-list or ask for a referral fee.

YOU CAN HELP YOUR CLIENTS BY STEERING THEM AWAY FROM THESE MISTAKES

Clients who fall in love with the deal rather than the property can avoid making costly mistakes. Some of the most common mistakes made by real estate investors are listed below. (You can probably think of others.)

Mistake # 1: Analysis paralysis

Many people never take the first step toward building wealth or making a living in real estate because they suffer from analysis paralysis. Regardless of whether you're in a seller's market or a buyer's market, a property that is a good deal will not stay on the market for long. It is important to get the property under contract before you put much time and effort into analyzing it. A good contingency would be "subject to inspection by contractor to determine remodeling costs satisfactory to buyer within ____ days upon acceptance of offer." The word "satisfactory" has different meanings for different investors.

Mistake #2: Fudging the fix-up cost

Some investors underestimate the fix-up cost to talk themselves into moving forward with a purchase while others overestimate it to justify backing away from the deal. Investors may also forget to include the carrying costs, insurance, interest, taxes, and so on. Help your clients to take a realistic view of the fix-up cost. Don't fudge the numbers to make the deal cash flow or the rehab pay off. Buying or not buying without good information or facts doesn't make sense. Take time to perform the appropriate due diligence.

Mistake #3: Overestimating the rent

Sometimes rents are overestimated. What is the current market rent for the area? Is the estimated rent for the property above or below market rates? If it is under market, can the rent be increased? It is better to buy a property with below-market rents than one with above-market rents. When a unit becomes vacant will it be easy to rent or will the rent have to be reduced?

Mistake #4: Overestimating the property's value

Don't overestimate what the property is worth. Can the property be purchased at a drastic discount or perhaps for a few thousand dollars less than the asking price? Plan for the unknown and be conservative in your estimate. If you know the area and the prices for similar properties it should be easy to determine whether the property is a good deal. If it is a multi-unit, different factors will come into play.

Mistake #5: Failing to recognize a great deal

A deal is a deal any way you look at it. Learn how to spot a great deal for yourself or your clients, and then act on it. See mistake #1.

Mistake #6: Not paying attention to a property's location

Remember the old adage about the three most important features of real estate: location, location, location. Is the property in the A, B, C, or D category? Failing to consider where it is located could be the costliest mistake of all. If an investor is selling the property and if it is such a good deal, why are they selling it? Perhaps they want to make a quick profit. Maybe they want to pass on the deal to another investor who can take the project to the next level. Maybe they just purchased it last week and are wholesaling it. I purchased several properties and made $10,000 in a few days without doing a thing to them.

Mistake #7: Underestimating the time required to fix up a property

Some investors underestimate how much time it will take to fix and flip a property, and therefore the project's objective may be in jeopardy. It is always better to plan for the unexpected.

Mistake #8: Letting fear hold you back

Nothing ventured, nothing gained. Arm yourself with knowledge and act quickly when you spot a great deal. Money and wealth are found on the other side of fear.

Mistake #9: Doing everything yourself

The biggest blunder of all is for the investor not to utilize the services of a knowledgeable real estate agent. I listed properties that were purchased from "for sale by owners" that needed a lot of work and they overpaid. What they thought was going to be a profit-making proposition turned out to be the opposite. Ouch!

HOW TO DETERMINE WHETHER A PROPERTY IS A GREAT DEAL

Your evaluation should consider the following aspects of a potential purchase: cash flow, leverage, equity, appreciation, and risk.

1. Cash flow

- What is the purchase price?
- What are the taxes?
- Will this property cash flow?
- What is the condition of the rental market in the vicinity of the property?
- What is the vacancy situation?
- What is the down payment?
- What is the interest rate?
- What is the net operating income (NOI)?
- Is the subject property a house, duplex, fourplex, or something else?

All of these factors should be considered in evaluating whether a property will provide income. How does the cash flow for this property compare with that of other potential investment properties? For example, does the $50,000 house that rents for $750/month have better income potential than a $100,000 duplex that rents for $525 per side for $1,050 total rent per month? How about a fourplex that costs $150,000 and brings $2,000 month in the same neighborhood? Which of these properties is the best investment?

Be sure to consider the financial circumstances of the investor when you are looking at cash flow:

- How important is income to them?
- Do they have other income?
- Are they more interested in reducing their taxes than in earning income?
- Do they need more income now or in the future?

There's no right answer to these questions, but they are all factors that should be analyzed when looking at a potential purchase.

2. Leverage

The lower the down payment, the more properties one may be able to purchase. Banks may no longer be open to financing 100% of the property value, but it is not uncommon for them to require a loan-to-value ratio of 70% to 85%. Keep in mind that the more solid the financial statement and assets of the borrower, the greater the likelihood that the bank will structure the loan with more favorable terms.

3. Equity

Your clients are expecting you to track down great deals for them. There are many ways to create equity, but the easiest one is to buy a property that is a great deal.

4. Appreciation

Buying in the right neighborhood will increase the likelihood of a successful investment. In today's market it is not uncommon to buy a property for 20% less than the price at which a comparable property would have sold just a few years ago. Under normal conditions the average rate of appreciation is 2% to 4% yearly, and it would take five to ten years for a property to appreciate 20%. There's no need to wait for a property to appreciate in value, because you should be able to find deals every day.

5. Risk

What happens if your client's assumptions are not correct? Will they be able to continue making the mortgage payment if there's a vacancy, for example?

WHAT INFORMATION IS NEEDED TO ANALYZE A PROPERTY?

The first step is to understand the factors that contribute to property value. Gathering accurate information can help you determine whether a property is likely to be a good investment, but ultimately the client must decide whether a property is the right investment for them.

1. Property details
   This information includes how old the property is, number of units, square feet, whether the utilities are separate or on a single meter, whether the property includes garages that can produce additional income, whether it has laundry facilities (coin-operated), and so on.

2. Purchase information
   What is the asking price, how much rehab work is needed, and how much deferred maintenance does the property have? The better the condition of the property, the more rent you can expect.

3. Financial details
   Will the client be purchasing the property with cash, or will they need to obtain a loan? If a loan will be needed, what are the loan amount, down payment, interest rate, and closing costs?

4. Income
   How much income does the property produce from rent payments and from the laundry, garages, and so on?

5. Expenses
   What are the costs to operate the property, such as maintenance, property taxes, insurance, property management, and so on?

DIFFERENCE BETWEEN PRO FORMA AND ACTUAL VALUE

The value of a property is closely tied to how much income it produces. Knowing this, some sellers will provide financial information that is inaccurate. For example, they may overestimate rental income and neglect to mention that the maintenance expenses are much higher than the estimate. This scenario makes the property seem more valuable that it really is.

One of the most important measures for determining property value is the NOI or net operating income, a topic that will be discussed later in this chapter.

The more complete the information you have gathered, the better your chances of making a good decision. How can you ensure that you have the information needed? Actual data is critical for making a good analysis, but there are some things that can easily change the picture. Initially you may be able to use the pro forma data, but the estimated numbers will need to be verified by actual numbers.

One common way to verify information is to ask the seller to provide tax returns and maintenance records. Don't be surprised if the seller refuses (in which case a red flag should go up). If they do provide the information, it will be similar to the pro forma.

What happens if the property's assessed value goes up or down? A big difference will make the property more or less valuable. Lower taxes mean higher income and higher taxes mean lower income. Small changes to income and expenses can make the difference between a poor, okay, or great investment.

WHERE CAN YOU FIND THE INFORMATION YOU NEED?

Property details: The seller should be very willing to provide whatever information is needed. If they don't, it is a lot easier to make yourself and the client comfortable when you don't have to force the issue. The assessor's office has the property details.

Purchase information: The seller has the property listed for a certain price (and as a savvy real estate agent that is where you come in to negotiate with the seller). The more important information that is critical is the assessment of deferred maintenance or updating needed in order for the property to meet or exceed the income requirement.

The better the property, the more updating it will have had, including big-ticket items such as a new roof, HVAC system, windows, appliances and so on. Such a property will have a higher purchase price than one that is the opposite. A property inspection is worthwhile even if the buyer is experienced, because you never know what kinds of defects may be hidden.

Financial details: How will the property be purchased? A cash offer is easy to deal with, but if the offer is subject to a loan it is important to talk to the lender (ideally, a local bank) to determine down payment requirements, term of loan, interest rate, and closing costs, and to obtain a preapproval letter or proof of funds.

Due diligence

It is imperative that seller provide any information that may be requested so that you can analyze the property to determine its investment potential.

Don't rely exclusively on the pro forma. If the seller uses a property management company, accurate information should be readily available from that source. Keep in mind that the owner of the property management company should also be a licensed broker so that there are no games played with information.

In addition, the home inspector/contractor can identify any potential repairs or big-ticket items that will need to be replaced in the future.

As a real estate agent you have to determine how involved you want to be in gathering the information that will be necessary to analyze a property to determine whether it is a good deal. If you are representing the buyer, then the listing agent should have access to the information. If you are representing the seller, you want to make sure the seller provides you with the information needed to do the analysis.

For a residential listing, a CMA (comparative market analysis) is fairly easy to do. Determining the value of a multi-unit is more complicated because it reflects the income that the property produces and the expenses involved in operating the property.

When I go on a listing appointment, my job is to gather the information needed to determine a range for a listing price. First and foremost I need information on the property's income and expenses. In addition, I ask the seller what he or she thinks the property is worth. If my analysis determines that the property is not worth as much as the seller thinks it is, the listing price will have to be adjusted downward. It is pointless to list a property that is unrealistically overpriced.

Determining property income

Net operating income (NOI) is the total income the property generates after expenses. It does not take into account the debt service (principle and interest payment to the lender).

A property's income could come from a number of sources including rents, laundry machines, vending machines, and garage rental, or it could come only from rents.

Since the majority of a property's income will come from rents paid by the tenants, it is imperative that vacancies are taken into consideration.

Depending on where the property is located, its condition, and other factors, vacancies may be higher or lower. It is next to impossible for any property to operate at 100% efficiency, and turnover will occur. Minimizing turnover is the key to maximizing income. Generally speaking, satisfied tenants tend to stay longer than dissatisfied ones.

The better the property is maintained and the more desirable its location, the lower its vacancy rate will be. Properties that have higher rates of tenant turnover are more costly to operate in terms of time and money.

If a property shows a much higher vacancy rate than similar properties in the same area or if the rents are lower than other properties, it is important to determine why this is so. Is the property in poor condition? What amenities does it offer? If similar properties have garages and new appliances while this one does not, this might explain why the rents are lower.

On the other hand the rents may be lower because the seller is not very savvy. Perhaps he or she has owned the property for a long time, has long-term tenants, and simply has not raised rents for many years. There are many unknowns that require further investigation.

As part of your due diligence, ask the listing agent to provide you with the rent roll for the property, which is a list of tenants, lease expiration dates, and monthly rents. Also ask to see the leases, as they can tell a lot.

If the buyer is experienced and savvy, there could be an opportunity to increase the value of the property simply by raising rents or by doing minimal updates that don't require spending thousands of dollars. Simple things such as new paint, countertops, ceramic tile in kitchen and baths, new carpet or refinishing the wood floors may make a difference.

Your due diligence should examine all the factors that will determine whether the property will serve the buyer's short- and long-term objectives.

Determining property expenses

The expenses for operating a rental property typically will break down into the following categories:

1. Property taxes (easy to determine)

2. Insurance (easy to determine through a quote from the agent)

3. Maintenance
   Maintenance expenses may include lawn care, painting, gutter repairs, plumbing, roof, HVAC, appliances, and any other repairs that are required to keep the property in good working order. A property's future expenses will be affected by its overall condition and the amount of deferred maintenance.
   As a real estate agent, you probably have formed a habit of assessing the overall condition of each property that you look at with your clients. A nice property attracts good tenants, and a property with a lot of deferred maintenance does not. Although not spending money on maintenance makes the property's income look better in the short term, in the end it is costly. It is impossible for a property to have no maintenance expenses. If the maintenance information provided for a property is minimal, you should include a 10% maintenance factor as an expense, based on the Gross Scheduled Income. You should ask a number of questions to assess the

condition of each property. How old is the roof? What about the HVAC system, appliances, and electrical system (fuses or circuit breakers)? Does it have new or old windows? Are the kitchen and bathroom original or have they been updated? Is the plumbing galvanized or copper? If these big-ticket items have been updated, future maintenance expenses will be lower.

But keep in mind that when a property has not been well maintained, there are dollar signs written all over it for the savvy investor. Such properties can sometimes be purchased at huge discounts, illustrating the truth of the saying, "You make your money when you buy."

4. Advertising
In all likelihood this should not be a major expense, particularly if the property has a low vacancy rate. How much does it cost in your area to place an ad in the newspaper? Advertising is also available online at little or no cost.

5. Supplies
This category of expenses involves anything needed to fix up a rental property to maintain its current value. Examples might include tools, drywall, plywood, paint and so on. The list could be endless.

6. Legal and professional fees
Most investors will utilize a tax professional to prepare their taxes and an attorney to assist in evicting a tenant or preparing legal documents such an LLC. These professional fees are tax-deductible business expenses.

7. Property management
   Will the buyer be managing the property themselves
   or using a property manager? You can check with local
   property managers to determine their fees. Some will
   charge 6% to 10% of rents, depending on the services they
   provide. Detailed information on property management
   is provided in Chapter 10.

8. Utilities
   Who pays for the gas, water, and electricity in the units?
   In houses or duplexes, utility bills are generally paid by
   the tenant. If the property owner pays for the utilities,
   this is a hard number to determine when budgeting from
   year to year. You can verify the cost of utilities by calling
   the utility companies, as it is public information. If the
   property is an apartment building it may have separate
   utilities for each unit (gas and electricity), but water will
   not be separated.

Among all of the expenses involved in operating a rental
property, two of the most powerful tax deductions are interest
and depreciation.

Interest. Any interest paid during the year is deductible.
Buyers who pay cash miss out on this huge benefit.

Depreciation. One of the largest tax benefits for an investor
comes in the form of depreciation. The IRS allows investors to take
a tax loss every year based on depreciation over the useful life of the
asset, known as the cost recovery period. Depreciation can reduce
an investor's taxable income by thousands of dollars each year.

The property itself can be depreciated at a steady rate for 27½
years for residential-type properties (four units or less) and 39
years for commercial properties.

Land that the property sits on is classified as a non-depre-
ciable asset.

Personal property, which includes things such as appliances and carpets in rental units, can be depreciated over 5 years.

Land improvements such as shrubs, fences, sidewalks, driveways, and landscaping can be depreciated over 15 years.

Anyone contemplating the purchase of an investment property should seek the advice of a competent and knowledgeable attorney and tax advisor.

SAMPLE PROPERTY ANALYSIS AND DEFINITION OF TERMS

After tracking down the numbers, you can analyze a property for every important financial measure to determine whether it is likely to be an okay, good, excellent, or poor investment.

To make it easy for you, I have included a "Running the Numbers Analysis Form" in the Resources section near the end of this book. In the sample form, the only sections you will need to change are in the highlighted areas. Use the "Cost Recovery Depreciation" table in the Resources section to figure out the depreciation for Year 1.

When you are analyzing a property, the outcomes that you can predict with some degree of certainty are only for the first year after purchase. Anything after that is speculative.

Here we go!

Sample Property: Parker Duplex

Purchase price	$120,000
Down payment	$ 24,000
Term	20 years
Interest	6.5%

Closing costs	$ 3,600
Total investment	$ 27,600
Income from rents	$850 monthly rent per side = $20,400/yr
Other income	None
Vacancy and credit loss	10% ($2,040)
Expenses	
Taxes	$ 2,997
Maintenance	$ 1,800
Insurance	$ 900
Repairs	$ 100
Lawn care / Snow removal	$ 200
Utilities	$ 100
Advertising	$ 50
Supplies	$ 200
Total expenses	$ (6,347)

FORMULAS FOR ANALYZING A RENTAL PROPERTY

Gross Scheduled Income: This is the total annual income that would be produced if all units were rented and rent was collected from every tenant. This number represents the highest possible income collection for the property in its current condition.
Example: $20,400 income potential

Vacancy and Credit Loss: This is the income that will be lost due to vacant units (vacancy) or non-payment of rent (credit loss).
Example: $20,400 x 0.10 = $2,040

Gross Operating Income (GOI): This is the gross scheduled income, less vacancy and credit loss, plus income from other sources such as coin-operated laundry equipment, vending machines, and garage rentals.
Example: $20,400 − $2,040 = $18,360

Operating Expense (OE): This is the cost associated with operating the property, including such things as property taxes, maintenance, insurance, repairs, lawn care / snow removal, utilities, advertising, supplies, trash removal, property management, and so on. Operating expense does not include debt service, income taxes, or depreciation.
Example: $6,347

Net Operating Income (NOI): This is one of the most important measures because it represents the return on the purchase price of the property. Additionally, NOI can be used to as a strategy to increase value. For example, you can improve NOI by increasing the rent and decreasing the expenses whenever possible. To calculate NOI, you simply take the gross operating income and subtract the operating expenses.
Example: $18,360 − $6,347 = $12,013
Note: **Do not include debt service or capital expenditures in NOI.**

Capital Expenditures: These are basically "one-time" costs that are not part of the day-to-day operations of the property. This category includes expenses such as installing new windows, replacing the roof, putting in a new driveway, and so on.

Cash Flow Before Taxes (CFBT): This figure is calculated by taking net operating income, subtracting debt service and capital expenditures, and adding loan proceeds (if any) and interest earned (if any). It represents the annual cash flow available before income tax deductions are considered. Cash flow is the money that the property generates. Even if the tax return shows a loss, the actual cash flow of the property may show profits, or vice versa.

Formula:
Net Operating Income – Debt Service – Capital Expenditures
+ Loan Proceeds (for loans to finance operations, if any)
+ Interest Earned (if any)
= Cash Flow Before Taxes
Example: $12,013 – $8,589 = $3,424

Taxable Income (or Loss): This is the net operating income, less interest, depreciation of real property and capital improvements, and loan costs, plus interest earned on property bank accounts. Taxable income may be negative or positive. If it is negative (a loss), it can shelter the investor's other earnings and result in a negative tax liability on the investor's income tax return.

Formula:
Net Operating Income – Interest Paid – Depreciation –
Amortization + Interest Earned
= Taxable Income or Loss
Example: $12,013 – $6,169 – $3,735 = $2,109

Tax Liability and/or Savings: This is the taxable income (or loss) times the tax bracket of the property owner.
Example: $2,109 × 30% = $633

Cash Flow After Taxes (CFAT): This is the amount of cash generated from the property after taxes have been taken into account. This figure is calculated by subtracting the tax liability from cash flow before taxes. It is the measure that determines the ability of the property to generate cash flow through its operations.

Formula:
Cash Flow Before Taxes – Tax Liability =
Cash Flow After Taxes
Example: $3,424 – $633 = $2,791

Gross Rent Multiplier (GRM): This calculation provides a simple way to estimate the market value of any income-producing property. It is the ratio of the price of the property to its annual rental income before expenses such as property taxes, insurance, utilities, and maintenance (see operating expenses).

Formula:

Price / Gross Scheduled Income = GRM

Example: $120,000 / $20,400 Potential Annual Gross Income = 5.9% GRM

Capitalization Rate: The Cap Rate (as it is more commonly called) is the rate at which you discount future income to determine its present value. It is used to estimate the potential return on the investment. This figure is calculated by dividing the net operating income by the proposed asking price. The higher the Cap Rate is, the better it is for the buyer (lower purchase price). The lower the Cap Rate, the better it is for the seller (higher asking price).

Formula:

NOI / Value = Cap Rate

Example: $12,013/ $120,000 = 10.0%

Cash on Cash Return (COC): This represents the ratio between the property's annual cash flow (usually the first year before taxes) and the amount of the initial capital investment (down payment, loan fees, and acquisition costs). It is a very important ratio to evaluate the long-term performance of a property investment. You can compare the COC to the annual return on a certificate of deposit.

Formula:

Cash Flow Before Taxes (CFBT) / Capital Investment = Cash on Cash

Example: $3,424 / $27,600 = 12.4%

Operating Expense Ratio (OER): This represents the ratio of the property's total operating expenses to its gross operating income (GOI). The operating expense ratio is a useful tool for comparing the expenses of similar properties.

A reasonable OER should fall between 30% and 45%. If a particular piece of property has an unusually high OER, an investor should view this as a red flag to look deeper into why expenses are so much higher for this property than for comparable properties. Perhaps maintenance expenses are unusually high, for example.

Formula:
Operating Expenses / GOI = Operating Expense Ratio
Example: $6,347 / $18,360 = 34.6%

Debt Coverage Ratio (DCR), also known as Debt Service Coverage Ratio (DSCR): This is the ratio between the property's net operating income and annual debt service for the year. A DCR of 1 indicates that the income is just sufficient to cover debt service payments (not a good situation). A DCR of less than 1 indicates that the property is unable to generate sufficient income to cover its payments.

A property with a DCR of 1.25 generates 1.25 times as much annual income as the annual debt service on the property. The greater the DCR is above 1.2, the more favorably it is viewed by lenders because this means the property generates more than enough income to repay the debt service. The higher the DCR, the better. Lenders typically require a DCR of 1.2 or more.

Factors that can affect the DCR may include such things as interest rate, down payment, vacancy rates in the area, over supply of properties, current economic outlook, overall demand for real estate, physical condition and location of the property, age, crime rate in the area, proximity to shopping and schools, property management, overall upkeep, and so on.

On another note, lenders are now starting to use what is called a global DCR. This is a ratio that combines an investment portfolio of properties with weak cash flow or lower Cap Rates so that the buyer will be able to qualify for a commercial loan.

Formula:

Net Operating Income / Annual Debt Service =
Debt Coverage Ratio

Example: $12,013 / $8,589 = 1.4

Break-Even Ratio (BER): This ratio measures the amount of money going out against the amount of money coming in, and it tells the investor what part of gross operating income will be used by all estimated expenses.

Lenders use the break-even ratio as one of their analysis methods when considering an investor's application for a loan. A high break-even ratio is a red flag that tells the lender that a property might be vulnerable to defaulting on its debt if the rental income declines.

The BER always must be less than 100% for an investment to be viable (the lower, the better). Lenders typically require a BER of 85% or less.

Formula:

Operating Expenses + Debt Service / Gross Operating Income
= BER

Example: ($6,347 + $8,589) / $18,360 = 81.4%

Loan to Value (LTV): This is the ratio of the loan amount to the appraised value of the property. It measures the percent of the property's appraised value or selling price that will be financed by the loan. A higher LTV means greater leverage for the investor (higher financial risk for the lender). A lower LTV means less leverage for the investor (lower financial risk for the lender).

Formula:

Loan Amount / Less of Appraised Value or Selling Price = LTV

Return on Investment (ROI) with Appreciation: This figure takes into account the four benefits of investing in real estate: income, principal reduction, appreciation, and depreciation. This measure will let you know how the potential investment compares against other properties that are under consideration.

Formula:

[Cash Flow Before Taxes (CFBT) + Principal Reduction – Taxes Paid + Appreciation Estimate] / Cash Invested = Return on Investment with Appreciation

Example: ($3,424 + $2,420 – $633 + $2,400) / $27,600 = 27.6%

Return on Investment (ROI) without Appreciation: This figure takes into account three of the four benefits of investing in real estate: income, principal reduction, and depreciation. This measure will let you know how the potential investment compares against other properties that are under consideration.

Formula:

Cash Flow Before Taxes + Principal Reduction – Taxes Paid / Cash Invested = Return on Investment without Appreciation

Example: ($3,424 + $2,420 – $633) / $27,600 = 18.9%

Annual Debt Service (ADS): This is the total amount paid on the loan (interest payments and principal) over the course of one year.

How to use these formulas
to help your clients

The formulas discussed in this chapter should help you iden-tify profitable investments so you can assist clients to make good investment decisions when choosing among different properties. Each investor will need to decide what level of results will allow them to accomplish their goals. Keep in mind that investors have different goals and objectives, so what may be good for one investor may not be good for another.

Although these formulas may seem a bit overwhelming at first, I promise you it is not rocket science. When you gain some practice applying them, you will be amazed at how useful they are.

You now have the power to assist those who are consider-ing investing and to help current investors analyze properties to determine whether a property is likely to be a good or bad investment. Using these formulas will help you assist clients to identify and minimize risk.

One of the biggest opportunities you now have is to bring the value and expertise investors are expecting from you. Your knowledge will be especially important for new investors.

Using these formulas will let you help your clients deter-mine what a property is worth. Keep in mind that when you are evaluating a property it should be for the first year only. We cannot accurately predict what the future holds for the property because there are too many variables involved, such as increases or decreases in property assessments, changes in rental rates depending on the local market situation, unexpected expenses, and changes in the client's personal tax situation. All of these factors and others may affect the return that the property is generating.

KEY POINTS TO REMEMBER:

- As an investor-friendly real estate agent, you will need to become familiar with various financial measures so you can help your clients make good investment decisions.

- Remember that investors base their decisions on money rather than emotion; they fall in love with a deal rather than a property.

- Having a gut feeling about whether a property will be a good deal is not enough; you need to run the numbers even if you are not a "numbers person."

- Some of the information you require for evaluating a property's investment potential will be easy to find, while other types of information will be harder to track down.

- Remember that investors have different goals, and what is good for one client may not be good for another.

CHAPTER 9

DO I FLIP OR DO I HOLD?

Have you ever flipped a property?

If your answer is yes, congratulations! You can be the perfect mentor for new investors because your first-hand experience will bring value to clients.

If your answer is no, you're in a difficult position. What advice can you offer to prospective clients who are interested in purchasing properties to flip? If they ask you whether a specific property is likely to be a good flipper, what will you tell them? And if they want to know how much money they can expect to make on an average flip, what will your response be?

Unless you have practical experience flipping properties, it will be challenging for you to work with clients who want to get into this multi-billion-dollar business. If you have never flipped a property before, you are not bringing much to the table.

Flipping houses has been extremely lucrative for me personally, so I find it easy to understand why more and more people are getting involved in flipping.

As the demand for properties with flipping potential has gone up, the supply has gone down. Competition among buyers has increased in recent years. The days of finding steals are long gone, and even my long-term clients who made serious money in 2005–2006 have been feeling the challenges. Do you find this to be true in your area?

Why are fewer properties available for flipping now than in the past? Mainly because foreclosures are way down. This is good for the economy, and it's the main reason the real estate market has seen a nice turnaround.

The norm now is for potential buyers to pay higher prices and to contend with competing offers. This is not a bad thing, because it means the selling price will be higher after a property has been improved.

Today's increasingly competitive flipping environment is proof that real estate has withstood the storm and proven itself to be one of the best options for hard-working people to earn money and build wealth. I make an average of $15,000 to $20,000 personally on each flip before taxes, and I have clients who make much more. The average profit from flipping a property in your community may be much higher.

Why has flipping become so popular? Here are a couple of possible reasons:

1. Warren Buffett, the "Oracle of Omaha" and one of the richest men in America, told reporters in 2012 that if there was a practical way for him to purchase "a couple hundred thousand single-family homes" and manage them, he would do it.

2. TV shows have made the flipping process seem easy. You find a cheap property, put some money and sweat equity into fixing it up, and then you resell the house for a huge profit.

It is true that experienced real estate investors can make enormous profits by flipping. Even though inventories are way down, this is still a great time to get into the flipping game or to start building wealth by purchasing income-producing properties.

---

*The most money I made on a flip was $90,000
before taxes, and that was in the fall of 2018.*

Flipping doesn't always bring big profits, though. Timing is important. I lost $25,000 in 2009 after holding a property for almost a year, purely because of greed. I could have made at least $50,000 had I taken an early offer. (You remember what happened in 2008, right?)

If you have thought about flipping but never pulled the trigger, now is the time to do it. If you have dabbled in real estate unsuccessfully in the past, now is the time to get re-engaged.

As an agent you are knowledgeable about real estate, so why not put your knowledge to use by working with investor clients? And why not become your own best client? If you buy a property to flip, you can get a commission check when you buy and when you sell. If you don't have the money right now, why not partner with an associate or family member? Could you use $10,000 or $20,000 additional income this year?

In all likelihood at some point a client will ask you to assist them in finding a property that they can fix up and sell for a higher price. Although individuals can be successful finding properties on their own, it may seem like they're looking for the perfect piece of corn in the field. Your guidance can help them avoid making costly mistakes. It is not necessary for them to do all the work by themselves when you are available to help.

Instead of paying thousands of dollars for "flipping"
programs, anyone looking to flip should use the money
as a down payment and/or for fix-up costs. This will get
them much closer to accomplishing their objective. The
best resource of all is to utilize a residential investment
specialist who understands the ins and outs of this
business and/or has flipped a number of properties.
Flippers will also benefit from using the "Remodeling
Cost Estimator" and "Real Estate Rehab Worksheet" in
the Resources section at the end of this book.

Anyone who is serious about this business should align them-selves with a knowledgeable and experienced real estate agent. You have your finger on the pulse of the local market and will know when a good deal comes up, maybe even before it gets listed.

I started flipping properties in the 1980s, before the term "flipping" was widely used. Since 2003 I have flipped over 50 properties and it has been a very large part of my income, so I understand the ins and outs of this game. Keep in mind that I did not do any of the work to fix up these properties myself. On occasion, I even sold a few properties without doing anything at all to them. I made $10,000 simply by wholesaling—passing on the deal to a flipper or to someone who wanted to fix up the property and earn rental income.

At this point you may be wondering whether I compete with my clients for properties. The answer is NO. Many times I have shown them a property and they decided not to buy it for one reason or another, so I ended up purchasing it myself.

I have continued to flip properties for ordinary income and to rely on my sizable rental portfolio for wealth building and retire-ment income. Real estate investors often have strong opinions about whether it is better to buy and flip or buy and hold, but I have found that both strategies can produce excellent results. The best choice is the one that fulfills the investor's needs.

Have you talked with anyone lately who is not a fan of real estate? What was their opinion on flipping or long-term rentals? If they tried one of these strategies and it didn't work well for them, perhaps they made a poor decision or worked with a real estate agent who lacked experience with investment properties. Or maybe they were speculators rather than investors. Did they have a business plan? Did they pay too much to purchase a property or to remodel it and end up losing money? Investors can minimize the risk involved in flipping if they follow a business plan and make their money when they buy.

To me, flipping is like being an artist who takes a blank canvas and creates a beautiful picture. There is nothing more rewarding than reconditioning a rundown property and helping to improve the neighborhood.

Even more rewarding is the fact that you or your clients are making the dream of home ownership possible for a family and at the same time earning a nice profit. It's an example of the Win-Win concept at work.

I am often asked whether it's a better option to flip or to hold properties. My answer is that it depends on the investor's needs and objectives. Flipping is a terrific way to make a living, while buying and holding rental property is a great way to build wealth for the future. Both options are certainly better than doing nothing at all.

I think doing some of both is the best way to go—flipping for ordinary income and holding long-term rentals to build wealth.

ADVANTAGES OF FLIPPING

1. The main advantage of flipping is that a nice profit can be made in a relatively short period of time. As I have been saying all along, the key to success is not to overpay for the property or to underestimate the work required. It

is critical to stay on budget and to complete the project on schedule. Most projects should be completed in three to six weeks.

2. When you flip properties, you are your own boss. You can reap the financial rewards of your decisions. If flipping is done correctly, it can easily replace your income from the workplace.

3. For people who are in another line of work, flipping can provide an additional source of income and an opportunity to partner with someone so that both of you can enjoy the benefits.

4. Flipping is available to anyone who is credit worthy and has a solid financial statement. There are limited investment options available in which substantial amounts of money can be made in a relatively short period of time, especially for those who have limited financial resources.

DISADVANTAGES OF FLIPPING

The only significant disadvantage of flipping is the risk of losing money, but any worthwhile venture involves risk. No risk, no reward. Money can be found on the other side of fear. Clients can minimize their risk and increase their chances of success by working with you. As their real estate agent, you can assist your clients to analyze upfront the anticipated expenses and to purchase the property at a price that makes sense. You can help them explore different scenarios. For example, if the property is purchased at a certain price and sold at a certain price (less the remodeling expenses, carrying costs, etc.), will the client make the desired profit?

Although there are always risks involved in anything we may do, I believe the benefits of flipping far outweigh the disadvantages and I would strongly recommend it for anyone who is looking to make extra money or even establish it as an ongoing business venture.

THE GOOD, BETTER, BEST SCENARIO

Flipping is often portrayed as a complicated process by people who write books, do seminars, and charge people substantial fees to buy their systems. Maybe you know someone who attended a seminar on real estate investment and ended up spending thousands of dollars on information that was not necessary. Or maybe they hired a coach or mentor who didn't even live in their community. In either case, they were spending money that could have been put to better use for a down payment or remodeling.

In talking with my clients about how to evaluate investment property, I always suggest that they envision three different scenarios for profit potential: good, better, and best.

A. The good price point is the highest price they should pay for the property and the lowest price it can be sold for to make what they consider a good profit. For example, a property may have a purchase price of $80,000 and a selling price of $120,000, and the total expenses for repairs, selling costs, etc., are $30,000, producing a profit of $10,000 before taxes. How many hourly wage earners do you know who must work for three to four months to earn $10,000? How much volume do you have to sell to make $10,000?

B. The better price point is the price they should pay for the property and the price it can be sold for to make what they consider a better profit. Example: $75,000 purchase price, $125,000 selling price, $30,000 total expenses for repairs, selling costs, etc., producing $20,000 profit before taxes. How

many hourly wage earners do you know who must work for
five to eight months to earn $20,000? How much volume do
you have to sell to make $20,000?

C. The best price point is the lowest price they could pay for the
property and the highest price it could be sold for to make
what they consider the best possible profit. Example: $70,000
purchase price, $130,000 selling price, $30,000 total expenses
for repairs, selling costs, etc., producing $30,000 profit before
taxes. How many hourly wage earners do you know who must
work a year or more to earn $30,000? How much volume do
you have to sell to make $30,000? (See form in Resources.)

Planning ahead is the most effective way to minimize risk.
What if the property doesn't sell? This outcome is unlikely when
your clients have these three scenarios in mind, but a property
that doesn't sell can also become a rental unit. Instant equity is
the result, and wealth building is the outcome.

Holding on to a property for a longer period of time has an
additional benefit: the profit will be taxed at a lower rate. When
a property is sold within the first year after purchase, the IRS
treats the profit as ordinary income and taxes it at rates that
can be very high, depending on your income tax bracket. If the
property is held for more than one year after being purchased,
the profits made by selling it are considered capital gains and are
taxed at a rate that is typically lower than for ordinary income.

As with any other aspect of real estate investment, people who
are contemplating flipping or owning rental properties should
seek the advice of a competent and knowledgeable accountant.

SELLING TIME

Flipping should happen within a relatively short period of
time. The longer a property is on the market, the less the profit
will be because the investor is responsible for paying utilities,
insurance, carrying costs, and so on until the property is sold.

CAPITAL REQUIREMENT

Although some people will say that a disadvantage of flipping is that you need a large amount of money to purchase and upgrade a property, I do not see it as a disadvantage at all. Anyone who is credit worthy can secure funds. Cash is always king, but investors can use other people's money (OPM) by opening a line of credit, taking out a bridge loan, or pooling resources with a partner. Earning money through flipping doesn't have to be a fantasy. It is a reality for me and for the clients I serve.

ADVANTAGES OF HOLDING

Holding onto a rental property over the long term is an excellent way to build wealth. While the tenant reduces the debt, property values continue to go up and residual income for the investor's retirement years is the outcome.

How can you help a client decide whether to buy and flip or buy and hold? You may want to ask them for more information:

1. What are they planning to do with the profits? Do they want to buy a car, take a vacation, pay off debt, pay for their children's college tuition, or use the funds for a down payment on their next flip or rental property?
2. Are they aware that their profits from flipping will be treated as ordinary income and taxes will have to be paid?
3. Is it better for them to earn income now (flipping) or residual income later on (buy and hold)?

My system for flipping properties is no different from that used for purchasing properties to hold; however, the investor may be able to pay more for a long-term rental property because of the power of leverage.

Flipping is all about the bottom line: Will the property bring the client enough money to make the project worthwhile?

MY SYSTEM FOR FLIPPING A PROPERTY:

1. Find a property with investment potential.

2. Analyze the property. If it is a single-family dwelling, comparables are the best indicator of the property's value after it has been fixed up. If it's a multi-unit, more information is needed to run the numbers. If the property passes this test, the next step is to write an offer.

3. Buy the right property that meets the client's needs and objectives.

4. Fix the property. Make repairs and/or updates to get optimum rents or profits. Be sure to stay on budget and on schedule.

Flip *quickly*.

Step 1. Find a property with investment potential

If a property is truly a great deal, your clients must act quickly before it is gone. Remind them that they are competing with other investors for limited properties that are available. They should choose a potential purchase based on numbers, not emotions. Will the property meet their financial objectives? If your client pays too much for a property or spends considerably more for the rehab than their budgeted amount, their desired profit may not become a reality. In other words, an investor should fall in love with the deal rather than with the property.

How to recognize a good deal

This is where you can bring tremendous value to your clients. As a real estate agent who understands how to analyze investment properties, you will be a tremendous resource for anyone who is contemplating flipping. Real estate agents who are also investors and flippers bring knowledge that only comes with experience, research, and education.

Knowing what is a good deal should not be left up to chance. Is a $50,000 or $100,000 property a good deal to flip? To find out, your clients will need the following information:

1. What are comparable properties selling for in the same neighborhood?

2. What is the expected selling price?

3. What are the expected repair costs and other expenses?

4. What is the expected profit?

5. Based on the above information, is the project worth doing?

Where to find properties

Although there are many ways to find properties for investment purposes, my top choice is the MLS. As I have mentioned, the competition is quite fierce for properties with investment potential. However, on any given day you can find properties that will meet most investors' criteria.

How often should you check the MLS for updates (new listings, price reductions, and so on)? I search probably four to five times a day, which increases the likelihood of finding properties that meet my clients' criteria.

Network with other real estate agents in your community (not just those who are affiliated with your company). When you are engaged in this niche market you will get to know other real estate agents who are doing the same thing you are doing. How about asking your fellow real estate agents to let you know when they are listing properties that may meet your clients' criteria? Get acquainted with agents who list foreclosures or short sales. Let other real estate agents know that you have potential buyers for properties that need work. These properties are great candidates for flipping or rentals.

Place an advertisement in the real estate section of your local newspaper saying that you have buyers for properties that need work, estate sales, and so on. You can also get a one-party listing or even a listing for a week and show the properties to your buyers. (This idea has worked well for me in the past, and I have made a few sales as a result.) Avoid gimmicks like claiming that you will buy houses in any condition. Look in the rental section of your newspaper, especially in the multi-unit section, and you may find ads for properties that meet the criteria.

Step 2. Analyze a property

The most important criterion for a potential flipper is the financial component. An offer is made based on analyzing whether the property is likely to produce the desired level of profits. At this stage of the process, your clients must decide whether they are comfortable writing an offer. If the deal doesn't make sense financially, it will not be a good property to flip.

Keep in mind that investors can write an offer that is subject to inspection by a contractor to determine whether remodeling costs are satisfactory to the buyer. The earnest deposit can even be submitted upon removal of the inspection, when the investors are satisfied with their due diligence. At the buying stage, a more detailed analysis is conducted.

It is important to know what factors contribute to the value of a property. As an agent, you know that kitchens and baths are the basics in upgrading a property. You know about looking for comps. What should the property sell for once it is fixed up?

Step 3. Buy the right property that meets the client's needs and objectives

Everything that needs to happen from the purchase agreement to closing takes place in step 3.

At this stage it is also important to do whatever due diligence is desired. This may include inspections by contractor(s) to determine whether the remodeling costs are satisfactory to the buyer. Due diligence can be a useful out because "satisfactory" will have a different meaning for each person. Are your clients comfortable with all the findings? If the property is a multi-unit rather than a single-family dwelling, the same due diligence may apply.

Depending on whether the property meets the investor's criteria, the offer is either written or not. If the property will be used as a rental, investors may be able to pay more than they could pay for a property that is purchased as a flipper.

How will the offer be written? Keep in mind that the preferred method of acquiring these types of properties is cash. Making an offer that is subject to a loan is still possible, but there is a very good chance that other buyers will offer cash for the property. Cash offers are viewed favorably by sellers because they don't involve appraisals or underwriting guidelines.

Other options for making cash offers include using a line of credit (which is still considered a cash offer) or bridge loan (also considered a cash offer). The credit line or bridge loan may be secured by collateral such as the investor's personal residence, securities, or other assets.

Investors can also use their self-directed or Roth IRAs to purchase properties. A self-directed IRA is the lesser known of IRA options and requires account owners to make active investments on behalf of the plan. To open a self-directed or Roth IRA, the owner of the account must hire a trustee or custodian to hold the IRA assets and be responsible for administering the account and filing the required documents with the IRS. For additional information about using IRAs to purchase investment properties, see Chapter 12.

Many real estate agents and investors are getting frustrated because it is becoming harder to find "deals." The most common complaint is that when a property that is priced right hits the market, there are multiple offers, a bidding war ensues, and ultimately the price it takes to buy the property is higher than it would have been a few years ago. However, the fact that deals are harder to find today doesn't mean that no deals are available. In addition, when property values are higher you may pay more for a property but it also means that rents are going up and so are the prices that you will receive for flipped properties.

You may need to help your clients understand that the real estate market has changed from what it was like a few years ago. In all likelihood low-ball offers are just a waste of time.

A strategy that you may not be aware of is to write an offer saying that the buyer will pay a certain amount (such as $500) more than the next-highest offer up to a certain maximum amount. With this strategy, the agent must be able to verify the next-highest offer. This strategy does not work well with foreclosures.

Step 4. Fix up the property

After buying a property, the next step is to make repairs and/or updates to bring optimum profits. Keeping the project on budget during this phase is key.

Although there may be an opportunity to purchase a property that is considered a good deal without any repairs, it is not likely that an investor will pay a high enough price for the property to compete with owner-occupied buyers who are probably willing to pay a lot more than the investor.

Based on my experience, the properties that owner-occupied buyers walk away from are those that need work and sometimes even major reconstruction. These types of properties offer the best opportunities for investors.

Some investors will walk away from certain properties that involve major remodeling tasks, but there are investors for every type of property. Some may consider re-roofing, a new furnace, bathroom, or foundation to be a major project while others may think nothing of such repairs.

Will an inexperienced investor who has no construction knowledge make an offer on a property that is considered to be a major project? Probably not.

I have shown the same property to different investors, and some have passed on it while one has ended up buying a great property that met their criteria.

Investors have different needs and objectives. Some may only want to do minor repairs to just get by and probably will not make much profit as a flipper. Other investors may be willing to take the property to a higher level. For example, one investor might paint the kitchen cabinets without replacing the original countertops, while another might install new cabinets, countertops, and so on. The outcome of more remodeling most likely will be higher profit for the flipper.

Taking things to the next level makes sense only if a property is considered to be a good deal. There is no need to buy the property if it would involve so much remodeling that the investor would end up paying the retail price. Keep in mind that the objective is to make money, not to break even.

How should an investor determine how much to spend on repairs or remodeling? The numbers should provide some direction.

For example, let's say your client has purchased a $60,000 property with $15,000 in repair costs for a total investment of $75,000.

Comparable properties in the same neighborhood sell in the $110,000 range and the investor bought this property to flip. Carrying costs and selling expenses are $12,000, for a total investment of $87,000.

The potential profit in this deal is $23,000 less tax consequences—not a bad return in just a few short months. The line of credit is paid back and the investor moves on to the next deal using the same procedure.

Flipping strategies

What steps should your client take to improve the property before putting it on the market?

Keep in mind that the majority of the remodeling budget should be devoted to updating the kitchen and bath(s). Does that mean your client should install granite counters instead of Formica? It depends on the price point.

What about replacing kitchen cabinets versus painting? Again, it depends on the price point of the expected sale.

Remodeling does not have to be expensive. It is not necessary to hire a high-end contractor who is likely to make more money than the investor does.

Investors should focus on making improvements that will increase the overall appeal of the property as well as its market value, thereby increasing the profit margin.

If the remodeling efforts will cost $25,000 and the value of the property will only increase by $18,000, then perhaps this would be a better wholesaling project than a flipper. The investor can sell the property to another investor and make money without doing anything to it. On the other hand, if the remodeling cost will be $18,000 and it will increase the value of the property by $25,000, then the fix-up project should move forward. There is no reason to spend $1 to make $1. Spending 50 cents to make $1 makes a lot more sense.

The investor must weigh the remodeling costs (including time and effort) against the potential for profit. If the project will make the property more appealing to a potential buyer and not cut into the profit, then it may be a great way to make a nice return on the property investment.

The best way to improve home values without overspending is to do exactly what needs doing and nothing more. Making the necessary improvements will increase the property's value and make it more attractive to a buyer.

There are numerous simple things an investor can do to increase the value of a property:

1. Pay attention to curb appeal. A good first impression can dramatically increase the value of the property.

2. Take care of landscaping and yard work (mowing, trimming, and weeding). The yard is the first thing potential buyers will see. Planting flowers is an inexpensive way to make a property more appealing.

3. Remove old carpet and refinish hardwood floors.

4. Refinish or reface kitchen cabinets and replace knobs. Replace lighting fixtures in the kitchen ceiling.

5. Paint interior/exterior.

6. Remodel bathroom(s).

Step 5. Flip quickly

Ideally, you should be the agent who lists the property that you helped your client to buy. If they don't ask you to do this, don't do business with them the next time they come to you for help.

To flip quickly, the listing price should be lower than the asking price for similar properties in the same neighborhood. Since an investor looks at the bottom line and is not emotional in making these decisions, a few thousand dollars plus or minus is not a big issue.

By contrast, owner-occupied sellers tend to be more emotional in their expectations. Their property may need updating, yet they want the buyer to pay a premium price. If an investor is offering a similar property in better condition for less money, buyers are likely to choose it instead. I like to tell my clients, "Let those properties help sell yours."

YOU CAN MAKE A DIFFERENCE

As a real estate agent, you can have more influence on your clients and your community than you ever expected. People need you to help them realize their dreams of becoming an entrepreneur.

How many people do you know who are not happy with their job? They may be working harder than ever and helping the owner of the company to get wealthy while they are making little or no progress toward their own financial goals.

Do you know anyone who would love to be their own boss and have the independence to do as they wish? Most logical people want to be in control of their own destiny, and in my opinion the ticket is real estate. Although this chapter has been all about flipping, building wealth by investing in one property at a time is within the reach of a lot more people than those who are currently involved in the investment game.

Your knowledge and experience can help clients turn their dreams into reality. At the same time you can help yourself and your loved ones by bringing in a very good income. Flipping properties or holding them can allow you to become financially independent so that you will no longer need to rely solely on commission checks for your livelihood. You can achieve your own dreams by working with investors and by becoming an investor yourself.

KEY POINTS TO REMEMBER:

- Flipping has become more popular at the same time that foreclosed properties have become harder to find, but good deals are still available.

- Flipping can allow your clients to make a substantial profit within a relatively short period of time, while owning rental property will help them build wealth over the long term. Doing both strategies is a good option.

- The IRS treats profits from short-term flipping (within a year of purchase) as ordinary income. If a property is held for more than a year before being sold, the profits are considered capital gains and taxed at a lower rate.

- To determine the potential profit from flipping a property, you have to run the numbers.

- Don't go overboard in remodeling a property. Establish a budget and stick to it.

CHAPTER 10

PROPERTY MANAGEMENT

Most of the investors you work with will choose to manage their own investment portfolio, so this chapter will just give you a brief overview of the services provided by property management companies.

Throughout this book I have emphasized that building wealth through real estate is within the reach of far more people than the ones who currently own investment properties. Depending on creditworthiness, real estate investing is within the reach of everyone from hourly wage earners to high-income professionals. Although each investor will have different needs and objectives, real estate is still one of the best ways to generate wealth, and property management should be part of the picture.

Be careful to avoid confusing high income with actual wealth. Some people make a lot of money but have little to show for all their hard work. Money comes in and money goes out, and very little is saved for the future.

Clients at different income levels need your help for different reasons. Hourly wage earners will want to invest in real estate to receive income from flipping or rentals. By contrast, high-income individuals often pay far more than their fair share of taxes, and real estate investing can help lighten their burden. They are often short on time and will be more likely to invest in real estate if they can hire a property management company to handle the day-to-day tasks of property ownership.

The role of a property management company is similar to that of a stockbroker or financial planner. For a fee, they manage their client's portfolio. Investors should not hesitate to hire a property management company, because the advantages are substantial.

A property management company has a primary responsibility to the landlord and a secondary responsibility to the tenant. They play a crucial role in fulfilling the expectations of both parties to the lease, since both parties have specific rights and benefits.

Hiring a competent and reputable property management company will go a long way toward ensuring a positive experience. This type of help is well worth the additional expense involved.

Keep in mind that property managers are businesslike and unemotional in doing their job. They don't get chummy with the tenants. They are friendly and cordial, but they treat all tenants the same. They can keep the investor out of trouble because they understand the landlord-tenant laws.

What are some of the ways a property management company can bring added value to an investor?

1. Generally they attract higher-quality tenants because they do the proper background screening, from landlord verifications to criminal checks. Of course, nothing is 100% guaranteed and a perfectly qualified tenant can eventually become a bad tenant. However, a property management company tends to have a better overall outcome in regard to tenants.

2. An experienced property management company regularly reviews hundreds of applications, so they have the expertise to quickly screen candidates and recognize warning signs. Any experienced landlord will tell you that it takes only one bad tenant to create costly legal fees and a financial burden.

3. The property management company is knowledgeable about the latest landlord-tenant laws. State laws cover many aspects of the landlord-tenant relationship, from security deposits to evictions and rules about landlord access to rental property. A summary of the state laws can be found at http://www.nolo.com/legal-encyclopedia/state-landlord-tenant-laws

4. Property managers also understand the mandates of the Occupational Safety and Health Administration (OSHA), Environmental Protection Agency (EPA), Americans with Disabilities Act (ADA), Fair Housing and Equal Opportunity (FHEO), and the Equal Employment Opportunity Commission (EEOC). They are well worth the expense, because avoiding one lawsuit will more than pay the annual fees charged by a property management company.

When you are analyzing a potential investment property for a client, be sure to include property management fees of 6% to 10% even if your client intends to manage the property. What happens if the investor has to move out of town unexpectedly due to a job transfer or finds that they don't enjoy dealing directly with tenants?

Sometimes the additional expense of a property manager makes the difference between positive and negative cash flow from an investment. However, hiring a property management company can still make sense because of the equity associated with owning the property.

Although a majority of "Ma and Pa" investors will manage their own portfolios, for other investors one of the biggest decisions they must make will be whether or not to use a property management company. In my case, I felt that my time would be better utilized by focusing on my work as a real estate agent than by handling all of the day-to-day responsibilities of being a landlord. One small commission check covers the property management fees.

WHAT DOES A PROPERTY MANAGEMENT COMPANY DO?

First and foremost, property managers deal directly with prospects and tenants. Some investors simply do not want anything to do with tenants, possibly because they lack the people skills to perform this role.

Additional services provided by property management companies include the following:

1. Leasing

2. Maintenance and repairs

3. Rent collection

4. Lease renewals

5. Record keeping

6. Payments

7. Responding to complaints

8. Evictions

Leasing

Property managers take care of everything related to ensuring that a rental property is continuously occupied, from advertising the property to conducting background checks on prospective tenants.

They know the best methods to advertise, improve, and prepare the property to be rented. They market the property and charge a finder's fee when they find a tenant—typically half a month or a full month's rent.

Property managers know the local rental market and will set the monthly rent accordingly. Rents that are too high could increase the time required to line up a tenant, and rents that are too low will ultimately reduce the investor's income. The property manager may choose to rent the property for a higher amount than the investor would have charged on their own. Higher rental income ultimately makes the investment worth more.

Maintenance and repairs

Property managers coordinate all aspects of maintenance, from preparing the property for a new tenant to handling general repairs, plumbing, HVAC, and re-keying the locks. They are available 24/7 to deal with emergency situations. They can also oversee major remodeling jobs.

Rent collection

The property management company is responsible for making sure tenants pay their rent on time or handling eviction proceedings in the event of nonpayment. The company's methods of handling rent collection or late payments may make the difference between success and failure for the investor.

I have seen many inexperienced or weak landlords who were manipulated by their tenants. By contrast, property managers establish expectations for tenants and enforce the terms of the lease.

The property management company is well aware that collecting the rent on time is vital to the livelihood of the client and the way to pay the mortgage.

Lease renewals

Property managers find out in advance whether a tenant is planning to renew the lease or move out when it expires. If the lease will not be renewed, they will show the property (assuming it is in showable condition) to prospective tenants so that a new tenant can move in quickly and minimize the loss of rent.

Record keeping

The property management company keeps the investor informed on a monthly basis about the property's income and expenses. They issue a detailed annual report that can be given to the investor's accountant.

Payments

Property managers make payments on behalf of the investor, ranging from monthly mortgage payments to utility bills.

Responding to complaints

A competent property manager responds promptly to tenants' complaints. A happy tenant stays longer than one who is dissatisfied, and tenant retention maximizes rental income.

Evictions

There is a right and wrong way to evict tenants who violate the terms of the lease. Noncompliance with tenant/landlord laws during the eviction process can create major problems for investors. Property managers understand how to handle evictions so as to achieve the best possible outcome.

QUESTIONS TO ASK A PROPERTY MANAGEMENT COMPANY

It's important to understand that property management companies are not all the same, just as real estate agents are not all the same.

A good property management company will help the investor have a successful experience. Their knowledge and experience can give your client the peace of mind that comes from knowing that their property is in good hands.

If your client has a bad experience with a rental property, they will be unlikely to turn to you for help in purchasing additional properties. The opposite is true as well.

The experience level of a property management company is a key factor in achieving a good outcome. To evaluate a company before recommending them to your clients, be sure to ask the following questions:

1. How many properties do you manage?

2. How long have you been in business?

3. Have you had any complaints from the state real estate commission?

4. How long does it take, on average, for you to rent a property?

5. What are your fees, and what services are provided?

6. Do you have your own employees who do the work, or do you use vendors? Is there an additional premium for the vendors, and if so, how much is it?

7. How do you handle evictions and what happens with money that is owed? Do you turn over the debt to collections? If so, what fees are charged?

Your clients always have the option of managing their own properties and not having to pay a fee to someone else, but they might want to think about how much their time is worth. If they are high-income professionals, they may find that it's much more cost-effective to hire a property management company than to handle everything themselves. In my own case, I believe it makes sense to leave the day-to-day duties to the experts.

Advantages and disadvantages of using a property management company

As I have been saying throughout this book, owning a worthwhile portfolio is one of the best ways to create wealth, assets, and residual income. One of the first discussions you should have with potential clients involves whether they intend to manage their own property or hire a property management company.

Let's consider the pros and cons of using a property management company. Keep in mind that many clients will want to manage their own properties if possible, but when it's not possible or the client simply doesn't want to deal with the day-to-day aspects of being a landlord, property management is the way to go.

Disadvantages

Probably the main disadvantage of hiring a property management company is the effect on the property's bottom line. The average property management company will initially charge half a month to one month's rent to line up a new tenant. They will charge 6% to 10% of each month's rent after that, depending on the services they provide.

The initial property management fee covers their expense for any advertising, showing the property, processing an applicant, verifying credit, and other general expenses that come with setting up a new account.

When you are analyzing a property to help your client decide whether or not it will be a good investment, it is imperative to include property management expenses in your calculations. You need find out whether the property will cash flow with the additional fees.

Advantages

Given the duties and responsibilities already mentioned, hiring a property management company is worth the expense for some investors. For them, the advantages of using a property management company far outweigh the disadvantages. Even if the numbers are tight it is still worth it.

Remember that real estate investors make their money when they buy. In that regard, the properties you are helping your clients to purchase should be good deals so that instant equity starts from day one. Does it make sense to buy a property that offers immediate equity and hire a property management company to manage it? Of course it does.

Personally, I would rather take advantage of all the benefits a career in real estate has to offer and utilize the services of a competent property management company to handle the day-to-day tasks involved in being a landlord. You may eventually reach the same conclusion, and so will some of your clients.

KEY POINTS TO REMEMBER:

- High-income clients are more likely than "Ma and Pa" investors to hire a property management company.

- Property management companies can provide a wide range of services to your investor clients.

- Property managers can improve tenant retention by responding promptly to complaints.

- The advantages of hiring a property management company are well worth the fees involved, particularly when it comes to avoiding lawsuits.

Chapter 11

Types of Real Estate

The majority of your potential clients will have some knowledge of investing and may have considered the possibility of investing in real estate. However, they may be reluctant to take the next step if they have been "burned" by other types of investments. For example, they might be leery of real estate investing if they have lost money in the stock market. (This happened to me.) Others may be hesitant to take the plunge because they don't know anything about investing in real estate.

The likelihood that someone would choose to invest in real estate without any background in this area is small. Most of your potential clients will already have at least a basic knowledge of real estate before they start working with you.

How knowledgeable are you regarding the details of the investments that you own? You probably need to rely on the expertise of your financial advisor when making decisions, correct? On the other hand, as an agent you are extremely knowledgeable about real estate. If you are not investing, what has held you back?

To bring value to your clients, you should at least become aware of the different options available to real estate investors. There's a lot more involved in being an "investor friendly" real estate agent than just writing an offer and moving on to your next client.

Real estate investors can choose from a variety of options, but most will want to specialize in a certain type of property.

The type of investment that is best for them will depend on their knowledge, experience, objectives, and risk tolerance.

The majority of your clients will be attracted to the residential investment market (single-family dwellings, duplexes, four-plexes, and small to medium-sized apartments under 24 units) and possibly some small commercial properties. The residential investment market will always hold the greatest appeal for the majority of investors because these properties are relatively easy to find, acquire, and manage.

As you know from previous chapters, my specialty is residential properties. My portfolio includes a variety of single-family dwellings and duplexes. I no longer own anything above a duplex, nor have I owned any commercial properties.

Keep in mind that there are real estate agents who specialize in each of the different types of properties. If a potential client asks you to list a property that is outside your specialty, it is best to make a referral or co-list with an agent who has that expertise. I have always subscribed to the motto "Only do the things that you know." I believe it is best for the client to have an experienced and knowledgeable listing agent as the lead agent, so I have co-listed with other agents.

Regardless of what types of properties one invests in, being a landlord or real estate investor is one of the greatest opportunities available for people who want to build wealth and have control over their financial future. There is no "Wall Street" or other outside influence that controls the financial future of real estate investors. They make their own decisions about everything from tenant selection to what type of real estate investment best suits their needs.

Below is a brief summary of the different types of real estate investments available, including residential, commercial, apartments, retail centers, hotels and motels, senior housing facilities, land development, golf courses, industrial properties, mixed-use properties, mobile home parks, and real estate investment trusts (REITs).

RESIDENTIAL PROPERTIES

The "residential" category includes properties such as houses, town homes, condos, duplexes, triplexes, fourplexes, and so on. Although duplexes and fourplexes are considered income-producing properties, they can be occupied by the owner so they are considered residential properties. You can use an FHA loan to buy anything from a single-family residence all the way up to a fourplex, as long as you use the property as your primary residence.

One of the greatest advantages of owning residential properties is that it requires a relatively small investment as a down payment and therefore this option is within reach of most people who want to get into the investment "game." This type of investment is ideal for the beginner or novice investor, as residential properties are relatively easy to rent.

COMMERCIAL PROPERTIES

This category consists mostly of office buildings that vary in size, style, and purpose. These properties may be leased to small local businesses or rented to national chains.

Investing in the commercial market is not recommended for beginners because it requires much more sophistication and knowledge than the residential market and the risk is much greater.

On the positive side, commercial properties can provide excellent cash flow and stability due to leases that may last as long as 25 years, providing consistent income for the duration of the lease.

On the negative side, there is a lot of risk involved. Office building occupancy is highly sensitive to changing economic conditions. If these properties become vacant, it may take months or even years to find a new tenant. Meanwhile, the mortgage payment still must be made.

SMALL APARTMENT BUILDINGS

These types of properties include everything from a five-unit building to one that has 50 units. The value of these types of properties is not based on comparables but rather on the income produced. This type of property is more difficult to finance than a residential property and will require a sizable down payment and different underwriting guidelines. Although small apartment buildings can provide significant cash flow, they require more day-to-day management than residential investments. Hiring a property management company is advisable.

Although this type of property is not listed often, it may represent an excellent opportunity for some investors. If a building is rundown and underperforming, a savvy and knowledgeable investor can purchase it at a low price and raise its value by improving it, increasing the income, decreasing the expenses, and managing it personally or with the help of a property management company.

LARGE APARTMENT COMPLEXES

This category encompasses very large complexes that often include a swimming pool, have a full-time, on-site management staff, and can cost in the millions of dollars.

At some point in your career you may lucky enough to represent a buyer or seller in this type of transaction. Wouldn't it be nice to receive a commission check in the hundreds of thousands?

This type of property may be owned by a hedge fund or insurance company or it may be purchased through syndication (a process in which a group of individual investors pool their financial resources). Rarely is it owned by one individual.

RETAIL CENTERS

This form of investment includes shopping malls, strip malls, neighborhood shopping centers, mega malls, storefronts, and so on. Many retail properties include a well-known anchor store that serves as the draw for shoppers. Leases for this type of property may include specialized language, such as stipulations that the landlord will receive a percentage of sales generated by the tenant in addition to monthly rent.

HOTEL AND MOTELS

This type of investment combines real estate (buildings) and businesses (restaurants and retail shops) to generate revenue. This category isn't the best place for a novice investor to get started. Many experienced investors find it to be a fun and profitable area until they lose a lot of money. One way to get started in this niche is to buy the real estate and lease it to another company that will operate the facility. Running a hotel is a business, not an investment, and running a business brings with it a whole new set of rules, regulations, and headaches.

SENIOR HOUSING FACILITIES

The three primary categories of senior housing facilities are independent living communities, assisted living communities, and nursing homes (or skilled nursing facilities). Continuing care retirement communities (CCRCs) generally provide all three housing types in one location, allowing residents to easily transition to higher levels of care as they age. Like a hotel or motel, a senior housing facility is a business as well as a building.

LAND DEVELOPMENT

This category of commercial real estate is exciting because it can bring high rewards. However, the risk of failure also is high and the outcome can painful if one jumps into land development without knowing what they are doing.

GOLF COURSES

Do you know anyone who is looking for a real estate bargain? They might want to consider investing in a golf course. Here's a web site that specializes in the sales of golf courses:

http://www.nationalgolfgroup.com/golf-courses-for-sale.cfm

According to a Wall Street Journal report, there are 16,000 golf courses with 18 or 36 holes, 4,500 courses with 9 holes, and fewer than 900 par 3 courses in the United States.

INDUSTRIAL PROPERTIES

Industrial real estate includes storage units, car washes, and other special-purpose real estate that generates income from customers who temporarily use the facility.

Although there are risks involved in this type of investment, research can reduce the likelihood of a negative outcome. For example, if you want to own a storage facility you should first research the number of storage facilities in your area, find out where they are located, and try to determine how full they are. Use phone book listings and Chamber of Commerce data to compile a list of competitors. You can make phone inquiries as a prospective renter to determine availability.

If you decide to invest in a storage facility, find a location that meets the objectives of your business plan. Units catering to businesses should be located near office parks or business centers. Personal units are best situated at the fringes of residential communities where renters can have easy and convenient access to their belongings. One benefit of owning and operating a storage facility is that tenants aren't going to call the owner at midnight to complain that their furnace broke down.

MIXED-USE PROPERTIES

An example of a mixed-use property might be a six-story building with retail space, a restaurant, or some other business on the first floor. The second and third floor could consist of individual offices. On the fourth floor a law firm might occupy the entire floor, and the fifth and sixth floors could be devoted to apartments or condos. Mixed-use properties are popular investments for those who have significant financial resources.

MOBILE HOME PARKS

Mobile home parks (or manufactured home communities) are one of the few investment properties where the buyer can immediately begin receiving cash flow. As with the storage unit scenario, the investor owns the ground and any permanent buildings on the facility. Tenants are responsible for making repairs to their mobile homes.

REAL ESTATE INVESTMENT TRUSTS

Real estate investment trusts (REITs) trade like stocks. Each REIT consists of a group of investors who jointly own a portfolio of real property or real estate mortgages.

TYPES OF NET LEASES THAT MAY APPLY TO SOME TYPES OF REAL PROPERTY

Nonresidential properties often have net leases that define the responsibilities of the landlord and the tenant differently from residential leases. Three types of net leases are described below:

- *Single net or "N" leases:* The tenant pays the basic monthly rent plus property taxes. The landlord or property owner pays operating expenses (also known as common area maintenance, or CAM) and property insurance.

- *Double net lease (NN)* – The tenant agrees to pay a basic monthly rent as well as the property taxes and property insurance. The landlord is responsible for all other operating expenses.

- *Triple net lease (NNN)* – The tenant agrees to pay a basic monthly rent as well as property taxes, property insurance, and maintenance expenses.

Generally, single-tenant office buildings are leased on a triple net basis (NNN). This type of lease calls for the tenant to be responsible for all costs associated with occupancy.

Regardless of the type of property that is being considered, potential investors should seek the advice of a competent CPA and attorney before moving forward with the purchase of a property. These professionals can assist your clients in fulfilling the legal requirements involved and in establishing financial goals. Of significant importance is how they intend to purchase the property. Will it be in their name, as an LLC, with a self-directed IRA or Roth IRA? Your job is to help clients with their purchase. Their CPA, attorney, and property management company can help them with everything else.

KEY POINTS TO REMEMBER:

- The majority of real estate investors specialize in residential properties because these properties are relatively easy to find, acquire, and manage.

- As an "investor friendly" real estate agent, you should familiarize yourself with the various investment options that are available to your clients, but you can always co-list nonresidential properties with an agent who has expertise in that type of property.

- Different types of real estate come with varying levels of risk and rewards.

CHAPTER 12

TREATING REAL ESTATE AS A BUSINESS

Real estate investment is a business that should be taken seriously, no matter whether it is done on a part-time or full-time basis. In addition to writing a business plan, investors need to decide who will hold ownership (if more than one person is involved in the business) and whether to operate as a sole proprietorship, partnership, or LLC (limited liability company). Real estate investors need to have an exit plan, and they should understand the advantages and disadvantages of using a Roth IRA to purchase real estate.

WHAT ARE THE BENEFITS OF WRITING A BUSINESS PLAN?

Writing a business plan can help your clients consider the details of their business, including aspects they may not have explored previously.

Looking at their business plan periodically can help investors monitor whether they are on track to meet their short- and long-term goals. What do they want their business to look like one year, five years, and ten years down the road?

Another great reason to prepare a business plan is that it will help tremendously if the client is trying to borrow money.

Having a plan will show the lending institution that the potential borrower is serious and wants to achieve success. The business plan should be based on realistic expectations, not pie in the sky.

Although it may take some time and energy to prepare a business plan, it is well worth taking the time to do it right.

The plan must include clear descriptions of the types of property the investor will consider and the types they will walk away from. Keep in mind that no two investors will think alike, and what may be an excellent property for one investor may not serve the needs of another.

REVIEW: ABCD CLASSIFICATION OF PROPERTIES AND AREAS

Along these lines, let's take another look at the ABCD classification of properties that was introduced in Chapter 7. Although assigning these letter grades can sometimes feel more like an art than a science, the property classes are typically characterized by the following features:

1. "A" properties
   These properties are like blue-chip stock. They tend to be newer properties built within the last five to fifteen years with the most up-to-date amenities and the highest rents. There is no deferred maintenance. Older properties in excellent condition that are located in extremely desirable areas also can fall in this category, as can properties located near universities.

2. "B" properties
   These properties may be a notch or two below an A property without the same amenities. They tend to be a bit older and will not command as much rent. They may have some deferred maintenance, and they usually

have appreciation potential. The savvy investor can quickly raise the property's value by making minor improvements.

3. "C" properties
   These are typically older properties built 30+ years ago with much fewer amenities. They may be a notch or two below a B. They may be located in up-and-coming neighborhoods. Rents are lower than for B properties. They usually have more deferred maintenance. The savvy investor can quickly transform a C into a B by making minor improvements.

4. "D" properties
   These properties are located in undesirable areas. They may be in very poor condition and located in high-crime neighborhoods. The neighborhood is a bigger problem than the condition of the property, because properties can be updated but little can be done about the neighborhood. These properties may have a lot of deferred maintenance. Rents are low, and the quality of the tenant may not be great. Unless the neighborhood turns around there will probably be little or no appreciation. These properties require intense management and are not recommended for the brand-new investor. A lot of money is being made with "D" properties, and although they are cash flow machines they require a lot of attention and repairs. These properties can be compared to penny stock.

Timing is everything. As a real estate agent you should be knowledgeable about areas that are improving as well as areas that are declining. Depending on changes in the neighborhood, what may be a D property today could become a B property in a few years and vice versa.

When you evaluate areas, you can use a similar classification system:

A – Newer growth areas
B – Older, stable areas
C – Older, declining, or stable areas
D – Older, declining, potentially rapidly declining areas

These guidelines will help you and your clients to determine the property types and locations they are looking for so they can include this information in their business plan. The key is to identify properties that will help them accomplish their investment goals.

In choosing a property, investors should focus on properties in areas that are equal to or better than the class of the property itself (for example, a B property in a B or A area) and avoid properties in areas that are lower than the property class (for example, an A property in a C area). The area class they invest in will have a great deal of influence on the stability of their portfolio over time and will determine whether it appreciates or declines in value during periods of economic fluctuation. An A property will have a much harder time performing like an A property if it is located in a C area, but a C property might perform better over time if it's in an A area.

If your clients are looking for investments with the highest appreciation potential and the best initial cash flow, they will want to look for A and B properties located in A and B areas or in the path of progress. They will want to avoid C properties in C areas. If they are not as interested in appreciation but are looking for investments with strong cash flow, then B and C properties in B and C areas would be the best fit.

SAMPLE BUSINESS PLAN

To give you a glimpse of the types of information that a business plan for a real estate investor should include, a sample business plan framework is included on the next few pages. You can use this example to create your own business plan. A filled-out business plan also is included in the Resources section near the end of this book.

Sample Business Plan Framework

Year (_____) Real Estate Business Plan for _____

Especially prepared for_____

BUSINESS GOALS

Mission: Our mission is to create income by purchasing undervalued properties to remodel and sell or retain as long-term investments.

_____ has over _____ years of experience as an investor and is (Provide background on each investor's employment, real estate background, and other qualifications to invest in real estate.)

Profit will be generated by:

(1) Performing cosmetic improvements to single-family homes and selling them to generate 40% to 50% profit

(2) Maintaining long-term rentals that generate a minimum of 10% cash on cash return

SHORT-TERM GOALS

We will create and uphold a reputation in our community for honesty in our business dealings, and we will aim to achieve win-win results. We will focus on acquiring distressed properties that can be fixed up and either sell them or use them as rentals.

During (year) we will purchase ___ properties to flip and ___ properties to rent. This will be the beginning of our long-term investment strategy to accumulate income-producing properties.

Actual number of properties purchased in (year):

flipped: _____ sold: _____ rentals: _____

LONG-TERM GOALS

Our objective in (year) and each year until (year) will be to purchase an average of ___ properties per year to fix up and sell and ___ properties per year to increase our rental portfolio.

Pursuing this strategy over a five-year period will add ___ properties to our portfolio (single-family dwellings and duplexes) to go along with the ___ units currently in our portfolio (mix of single-family dwellings and multi-units, each returning an average of $_____ positive annual cash flow for a total annual income of $_____ per year and annual asset appreciation of ___%.

Also, during this five-year period, it is our objective that more than ___ properties will be sold for an average of $____ profit each, for a total of more than $____ cash income.

OWNERSHIP

(Name of business)

We intend to be highly leveraged. All renovations will be done by licensed contractors.

DEVELOPING KNOWLEDGE OF THE MARKETPLACE

Target Neighborhoods

We will operate in the _____ neighborhoods of the _____ metro area. This area was chosen because properties can be purchased in the price range of $_____ to $_____ and because of our significant knowledge of the area.

Selecting Properties

We have developed our strategy by purchasing properties in the $_____ to $_____ price range. This price range represents the lower end of what properties are selling in the area, at least 20 to 40% less than average.

1. $_____ between our purchase price and typical sales price is necessary to achieve our profit margin of approximately _____

2. For our rental portfolio, a purchase price of at least _____% price differential from market value is necessary for each purchase.

In order to appeal to homeowners and renters, these properties should be 3 bedrooms for resale and a minimum of 2 bedrooms for rentals. Properties should be located close to schools and shopping, and should include amenities that will attract young families and first-time buyers.

Locating Flexible / Distressed Sellers

Our target market will be sellers who are highly motivated and may be having financial difficulties, or those whose properties have been on the market for at least _____ months.

Properties that initially will meet our criteria include:

1. Foreclosures

2. Properties in disrepair

3. Property management problems

4. Estate sales

5. Absentee ownership

6. Tenant problems

7. Retirement or relocation

It is anticipated that these sellers will be willing to negotiate to meet our minimum criteria for purchases.

Developing a Network

To be successful with our strategy, we will establish strong partnerships with real estate agents, banks, and others.

BUSINESS OPERATIONS

Target Customer

Age group: _____ to _____ years

1. Resale Properties
   Our target buyer is a young, dual-income family. These buyers will have adequate to good credit but may lack significant cash reserves for a down payment or closing costs. Purchase price: $_____ to $_____
   Our approach to these buyers will be to utilize programs such as FHA, VA, and others.

2. Rentals
   For our rental portfolio, our target market for tenants will include students, young couples, single parents, and dual-income families. The target rent will be $_____ to $_____ per month. These tenants will also serve as perfect candidates to purchase the property in the future.

Performing Market Analysis

The source we will use to determine the value of a property will be market analysis available through the Multiple Listing Service and our own experience over the past ___ years.

Financial Analysis

Each property to be purchased will be analyzed to determine the value of the property, appropriate purchase price, estimated cost of potential renovation, acquisition costs, and potential selling price as well as anticipated profit.

Financial Arrangements

We have established relationships with the following banks: _____ so we will know in advance of our ability to purchase properties that meet our criteria.

As we will only purchase undervalued properties, after the renovations are completed we will seek permanent financing based on appraisal.

Renovation Process

We intend to purchase properties that are sold well below market value and will require minimal cosmetic updates and improvements. We anticipate that every property will require at least some cosmetic improvements to increase its value. It is our intent for these properties to be sold within a 90- to 120-day period encompassing acquisition, remodeling, and purchase by buyer.

To perform these renovations as quickly and efficiently as possible, we have assembled an experienced crew that we have used extensively over the past _____ years. Additionally, we have sufficient experience and knowledge to determine the estimated costs and time frame required to complete each project. We anticipate that each project should be completed within 45 days from start to finish.

Based on our experience, the following improvements will significantly increase the value of each property:

1. Update kitchen: Install new cabinets if necessary, ceramic tile floor, new countertops, dishwasher, and other appliances.

2. Replace carpet, refinish wood floors, install new blinds.

3. Update bathroom fixtures including vanities.

4. Paint interior/exterior as necessary.

5. Perform landscaping to improve exterior appearance.

6. Perform general overall polishing of property. We will keep in mind that our target sale price is in the $100,000 to $120,000 range.

Each property will be evaluated on its own merits, but typical renovation costs are expected to range between $_____ and $_____. Properties that are purchased at $_____ to $_____ below market value will provide adequate profit to achieve our desired return within ____ to ____ days from acquisition.

Our renovation process model assumes that the six key tasks stated above represent the entire work to be completed. This assumption will be validated prior to purchase by means of a thorough inspection process. Our inspections will be done by contractors so there will be no surprises regarding the renovation costs.

On occasion, however, a property may be available that may require a much higher remodeling price that would be justified by an opportunity to make a lot more money. These properties may require structural improvements or other major remodeling. These could be properties that are in terrible disrepair.

Another exception to our typical purchase criteria may be a small property that is surrounded by much larger and more expensive homes in a very desirable neighborhood. These scenarios do not meet our investment strategy but may be considered depending on the money needed to complete the project.

Selling Properties

After each property has been renovated it will be listed for sale. As our target market consists of ____- to ___- year olds who may only have enough of a down payment for an FHA mortgage, we expect to offer assistance with closing costs.

Rental Portfolio

Careful attention will be given during the purchase process to find potential rental properties that would meet the criteria for our long-term investment portfolio. In order for these properties to meet our standards, they must pass the following performance measures:

1. We must be able to buy and fix up the property with minimal cash outlay.

2. The property must be located in a desirable area (family-friendly neighborhood) to ensure better than average appreciation and better tenants, and it must be purchased at a price below market value.

3. The income and expense streams must be favorable to net a positive cash flow of at least $_____ per year from each property.

Timeline

In summary, following the timeline identified throughout this document, we expect to purchase an average of _____ to _____ properties per month.

Managing Our Properties

We are a very successful enterprise with over _____ years of experience as investors. We have an excellent system in place to continue to monitor our portfolio. We know every month how each property is performing. This is accomplished by our monthly profit and loss statement. We are confident that our experience and success over the years merit strong consideration for approval of a working line of credit in the amount of $_____. Thank you very much for your consideration, and we look forward to establishing a mutually beneficial relationship.

For a completed sample business plan, see Resources page 311.

How should investors take title to an investment property?

I am confident that you now fully understand the benefits of owning real estate so you can do a great job explaining these benefits to your potential clients.

A very important decision that should be made as part of an investor's business plan is how to take title to a property. How title is held has many consequences. The most important thing you can do for your clients is to advise them to consult with an attorney to determine which of the many ownership options will be best for them. Keep in mind that some states have additional laws or restrictions regarding how one may hold title. The title company you use can be a tremendous resource for you.

The most common ways of taking title to an investment property are sole ownership, joint tenancy with right of survivorship, tenancy in common, revocable living trust, and establishment of a limited liability company.

Sole ownership

The simplest way to hold title is by sole ownership of the property. As the name implies, the sole owner hold all rights to the property. Although this form of ownership is mostly utilized by singles, theoretically speaking a married person can claim sole ownership of a property if his or her spouse is willing to sign a quit claim deed, which is a document that effectively denies the spouse any rights to the property. (Very few spouses are willing to do this.)

Joint tenancy with right of survivorship

Two or more people may hold title together in a form of ownership called joint tenancy. In this form of ownership, each owner has equal rights to the property as a whole. "Right of survivorship" means that if one owner dies, the deceased person's share will be automatically transferred to the co-owner(s) of the property rather than to the heirs of the deceased.

Tenancy in common

This structure is primarily used when there are partners involved. Under tenancy in common, multiple partners can hold either equal or unequal portions of the same property. For example, two people can each own 50% of the property, or they could split ownership 70% and 30%, or one person could own 50% and the other 50% could be split between 10 additional partners who each hold 5% ownership. Any combination of percentages is acceptable.

You may wonder what would keep one partner from independently selling his or her percentage without consulting the other partners. It is standard procedure to have a written agreement between the owners specifying how a partner can transfer his or her interest in the property.

Revocable living trust

In a living trust, title is held in the name of the trustee of the trust. Usually the person who establishes the trust serves as its trustee in order to keep full control of the property. The owner can buy, sell, and refinance just as if the property is not being held in the trust. One of the benefits of establishing a revocable trust is that if the person is no longer capable of performing the duties of trustee, the successor trustee (who was named when the trust was set up) will take over as trustee. For additional information on establishing a revocable trust, go to http://www.aarp.org/money/estate-planning.

Limited liability company (LLC)

Many investors choose to operate their real estate business as a limited liability company (better known as an LLC). Like a corporation, an LLC protects its members from liability. This means that members theoretically are not personally liable for debts incurred by the business. However, in my experience lenders will not loan money to an LLC unless the loan is also personally guaranteed by the members.

One of the major benefits of an LLC is that often court judgments incurred by the LLC do not affect the personal assets of the individual members. This protection is not provided by a sole proprietorship or traditional partnership.

Advantages of an LLC

1. Tax flexibility

   The IRS does not consider an LLC to be a distinct, separate entity for tax purposes. This means that (at least initially) the IRS will not tax the LLC directly. Instead, members of the LLC get to determine how they want to be taxed. There are several options:

   Single-member LLC: This structure is taxed like a sole proprietorship. Profits or losses from the business are not taxed directly but instead are taxed through the single member's personal tax return.

   Partners in an LLC: Same as above, and profit and losses based on the percentage of ownership for tax purposes are taxed through the member's personal tax return.

   Generally, members of an LLC will create an Articles of Organization and Operating Agreement that outlines how the LLC will be treated for tax purposes and so on. Further information on how the IRS classifies some LLCs can be found at http://www.irs.gov/

2. Less paperwork

   Compared with C-Corps or S-Corps, LLCs are very flexible.

   With less stringent requirements for compliance and reduced paperwork, LLCs are easier to form and easier to keep in good legal standing. (On a side note, if you want to find out more about the differences between an S Corp and a C Corp, go to http://www.bizfilings.com.)

Disadvantages of an LLC

3. Self-employment taxes
    Unless the LLC chooses to be taxed like a corporation,
    members of an LLC are usually subject to self-employ-
    ment taxes. This means that the profits of the LLC won't
    be taxed at the corporate level, but will pass through to
    its members who will account for those profits on their
    personal federal tax returns. Often these taxes are higher
    than they would be at the corporate level. Individual
    members will pay for their own Medicare and Social
    Security.

4. Confusion about roles
    Corporations have specific roles (like directors, manag-
    ers, and employees), but LLCs generally do not. This can
    make it hard to figure out who's in charge, who can sign
    certain contracts, and so on. This type of confusion can
    be avoided if roles of the members are outlined in the
    LLC's articles of organization and operating agreement.

5. Limited life
    Corporations can live forever, whereas an LLC is dis-
    solved when a member dies or undergoes bankruptcy.
    In summary, LLCs provide a great degree of flexibility
    and protection to their members. They shield members
    from personal liability while providing many tax options.
    The most important thing you can do for your clients is
    to advise them to consult with an attorney to determine
    which of the many options for taking title will best serve
    their needs.

The preceding information is intended only as a brief overview of the different ways of taking title to a property. Specific details should be discussed with an attorney or accountant.

WHY DO INVESTORS NEED AN EXIT PLAN?

In *The 7 Habits of Highly Effective People*, author Stephen R. Covey calls the second habit "Begin with the End in Mind." I could not think of more appropriate advice for real estate investors. What is the plan for each property? Why should investors start with the end in mind? Because every property should be purchased with a goal in mind.

When I started investing some 40 years ago, the idea of an exit strategy was the furthest thing from my mind. Now that I am in my sixties it is time to ask "Now what? I'm not going to be around forever, so what should I do with my real estate portfolio?" The easiest answer is to hand it over to my kids. Unfortunately, I'm not sure whether I would be doing them a favor if I did that, because they might not have the same level of interest or commitment as I do.

At this point, you probably will agree that owning a worthwhile real estate portfolio is one of the better options for accomplishing financial prosperity. If your real estate business is successful, eventually you will have a sizable portfolio that provides substantial income and cash flow. Some investors will follow the exit strategy of "I'll hold onto my portfolio until I die," and depending on the size of the estate there may be significant tax consequences. Most of us, however, will choose different strategies that are more realistic and will sell some of our properties for one reason or another. Having an exit strategy is just as important as buying the property at a great price.

Why would an investor want to have an exit plan as they are rolling along in the accumulation mode? Simply stated, the answer is that the end can come sooner than expected.

Investors should ask themselves how long they intend to own a property. Earlier in this chapter, we reviewed the definitions of A, B, C, or D properties and areas. With this information in mind, who would be the likely buyer when it's time to sell?

What about tax consequences? Unfortunately Uncle Sam wants a piece of the action, so tax planning is critical. This is probably the most important strategy of all, because we only want to pay our fair share of taxes.

POSSIBLE EXITS

There are a number of different ways to sell a real estate investment and collect your profits. These may include the following:

1. Wholesale: Buy the property and sell it quickly to another investor.

2. Sell/Flip: Buy the property, improve it, and sell it to someone who wants to live in it (owner-occupied property).

3. Rental: Use the property as a long-term rental and then sell it.

4. Lease option: Lease it with the idea that in a year or two the renter may be in a position to buy. Perhaps they have good income but poor credit and in time they may be able to improve their credit score. With a lease option, tenants accept responsibility for repairs and maintenance. As a result, they tend to take their rental obligation seriously.

5. Seller financing: If the owner has the property paid in full, seller financing for the right buyer may be a good option. This strategy alleviates paying capital gains all at once. Seek the advice of a CPA to see if this option makes sense for you.

6. 1031 tax exchange: Thanks to IRC Section 1031, a properly structured 1031 exchange allows an investor to sell a property, reinvest the proceeds in a new property, and defer all capital gain taxes. This is probably the best exit strategy from a tax standpoint.

7. Charitable giving: Charitable giving is always an option. There are many methods of making a contribution, so it is best to seek the advice of an attorney or CPA.

Many real estate investors have spent a lot of time and energy building their portfolios but have paid very little time attention to designing their exit strategy. Having a plan now will help you make better decisions for the future. A good exit strategy takes account of personal goals for income, family, retirement, lifestyle, wealth preservation, income tax, and estate planning.

It is imperative to have a competent attorney or CPA on the team to assist in making these decisions.

DETAILS ON THE 1031 EXCHANGE

For real estate investors, the 1031 exchange is a powerful tool for managing tax liability when selling and purchasing investment properties.

Normally, when property is sold, any gain on the sale will be taxed. However, the 1031 exchange allows an investor to defer capital gains tax on the sale of a business or investment asset when the investor uses the proceeds to purchase an asset of like-kind.

This tax deferral provides investors with more capital to invest in their subsequent purchase. Although the 1031 exchange can be used in a variety of ways, it is most commonly associated with real estate transactions.

To understand the advantages a 1031 exchange offers, consider the following example:

An investor has a $200,000 capital gain and incurs a tax liability of approximately $70,000 in combined taxes (depreciation recapture, federal and state capital gain taxes) when a property is sold. Only $130,000 remains to reinvest in another property. Assuming a 25% down payment and a 75% loan-to-value ratio, the seller would be able to purchase a new property worth $520,000.

If the same investor chose a 1031 exchange, however, he or she would be able to reinvest the entire $200,000 of equity in the purchase of $800,000 in real estate, assuming the same down payment and loan-to-value ratios.

Anyone contemplating using a 1031 exchange should seek the advice of a competent attorney or CPA.

USING SELF-DIRECTED OR ROTH IRAS TO BUY REAL ESTATE

Want to have more control over your financial future? Consider using a self-directed or Roth IRA to purchase real estate.

Many investors and real estate agents are unaware that retirement funds such as self-directed and Roth IRAs can be utilized to invest in real estate such as rentals for long-term income or properties to fix and flip for quicker profits. Investors can even benefit from real estate without owning the property itself by using IRA funds to purchase mortgage notes and trust deeds secured by real estate.

A real estate IRA is technically no different from any other IRA (or 401k). The government created the IRA to allow investments to grow tax-free or tax-deferred with the proceeds compounded over time to maximize growth. The IRA provides asset protection so that assets can be passed down to future generations.

What kinds of real estate can be purchased using an IRA?

With an IRA, an investor has the freedom to invest in almost any form of real estate, including the following:

- Homes, apartments, and condominiums

- Commercial properties such as retail stores, hotels, and office complexes

- Trust deed notes, mortgages, and tax liens

- Undeveloped land, lots, and farmland, to name a few

Key differences between purchasing real estate with an IRA and making a traditional investment

Purchasing and maintaining real estate in a retirement account differs from traditional property investments in a few important ways:

- The property's buyer is the IRA, not the investor. That's why paperwork must flow through an IRA custodian like Pensco, New Direction IRA Inc., Equity Trust, Broad Financial, and others. I am mostly familiar with Pensco because a couple of my clients use their services.

- All expenses and revenue must go through the IRA. Expenses must be paid by the IRA, and any revenue must come into the IRA.

- The investor cannot use the property for personal reasons. The property must be treated as investment, not used for the immediate benefit of you, your business, or your family.

- Maintenance and repairs must be done by a third party. If the IRA owner provides any "sweat equity" activities – even something as minor as changing a light bulb — there could be significant tax penalties.

What is a self-directed IRA?

A self-directed IRA allows the account owner to direct the account trustee to make a broader range of investments than other types of IRAs.

Internal Revenue Service (IRS) regulations require that either a qualified trustee, or custodian, hold the IRA assets on behalf of the IRA owner. Generally the trustee/custodian will maintain the assets and all transactions and other records pertaining to them, file required IRS reports, issue client statements, help clients understand the rules regarding prohibited transactions, and perform other administrative duties on behalf of the self-directed IRA owner for the life of the IRA account. The custodian of a self-directed IRA may offer a selection of standard asset types that the account owner can select to invest in, such as stocks, bonds, and mutual funds, but the account owner also can make other types of investments, such as real estate. The range of permissible investments is broad but regulated by the IRS.

What is a Roth IRA?

A Roth IRA is a self-directed retirement account that is funded with post-tax dollars. Although contributions are not tax-deductible, the tax benefit of a Roth IRA is that all earnings, including interest, capital gains, and dividend income, grow tax-free. Income taxes are paid on initial contributions in the year they are made, but the account holder can withdraw the earnings tax-free if certain requirements are met.

In addition, direct contributions can be withdrawn at any time without penalty because these funds have already been taxed. Account holders can begin withdrawing earnings at age 59½ but are not required to take distributions at any age.

A Roth IRA gives the account holder the freedom to invest in almost any form of real estate. The key: It is all tax-free.

Anyone who is contemplating using their IRA to purchase real estate should seek the advice of a competent CPA and attorney and consult with the appropriate custodians.

KEY POINTS TO REMEMBER:

- Real estate investing should be treated as a business.

- Writing a business plan helps investors chart their progress toward short- and long-term goals and also makes it easier to borrow money from banks.

- How a business is owned and operated affects taxation and estate planning.

- As with any other business, real estate investors should have an exit strategy.

- Using a 1031 exchange defers taxation of capital gains and gives investors greater purchasing power.

- Investors can purchase real estate using funds from a self-directed or Roth IRA, and this type of financing brings both advantages and disadvantages for the investor.

CHAPTER 13

PUTTING IT ALL TOGETHER

I decided to write this book because I wanted to share strategies that have worked well for me during my 45 years as an investor and 20 years as a real estate agent. The financial benefits of investing in real estate have been substantial, but money has not been the only reward I have received from investing in real estate and working with investors. My life has also been enriched through longtime friendships with many of my former clients, tenants, and colleagues.

If you have been sitting on the sidelines while some of your associates are reaping the financial benefits of working with investors, I hope reading this book has helped you decide to get in the "game." You are ready to bring the value and expertise investors expect from their real estate agent. I am confident that your income stream will grow, as well as your client base.

Just as I have developed meaningful relationships with my clients, so will you. There's no better feeling than being able to play a significant role in your client's success as an investor.

PUT YOUR NEWFOUND KNOWLEDGE TO USE

You are now able to do more than just talk about investing. You have enough knowledge to effectively guide your clients every step of the way:

- You can assist them to identify their short- and long-term objectives.

- You can guide them in making good business decisions.

- You can identify properties that have investment potential.

- You can analyze whether a property is likely to be a poor, good, or great investment. (Remember that price alone doesn't determine whether a property is a good deal.)

- You can connect your clients with contractors, property management companies, bankers, accountants, attorneys, and people in the trades.

Armed with this knowledge, you will be the most important person on the investor's team. You can play a huge role in finding good deals and making sure their offers are accepted. If they don't work with you, they will never find out about the best deals.

For me, the past few years have been extremely rewarding financially. I have bought and flipped an average of six properties a year and also helped my clients buy and sell about 90 properties a year.

Although great deals are not as readily available today as they were in the past, you should be able to generate an additional $50,000 to $100,000 of income if you commit to making this a priority as part of your overall business plan and goals. If an investor is purchasing a property as a long-term rental and they have to pay another $5,000 to $10,000 more for it at 5% interest, this is an additional $33 to $66 per month. If this amount makes a big difference to their cash flow I understand, but if they are looking for long-term wealth and this is an issue, then they have other financial issues and probably should reconsider this business. Always keep in mind who is paying down the mortgage.

There's no doubt that you now have the experience to outperform your competition. Clients will see you as the go-to real estate agent in your area, and you will have more business than you ever thought was possible.

You now understand the different strategies for buy-and-hold versus buy-and-flip, so you should be able to assist clients in selecting properties that will meet their financial objectives. Additionally, you are familiar with some of the tax benefits available to investors, so you can help them make sure they are paying no more than their fair share of taxes.

You are an extremely talented real estate agent, yet maybe for one reason or another you haven't found as much success as you had hoped to find in this business. Finally you will be able to reap the benefits this industry has to offer.

WHAT'S NEXT?

To crystallize what you've learned from reading this book, how about creating mission, vision, and values statements that will separate you from other real estate agents? Here are some examples.

Mission

- To go above and beyond my clients' expectations by serving as a wealth advisor, coach, and mentor.

- To be a one-stop source of information for my clients' real estate investment needs.

- To bring knowledge and service beyond my clients' expectations.

Vision

- To help my clients generate wealth so they can become financially independent.

- To be a real estate agent that everyone wants to work with because otherwise they would be missing out.

Values

- I will strive to be 100% honest and put my clients' interests ahead of my own.

- I will no longer need to worry about the size of my next commission check. When my clients are successful, I will be successful.

AN ACTION PLAN FOR SUCCESS

Believe in yourself. Understand that you are a difference maker. You are not just an ordinary real estate agent but someone who is extraordinary because of your specialized knowledge.

Know that you can play a very integral part in helping clients generate wealth beyond what they have achieved with any other financial advisor they may have consulted. Remember that real estate is one of the better vehicles for wealth building and one of the few options that can provide tax benefits.

There has never been a better time to set some attainable goals for expanding your client base. How about meeting with 20 current or potential clients monthly for the next three months?

To reach your goal of twenty contacts in the next month, you could start by meeting with five people next week to talk about real estate investing. They can come from current/past clients, your sphere of influence, and anyone else in your circle of potential clients. Keep in mind that they are not doing you a favor by meeting with you; you are showing them a path to wealth-building that is realistic and attainable. They don't know what they have been missing by not investing, and if you don't lead the way they will remain in the dark.

One month from today, you will have reached out to twenty people and shared your enthusiasm and passion for real estate investment. You will have given them a number of compelling reasons why they should utilize your services. Do you know of anyone who would not enjoy paying fewer taxes and at the same time generating wealth? Three months from now, you will have met with sixty people to have a conversation about the benefits of investing in real estate.

Next, why not set a goal of converting twenty of these contacts to buyers of just one property within the next year? This would equal twenty additional sales. If the average sales price is $100,000 at 6% with a 60/40 split, this would bring you an additional $48,000 over the next year. Or if each of those twenty clients generated an average commission of $3,000 to $6,000, you would bring in $60,000 to $120,000 of additional income.

Your success in working with new investors will have a snowball effect by attracting additional clients. Think about how powerful this can be for you. If each of your past clients knows fifty people, and each of the twenty people you met with in one month decided to become an investor, you could potentially reach a thousand new clients. The nicest thing about this scenario is that you will not have to hound them or bug them to work with you. Rather, new clients will eventually seek you out. What a concept—finally getting calls instead of making them.

YOU HAVE A VALUABLE
SERVICE TO OFFER

The real estate industry is filled with get-rich-quick programs that make big promises and never deliver. There are no secrets in this business that are worth asking someone to pay $10,000 or more to attend a seminar. You are the coach, mentor and advisor for your clients, and you don't charge a dime for your services if you are working with the buyer. Who knows more about your community—you or someone who comes to town for a one-night-stand and leaves the next day?

Commit to taking the next step and begin having conversations about investing in real estate. The actions you take during the next 30 days could change your life. (You can use the "30-day Action Plan Worksheet" and "My Top 30 Potential Clients" in the Resources section to get started.)

Knowledge is powerful, and you have enough expertise to succeed and grow your business. Real estate agents who don't have your knowledge are working with investors, and you are much more qualified than they are.

Any real estate agent can look on the MLS to find properties and open doors, but how many agents can determine Cap Rates or Cash on Cash? Now that you are in the know, network with other agents (even agents at other companies) who are also specialists. They can tell you about properties that are not even listed if they don't have a buyer, and you can do the same for them. It is a win-win proposition for you and your clients.

Always keep in mind that when your clients achieve their goals, you will also achieve your goals as well.

You are well on your way to achieving success as an investor-friendly real estate agent. Congratulations!

Resources

Purchasing this book entitles you to download the documents in this section at no additional charge. To download, go to:

www.realestateclientsforlife.com

30 DAY ACTION PLAN WORKSHEET

Name:

MY ANNUAL GOAL   YEAR _____

MY MONTHLY GOAL   MONTH OF_____

MY ONE MONTH GOAL

WEEK 1	WEEK 2	WEEK 3	WEEK 4

My Top 30 Potential Clients

Name

1. _____
2. _____
3. _____
4. _____
5. _____
6. _____
7. _____
8. _____
9. _____
10. _____
11. _____
12. _____
13. _____
14. _____
15. _____
16. _____
17. _____
18. _____
19. _____
20. _____
21. _____
22. _____
23. _____
24. _____
25. _____
26. _____
27. _____
28. _____
29. _____
30. _____

Notes

_____
_____
_____

Questions to Ask Potential Clients
Sample questions you may consider asking
potential clients (not in any special order)

Name_____

Address_____

Phone number_____

Email_____

1. Do you own any rental properties? _____
2. Do you own them by yourself or with partners? _____
3. Any special reasons you want to invest or expand your portfolio:
   _____
   _____
   _____

4. What are your short-term and long-term objectives for investing?
   _____
   _____
   _____

5. How did you buy or are you planning on buying?
   ___ Cash ___ LOC ___ Loan
   How much cash do you have to invest? _____
6. Do you have an IRA?
   __Yes ___No ___Self-directed____ Roth
7. Price range and areas – Are there any areas you won't consider?
   _____
   _____
   _____

8. What types of properties will you consider?
   ____House ___Duplex ___Apt. Other:_____
9. Are you looking to flip or rent out? _____
10. Looking for properties that need work? _____
    or properties that are ready to go? _____
    Cosmetics_____

11. Are you planning to do your own work or hire out? _____

_____

12. Are you more interested in cash flow, tax benefits, or long-term wealth building?

13. Do you have a business plan?
    ___Yes ___No

14. Are you planning to manage your own properties or to use a property manager? _____

15. Are you on track to accomplish your retirement objectives?
    __Yes __No

16. How did you come out on your taxes last year? Did you pay more than you wanted? _____

17. What are you planning to do differently this year?_____

_____

18. Any major concerns with your current economic situation? _____

_____

_____

19. How much longer do you plan on working? To retirement age?

_____

20. Will you have enough money to maintain your current lifestyle in retirement with your current income and/or investments? _____

_____

21. Are you prepared for life after work? _____

22. What would happen if you got sick or no longer could earn a living at the workplace? _____

23. What is your current financial situation? _____

24. Are you saving enough money regularly or are you comfortable with your current savings? _____

25. Do you have enough disposable income? _____

26. Are you more in debt than you would like? _____

27. Do you have a college savings plan for your children? _____

_____

28. Are you satisfied with the return from your current investments/?

_____

Notes _____
_____
_____
_____

Property Checklist

Print out a few copies of this checklist to use as you visit prospective properties. Having information on each property can help you to compare properties and will make your final decision much easier.

Date _____

Address _____ Price _____

Property taxes _____

How long has it been on the market? _____   Foreclosure _____yes _____no

Other_____

_____

Age of property _____   Neighborhood/Subdivision _____

Corner lot __ yes __no

Overall impression of Area/Neighborhood __Acceptable __ Not acceptable

Overall impression of properties on either side and /across from subject property __Acceptable __ Not acceptable

Other_____

_____

Style

__ 2.5 Story __ 2 Story__1.5 Story   __Bungalow __Multi level __ Ranch

__ Split entry   __ Raised ranch

__ Tri level __ Cape Cod __ Townhouse __ Condo __Other

Type of Construction

__ Wood __ Brick __Stone __ Stucco __ Vinyl siding __ Aluminum siding __ Other

Exterior Features

Roof type _____

Roof condition ___ Good ___ Fair ___ Acceptable __ Needs replaced

Fenced ___yes ___no   Porch ___yes ___no   Deck __yes ___no

Patio __yes __no   Deck __yes ___no

Other_____

Paint ___ Acceptable ___ Needs painted

Other_____

_____

Garage

____ 1 car __ 2 car __Attached __Detached __ Carport

____ no garage __off-street parking

Central AC __ yes __no   Window units __yes __no # of units _____

Interior Features

Kitchen
Eat-In __yes__no_____Size _____
Type of flooring __Ceramic tile __Wood floors__ Linoleum __Other _____
 Appliances __ yes __no   Stove__yes __ ___ no
Refrigerator __yes __ no   Dishwasher __yes __ no   Other _____
Condition of cabinets ___ new___old ___   Painted: yes __no ____
Needs replacing __yes __no

Dining Room
___yes ___no   Size _____   Carpet yes___no___ Wood floors yes___no___

Living Room
 Size _____ Carpet ___yes __ no   Wood floors yes __no
Other_____

Den/Family room Size _____
Carpet __yes __no   Wood floors___yes __ no

Other rooms_____

Total bedrooms_____

Bedroom 1 size _____ Carpet __yes __no Wood floors yes __ no
Other _____

Bedroom 2 size _____ Carpet __yes __no Wood floors yes __ no
Other _____

Bedroom 3 size _____ Carpet __yes __no Wood floors yes __ no
Other _____

Bedroom 4 size _____ Carpet __yes __no Wood floors yes __ no
Other _____

_____
_____

Total bathrooms _____
 Full_____ 3/4_____ 1/2_____ 1/4 _____
Master bath ___ yes ___ no Flooring type_____
Guest/powder bath ___ yes ___ no   Flooring type_____
Other_____

Laundry room
Location _____   Washer ___yes ___no Dryer ___yes ___no
Other _____

Basement ___yes ___no   Finished ___yes ___no _____
Flooring   Carpet _____Tile _____   Other _____

Utilities
Type of Heating
_____Gas_____Steam ___Hot water _____Electric _____ Oil
Age of System _____

Age/Capacity of water heater_____ Gas_____ Electric_____

Electrical service
_____Fuses   _____Circuit breakers

Plumbing
Galvanized _____Copper _____Other _____
Sump pump/Drainage system: ___yes ___no
Sewer connected to public sewer ___yes ___no   Septic _____yes _____no
Other_____

Proximity to:
_____ Schools_____ Shopping _____Highways _____Religious institutions
_____Downtown _____ Hospitals
Other_____
_____
_____

Other things of interest nearby:
_____
_____
_____
_____

272

FRED TICHAUER

Recent sales of comparable properties in neighborhood

Address _____   Sq. Ft _____
              Price _____
# of bedrooms _____ # of baths_____
Other features_____
_____

Address _____   Sq. Ft _____
              Price _____
# of bedrooms _____ # of baths_____
Other features_____
_____

Address _____   Sq. Ft _____
              Price _____
# of bedrooms _____ # of baths_____
Other features_____
_____

Notes

_____
_____
_____
_____
_____
_____
_____
_____
_____
_____
_____
_____
_____
_____
_____
_____
_____
_____

Multi-unit due diligence checklist

Due diligence involves much more than doing an actual property inspection with an inspector. Inspections are important, but they are only a tiny part of the process. Leaving no stones unturned will go a long way toward uncovering most potential problems.

When you are considering the purchase of a multi-unit, it is critically important to gather as much information as possible. The financial details are especially important, because you will need to use them when you run the numbers to see whether the property is a good investment.

In summary, the physical and financial due diligence process will uncover critical information that will help you decide to either move forward or to back out of the deal. Carrying out due diligence can save you from making a costly mistake.

Property details
Property address:

_____
Asking price: $_____
Type of property: A__ B__ C__ D__
Legal description:

_____
Parcel no. _____
Tax assessed value (year) _____
Land value _____
Bldg. value _____
Existing financing (if any):
Lender (1st): _____ (2nd):_____
Interest rate: _____
Term of loan: # of years _____
# of years remaining on loan _____
Is property being managed property management company?
_____ by a _____
Contact: _____
% charged monthly: _____

Financial details
It is important to obtain as much of the following financial information as possible.
- Profit and loss statements (P&L) for past 2-3 years   [ ] Yes [ ] No

   Any concerns noted:

_____

_____

_____

- Year to date income and expense statement   [ ] Yes [ ] No
  Any concerns noted:

_____

_____

_____

- Tax returns for past 2 to 3 years   [ ] Yes [ ] No

  Any concerns noted:

_____

_____

_____

- Secure and review rent rolls for past 2-3 years   [ ] Yes [ ] No

  Any concerns noted:

_____

_____

_____

- Secure copies of all leases   [ ] Yes [ ] No

  Any concerns noted:

_____

_____

_____

- Number of units that will become vacant in the next 3 months ___

  6 months___ 9 months___

  Any concerns noted:

_____

_____

_____

- Secure copies of any service agreements (i.e., washer and dryer ,
  security system, cable, other)?   [ ] Yes [ ] No
  If yes, do any of them commit new buyer to be assumed?
  [ ] Yes [ ] No

- Does seller own washers / dryers? [ ] Yes [ ] No
- Any snow removal/ lawn mowing contracts? [ ] Yes [ ] No
- Secure copies of any major improvements/updates for past 2-3 years? [ ] Yes [ ] No
- Any concerns noted:

_____
_____
_____

- Secure list of personal property to be included in the sale? [ ] Yes [ ] No

_____
_____
_____
_____
_____
_____
_____

- Secure report of most recent accounts receivable? [ ] Yes [ ] No
- Secure report of delinquent rents/possible evictions? [ ] Yes [ ] No
- Are there any tenants with concessions (reduced rent, free rent, etc.)? [ ] Yes [ ] No   If yes, how many of tenants fall in this category? _____
- Secure current listing of vendors, contractors handyman, electrician, plumber, other? [ ] Yes [ ] No

_____
_____
_____
_____

- Pet policy and rules: .Are pets allowed? [ ] Yes [ ] No
  If yes, how many units have pets? _____

Other details
- Any known code violations? [ ] Yes [ ] No
- Any environmental concerns? [ ] Yes [ ] No
  Mold: [ ] Yes [ ] No
  Lead paint: [ ] Yes [ ] No
  Asbestos: [ ] Yes [ ] No
  Any other concerns noted:

_____
_____
_____

Insurance

- Secure a copy of current insurance policy and agent to compare /
  verify that you can obtain a satisfactory insurance quote?
  [ ] Yes [ ] No

Interior inspection

- Number of units__ How many: Efficiency __ 1 bedroom ___
  2 bedrooms ____ 3 bedrooms
- Checked interior of all units? [ ] Yes [ ] No
- Overall condition of units: Excellent ___ Good___ Poor___
  Needs lots of attention____
  Any repairs that will require immediate attention:

_____
_____
_____

- Any vacant units noticed? [ ] Yes [ ] No If yes, which ones?

_____
_____

- Any repairs to units that will require immediate attention? Which
  units?

_____
_____
_____
_____
_____

- Any pest/rodent/ problems noticed? [ ] Yes [ ] No
- Condition of appliances: Excellent ___ Good ___ Poor ___
  Appliances that need to be replaced:

_____
_____
_____

- Any water/fire damage noted? [ ] Yes [ ] No If yes, which unit(s)?_____
  _____
  _____

- Any problem tenants noticed? [ ] Yes [ ] No
- Security system? [ ] Yes [ ] No

Basement
- Are units separately metered for gas? [ ] Yes [ ] No
- Are units separately metered for electricity? [ ] Yes [ ] No
- Service panel fuses? [ ] Yes [ ] No
- Service panel circuit breakers? [ ] Yes [ ] No
- Is heating system boiler? [ ] Yes [ ] No
- If no, how many furnaces? _____ Age if known_____
- Number of water heaters_____ Age if known_____.
  Any recent updates?
  _____
  _____
  _____
  _____

Exterior details
- Condition of roof (age if known _____) Excellent ___
  Good___ Poor___ Needs to be replaced [ ] Yes [ ] No
- Condition of windows and doors: Old or new? ____ Excellent ____
  Good___ Poor___ Need to be replaced_____
  Anything else of concern:
  _____
  _____
  _____
  _____

- Condition of soffits and fascia: Excellent ___ Good___ Poor___
  Needs work_____
- Condition of paint: Excellent ___ Good___ Poor___ Needs
  repainting_____
- Condition of gutters and downspouts: Excellent ___ Good___
  Poor___ Needs to be replaced____
- Condition of chimney: Excellent ___ Good___ Poor___ Needs
  repair ___

- Condition of yard: Excellent ___ Good___ Needs lots of attention_____

  _____

  _____

- Parking situation: Is it on street parking? [ ] Yes [ ] No
- If off street, for how many spots? ____
- Overall condition of exterior: Excellent ___ Good___ Poor___
  Any potential issues? [ ] Yes [ ] No

Area

- Overall impression of area: Excellent ___ Good____ Poor___
  Area/neighborhood rating: A__ B__ C__ D___
- Anything else positive or negative that could cause you to walk away or move forward?

  _____

- How many apartments within a two-block area? _____
- Overall conditions and general appearance of the area within a two-block area of the property under consideration:

  _____

- Any recent updates to exterior? [ ] Yes [ ] No
  If yes, describe:

  _____

  _____

- Any trends and changes in the area that could have a positive or negative influence in the future (i.e., new condos, apartments, offices, commercial buildings, etc.)? [ ] Yes [ ] No
  If yes, describe:

  _____

  How many new buildings are being constructed in the area? _____

- Other observations:

  _____

_____

_____

Inspections

- Any structural inspections needed? [ ] Yes [ ] No
  If yes, what type?

  _____

  _____

  _____

  _____

- Any contractor inspections needed? [ ] Yes [ ] No
  If yes, what type?

  _____

  _____

  _____

  _____

- Any mechanical inspection needed? [ ] Yes [ ] No
  If yes, what type?

  _____

  _____

  _____

  _____

Remodeling Cost Estimator

Property Address _____ **Date** _____

Remodeling to be completed

Kitchen	Item	Cost	Subtotal
1.	_____	_____	_____
2.	_____	_____	_____
3.	_____	_____	_____
4.	_____	_____	_____
5.	_____	_____	_____
6.	_____	_____	_____
7.	_____	_____	_____
8.	_____	_____	_____

Bathroom	Item	Cost	Subtotal
1.	_____	_____	_____
2.	_____	_____	_____
3.	_____	_____	_____
4.	_____	_____	_____
5.	_____	_____	_____

Living Room	Item	Cost	Subtotal
1.	_____	_____	_____
2.	_____	_____	_____
3.	_____	_____	_____
4.	_____	_____	_____
5.	_____	_____	_____

Dining Room	Item	Cost	Subtotal
1.	_____	_____	_____
2.	_____	_____	_____
3.	_____	_____	_____
4.	_____	_____	_____
5.	_____	_____	_____

Bedroom 1	Item	Cost	Subtotal
1.	_____	_____	_____
2.	_____	_____	_____
3.	_____	_____	_____
4.	_____	_____	_____

Bedroom 2	Item	Cost	Subtotal
1.	_____	_____	_____
2.	_____	_____	_____
3.	_____	_____	_____
4.	_____	_____	_____

Bedroom 3	Item	Cost	Subtotal
1.	_____	_____	_____
2.	_____	_____	_____
3.	_____	_____	_____
4.	_____	_____	_____

Basement   **Item**   **Cost**   **Subtotal**

1. _____ _____ _____
2. _____ _____ _____
3. _____ _____ _____
4. _____ _____ _____

Exterior   **Item**   **Cost**   **Subtotal**

1. _____ _____ _____
2. _____ _____ _____
3. _____ _____ _____
4. _____ _____ _____

Misc.   **Item**   **Cost**   **Subtotal**

1. _____ _____ _____
2. _____ _____ _____
3. _____ _____ _____
4. _____ _____ _____
5. _____ _____ _____

                                                    Total   _____

Real Estate Rehab worksheet

Address

1.PURCHASE COSTS		
Loan Origination	$	1,000.00
Appraisal	$	400.00
Credit Report	$	70.00
Title Insurance	$	425.00
Escrow Fee	$	175.00
Recording Fee	$	50.00
Other		
TOTAL PURCHASE COSTS	**$**	**2,120.00**

	Good	Better	Best
PURCHASE PRICE	$ 85,000.00	$ 80,000.00	$ 75,000.00
PURCHASE COSTS	$ 2,120.00	$ 2,120.00	$ 2,120.00
HOLDING COSTS	$ 4,775.00	$ 4,775.00	$ 4,775.00
RENOVATION COSTS	$ 6,150.00	$ 6,150.00	$ 6,150.00
	$ 98,045.00	$ 93,045.00	$ 88,045.00

2.HOLDING COSTS		
Interest	$	3,600.00
Property Taxes	$	600.00
Insurance	$	150.00
Utilities		
Gas, Water, Sewer, Electrical	$	350.00
Trash service	$	75.00
Other		
TOTAL HOLDING COSTS	**$**	**4,775.00**

PROPOSED SALES PRICE	$ 120,000.00	$ 125,000.00	$ 130,000.00
Commission	$ 6,000.00	$ 7,000.00	$ 8,000.00
Title Insurance	$ 500.00	$ 500.00	$ 500.00
Document Stamps	$ 300.00	$ 300.00	$ 300.00
Other			
Other			
Other			
Net Proceeds To Seller	$ 113,200.00	$ 117,200.00	$ 121,200.00
Total Profit / Loss	$ 15,155.00	$ 24,155.00	$ 33,155.00

3.RENOVATION COSTS		
Clean up/Demolition	$	350.00
Electrical	$	500.00
Plumbing	$	500.00
Painting/drywall	$	1,000.00
Kitchen Remodel		
Bathroom Remodel		
Flooring	$	800.00
Carpet	$	2,500.00
Roof, Siding, Windows		
Landscape/Lawn	$	500.00
Other		
SUBTOTAL RENOVATION COSTS	**$**	**6,150.00**
TOTAL COSTS(1,2,3)	**$**	**13,045.00**

NOTES:

(Only change highlighted areas)

Real Estate Rehab worksheet

Address

1.PURCHASE COSTS	
Loan Origination	
Appraisal	
Credit Report	
Title Insurance	
Escrow Fee	
Recording Fee	
Other	
TOTAL PURCHASE COSTS	$ -

	Good		Better		Best	
PURCHASE PRICE						
PURCHASE COSTS	$	-	$	-	$	-
HOLDING COSTS	$	-	$	-	$	-
RENOVATION COSTS	$	-	$	-	$	-
	$	-	$	-	$	-

2.HOLDING COSTS	
Interest	
Property Taxes	
Insurance	
Utilities	
Gas, Water, Sewer, Electrical	
Trash service	
Other	
TOTAL HOLDING COSTS	$ -

	Good		Better		Best	
PROPOSED SALES PRICE						
Commission						
Title Insurance						
Document Stamps						
Other						
Other						
Other						
Net Proceeds To Seller	$	-	$	-	$	-
Total Profit / Loss	$	-	$	-	$	-

3.RENOVATION COSTS	
Clean up/Demolition	
Electrical	
Plumbing	
Painting/drywall	
Kitchen Remodel	
Bathroom Remodel	
Flooring	
Carpet	
Roof, Siding, Windows	
Landscape/Lawn	
Other	
SUBTOTAL RENOVATION COST:	$ -
TOTAL COSTS(1,2,3)	$ -

NOTES:

(Only change highlighted areas)

Instructions For Using Property Analysis Buy and Hold

Only change highlighted categories on the form:

1. Fill in "Property Address" and "No. of Units"
2. Fill in "Purchase Cost," "Down Payment," and "Closing Costs," and then add these amounts to get "Total Investment"
3. Financing: Fill in "Term," "Amount," "Rate," and "P & I" for first mortgage and second mortgage (if applicable)
4. Depreciation: Refer to "Cost Recovery – Depreciation" schedule provided. Analysis applies to Year 1 only, because it is difficult to predict depreciation beyond the first year.
   a. Land Value: Use County Assessor values (can't depreciate land).
   b. Personal Property: If appliances such as stove, refrigerator, dishwasher, washer, dryer are included in the purchase, estimate a value for each appliance and add all values.
   c. Land Improvement Value: Includes fencing, landscaping, sidewalks, driveways, etc.
   Building Value is the difference between the purchase price and the sum of a, b, c above.
5. Annual Rent: Assume vacancy of 10%.
6. Annual Operating Expenses: Change and/or add categories as needed. You can include other expenses in the "Misc." category.
7. Annual Debt Service: Interest is only for Year 1. (Use any amortization schedule.)
8. Net Operating Income: Tax bracket can be changed as needed. Use client's tax bracket from previous year or estimate 28%.
9. Appreciation Estimate: It is better to estimate on the low side even though appreciation has been relatively high (3% to 4%) for the past couple of years.

Note: The "Property Analysis Buy and Hold" form is for informational purposes only. Client should consult his or her attorney or CPA.

Property Analysis Buy and Hold

1) Property Address	Parker Duplex (Randall)		No. of Units			2
2) Purchase Cost	$	120,000				
Down Payment	$	24,000				
Closing Costs	$	3,600				
Total Investment	$	27,600				

	TERM	AMOUNT	RATE		P & I	
3) FINANCING 1st Mortgage	20	$96,000.00	6.50%	$	716	
FINANCING 2nd Mortgage	10		7.50%	$	-	

4) Depreciation				Year 1		
a. Land Value		0.00%	$	22,600	$	22,600
b. Personal Property		20.00%	$	2,000	$	400
Building Value		3.48%	$	94,400	$	3,285
c. Land Improvement Value		5.00%	$	1,000	$	50
Total Depreciation			$	120,000	$	3,735

5) Annual Rent	$850 per side	$	20,400
Less Vacancy Rate (10%)		$	2,040
Gross Operating Income		$	18,360

6) Annual Operating Expenses		
Real Estate Taxes	$	2,997
Maintenance	$	1,800
Insurance	$	900
Repairs	$	100
Management	$	
Misc.	$	
Lawn and snow	$	200
Utilities	$	100
Advertising	$	50
Supplies	$	200
TOTAL	$	6,347

I.	Gross Operating Income		$	18,360	
	minus	Operating Expenses	$	6,347	
	equals	Net Operating Income	$	12,013	
	minus	Annual Debt Service	$	8,589	
	equals	Cash Flow Before Taxes	$	3,424	
II.	7) Annual Debt Service		$	8,589	
	minus	Interest	$	6,169	
	equals	Principal Reduction (PR)	$	2,420	$	(93,580)
III.	8) Net Operating Income		$	12,013	
	minus	Interest	$	6,169	
	minus	Total Depreciation	$	3,735	
	equals	Taxable Income	$	2,109	
	times tax bracket	Tax Bracket		28%	
	equals	Taxes Paid (TP)	$	590	
IV.	9) Appreciation Estimate (AE)			2.00%	$	2,400
V.	ROI with Appr. (CFBT+PR-TP+AE/cash inv.			27.73%	
VI.	ROI without Appr. (CFBT+PR-TP/ cash inv.			19.03%	
VII.	Capitalization Rate (NOI divided by purchase price)			10.01%	
VIII.	Cash on Cash (cash flow bef. taxes div. by cash inv.)			12.41%	
IX.	Gross Rent Multiplier (sale price div. by annual rent)			5.88%	
X.	Debt Coverage Ratio (NOI div. by debt service)			1.399	
XI.	Operating Exp. Ratio (op. exp. div. by gross op. inc.)			34.57%	
XII.	Break Even Ratio (BER) = Op. Exp. + Debt Service/Gross Op. Inc.			81.35%	
	Cash Flow After Taxes (CFAT) =				
XIII.	CFBT - Taxes Paid		$	2,834	

This form is designed to assist in estimating the first-year benefits of a real estate investment. It does not consider the effects of selling or exchanging the property in the future. This form is not a substitute for legal advice. Anyone contemplating the purchase of real estate investment property should seek the advice of competent legal and tax professionals.

Property Analysis Buy and Hold

1) Property Address		No. of Units		

2) Purchase Cost	$_____			
Down Payment	$_____			
Closing Costs	$_____			
Total Investment	$_____			

	TERM	AMOUNT	RATE	P & I
3) FINANCING 1st Mortgage		$_____	_____ %	$_____
FINANCING 2nd Mortgage		$_____		
4) Depreciation				Year 1
a. Land Value		0.00%	$_____	$_____
b. Personal Property		20.00%	$_____	$_____
Building Value		3.48%	$_____	$_____
c. Land Improvement Value		5.00%	$_____	$_____
Total Depreciation			$_____	$_____
5) Annual Rent		$_____		
Less Vacancy Rate (10%)		$_____		
Gross Operating Income		$_____		

6) Annual Operating Expenses	
Real Estate Taxes	$_____
Maintenance	$_____
Insurance	$_____
Repairs	$_____
Management	$_____
Misc.	$_____
Lawn and snow	$_____
Utilities	$_____
Advertising	$_____
Supplies	$_____
TOTAL	$_____

I.	Gross Operating Income		$_____	
	minus	Operating Expenses	$_____	
	equals	Net Operating Income	$_____	
	minus	Annual Debt Service	$_____	
	equals	Cash Flow Before Taxes	$_____	$_____
II.	7) Annual Debt Service		$_____	
	minus	Interest	$_____	
	equals	Principal Reduction (PR)	_____ %	$_____
III.	8) Net Operating Income		$_____	
	minus	Interest	$_____	
	minus	Total Depreciation	$_____	
	equals	Taxable Income	$_____	
	times (8)	Tax Bracket	_____ %	
	equals	Taxes Paid (TP)	$_____	
IV.	9) Appreciation Estimate (AE)		_____ %	$_____
V.	ROI with Appr. (CFBT+PR-TP+AE/cash inv.		_____ %	
VI.	ROI without Appr. (CFBT+PR-TP/ cash inv.		_____ %	
VII.	Capitalization Rate (NOI divided by purchase price)		_____ %	
VIII.	Cash on Cash (cash flow bef. taxes div. by cash inv.)		_____ %	
IX.	Gross Rent Multiplier (sale price div. by annual rent)		_____ %	
X.	Debt Coverage Ratio (NOI div. by debt service)		_____ %	
XI.	Operating Exp. Ratio (op. exp. div. by gross op. inc.)		_____ %	
XII.	Break Even Ratio (BER) = Op. Exp. + Debt Service/Gross Op. Inc.		_____ %	
XIII.	Cash Flow After Taxes (CFAT) = CFBT - Taxes Paid		$_____	

This form is designed to assist in estimating the first-year benefits of a real estate investment. It does not consider the effects of selling or exchanging the property in the future. This form is not a substitute for legal advice. Anyone contemplating the purchase of real estate investment property should seek the advice of competent legal and tax professionals.

Cost Recovery – Depreciation

Cost recovery (depreciation) is the periodic allocation of the cost of qualified assets. When a taxpayer, or in some cases a lessee, purchases a qualified asset they are allowed to recover the acquisition cost of the asset through certain deductions set forth in the Internal Revenue Code. The method and length of recovery periods depends on the type of property purchased. Below are the cost recovery tables for the various types of property. These tables are rounded to two decimal points for simplicity. Check with your tax advisor for the actual percentages.

Recovery Percentages for Residential Rental Property (27.5 Years)

Recovery Year	Jan	Feb	March	April	May	June
1	3.48	3.18	2.88	2.58	2.27	1.97
2–27	3.64	3.64	3.64	3.64	3.64	3.64
28	1.88	2.27	2.57	2.87	3.18	3.48
29	0.00	0.00	0.00	0.00	0.00	0.00

Recovery Year	July	Aug	Sept	Oct	Nov	Dec
1	1.67	1.36	1.06	0.76	0.45	0.15
227	3.64	3.64	3.64	3.64	3.64	3.64
28	3.64	3.64	3.64	3.64	3.64	3.64
29	0.15	0.45	0.75	1.06	1.36	1.66

Recovery Percentages for Non-Residential Real Estate Property (39 Years]

Recovery Year	Jan	Feb	March	April	May	June
1	2.46	2.24	2.03	1.82	1.60	1.39
2–38	2.56	2.56	2.56	2.56	2.56	2.56
39–40	Pro-rated					

Recovery Year	July	Aug	Sept	Oct	Nov	Dec
1	1.18	0.96	0.75	0.53	0.32	0.11
2–38	2.56	2.56	2.56	2.56	2.56	2.56
39–40	Pro-rated					

Cost Recovery – Depreciation *(continued)*

Recovery Percentages for 15-Year Land Improvements

Recovery Year	Percentage	Recovery Year	Percentage
1	5.00%	9	5.91%
2	9.50%	10	5.90%
3	8.55%	11	5.91%
4	7.70%	12	5.90%
5	6.93%	13	5.91%
6	6.23%	14	5.90%
7	5.90%	15	5.91%
8	5.90%	16	2.95%

Recovery Percentages for Five-Year Personal Property

Recovery Year	Percentage
1	20.00%
2	32.00%
3	19.20%
4	11.52%
5	11.52%
6	5.76%

SAMPLE LEASE AGREEMENT
THIS IS A LEGALLY BINDING DOCUMENT

IF NOT UNDERSTOOD, CONSULT AN ATTORNEY

Agreement of lease executed this ___ day of _____
20___ between

_____ (Landlord),
and _____ (Tenant(s) whether one
or more:

1. PREMISE: _____ Street: Landlord
hereby leases said premises to the Tenant in consideration of the
following rent to be paid by the Tenant to the Landlord. The Tenant
agrees to use and occupy said premises only as a residential premise,
and not for any commercial purposes. Tenant furthermore agrees not
to participate in or allow any illegal activity on or near the leased
premises, and understands that the Landlord may terminate this lease
if any illegal activity is found or discovered. No other persons may
occupy the premises without written consent of the Landlord.
Subletting and/or assignment of the lease without written consent of
the Landlord is prohibited. A guest may be any temporary visitor for a
period not to exceed seven (7) days. Any additional persons other
than children occupying the premises shall entitle the Landlord to an
additional amount of monthly rental in the amount of $50 per person,
per month. (Not allowed)

2. RENT: The Tenant shall pay rent for said premises as follows
___ Estate for Years or ___ Month-to-Month:

    a. ESTATE FOR YEARS: For a term to commence on
    _____ and end on
    _____ unless sooner terminated as
    hereinafter provided, the Tenant paying rent to the Landlord
    at his/her office $_____ in monthly
    installments of $_____, with the first such
    monthly installment due and payable to the Landlord on the
    ____ day of the month with a like payment on the ____ day
    of each and every month thereafter for the entire term of this
    lease. This Lease Agreement shall automatically renew for

successive one-month terms unless superseded by a new written lease agreement, or terminated by either party in writing at least 30 days before the expiration of the initial term or successive term.

b. MONTH-TO-MONTH: Tenant and Landlord agree that Tenant shall be a month-to-month tenant, and shall pay the Landlord a monthly rental amount of _____ dollars ($_____), payable in advance on the ____ day of each and every month at the Landlord's office, the first such monthly rental payment being made herewith.

3. LATE CHARGE: If the rent is not received by the Landlord within three (3) days from the date it is due, the Tenant shall pay, in addition to the rental as herein above described, a late charge of $25.00, and in addition the sum of $5.00 for each and every day thereafter that the rent remains unpaid. Landlord and Tenant agree that the Landlord may accept and deposit a rental payment from the Tenant without said late charge, and that the same will not constitute a waiver of the Landlord's right to collect said late charge for the current month or serve to waive the Landlord's right to collect any future late charge in any future month.

Any check not honored by the Bank on which it is drawn will be considered by the Landlord and Tenant to be non- sufficient fund check and an additional fee in the amount of $40.00 plus any and all applicable late charges shall be immediately due and payable to the Landlord. If more than one non-sufficient fund check is received in a twelve-month period, all future payments will be made via cash, a cashier's check or money order.

4 SECURITY DEPOSIT: The Tenant has deposited, and the Landlord hereby acknowledges receipt of a security deposit in the sum of $_____ for the faithful performance of all of the terms of this lease. In no event shall Tenant be entitled to apply such security deposit as rent due hereunder. In the event of Tenant's breach of or the termination of this lease, the Landlord may apply all or any portion of the security deposit to payment of rent and any other

costs, expenses and/or damages suffered by Landlord as a result of Tenant's noncompliance with this lease. Said security deposit shall not be kept in escrow or in a separate fund and shall not bear interest. Under no circumstances can said deposit be used or applied by the Tenant for the payment of rent.

It is understood between the parties hereto that the security deposit will not be returned to the tenant unless the following conditions have been met:
    a. Tenant has occupied premises for the full term of the lease.
    b. Tenant has given thirty (30) days' notice from the first day of the month of his or her intention to vacate the premises.
    c. Tenant has not damaged the premises, its contents, or its yard.
    d. Tenant has left the premises, including the yard, in a clean condition.
    e. Tenant has returned all keys.

5. UTILITIES: The following utilities are to be paid by the party whose name appears opposite each utility as indicated:

Gas	Tenant
Water & Sewer	Tenant
Electric	Tenant
Telephone	Tenant

In the event Tenant is paying utilities, Tenant agrees to apply for utility services prior to moving into the property and to register utilities in his/her name by not later than the commencement date as set forth in paragraph 2.
Failure of the tenant to place utilities in his/her name by commencement date will cause this lease to be construed as never having taken place, and any monies paid to Landlord, as deposit or otherwise, will be forfeited by the Tenant to the Landlord. Tenant further agrees that trash removal service is for Tenant's personal use only and is not to be used for the disposal of hazardous materials or any furniture/ appliance.

6. LOCKS: Tenant acknowledges and receipts for one set of keys to the premises, and agrees to return the same number of keys to the Landlord upon the expiration of this lease. Tenant will not duplicate

any of the keys without notice to the Landlord. UNDER NO CIRCUMSTANCES will the Tenant be allowed to replace any lock of lockset without the express written consent of the Landlord. In the event any locks or locksets are changed by the Tenant, the Tenant hereby gives the Landlord permission to immediately, without notice, remove said unauthorized lock or lockset, and replace the same with a lock or lockset installed by the Landlord.

7. RULES AND REGULATIONS: The Tenant agrees for him/herself and his/her family, licensees, invitees and guests, to conform to the Rules and Regulations governing the premises and to any reasonable changes or new regulations that the Landlord may deem necessary.

8. ACCESS: The Landlord, or his or her agent, with one (1) day's notice to the Tenant, shall have free access at all reasonable hours to the premises for the purpose of examining, exhibiting or making repairs and/or alterations. The Landlord may have immediate access in the event of an emergency for the purpose of making repairs. In the event rightful access is denied to the Landlord, this lease, at the option of the Landlord, shall terminate, and the Landlord may take action accordingly.

9. ALTERATIONS: Tenant acknowledges that he/she shall make no alterations, decorations or improvements without the express written consent of the Landlord. In the event any of the foregoing is made, irrespective of the identity of that party making the same, the same shall become the exclusive property of the Landlord. The Tenant shall not make any holes in the wall, without repairing the same upon vacating.

10. EQUIPMENT: All appliances and equipment in the Premises may be used by Tenant, but only in a reasonable, safe, and non-destructive manner. In the event of temporary interruption, of electricity, water, gas telephone or trash removal service, or failure or breakdown of heating, air conditioning, kitchen appliances, plumbing or electric equipment, Landlord shall not be liable to tenant. Tenant shall notify Landlord of such interruption or failure, and Landlord shall make repairs with reasonable promptness and rent shall not abate during said periods.

11. TENANT DAMAGES: Tenant agrees that he/she is fully responsible for any breakage, damage, destruction, and/or soilage, which may be caused by Tenant or tenant's family, which occurs during Term of this lease or any extension or renewal Term. Tenant shall reimburse landlord as additional rent, for all expenses, damages, or costs incurred by Landlord by reason of said breakage, damage, destruction and/or soilage. Landlord shall have the option, but not the obligation, to cause repairs for which the tenant is responsible to be done at Tenant's expense

12. CONDITION OF THE PREMISES: The Tenant hereby acknowledges that he/she has examined the premises and that no representations as to the condition or states of repairs thereof have been made by anyone.
Tenant further acknowledges that the Landlord has promised no repairs, and the Landlord is not responsible for any repairs except those specifically written into this contract.
Tenant furthermore agrees to keep the premises in good repair, and upon vacating the same, deliver the premises to the Landlord in the same good condition as when leased, normal wear and tear excluded. Tenant acknowledges that all light bulbs and sink strainers are in place, and agrees that upon termination, all light bulbs and sink strainers will be in place and in working order.
Tenant agrees to regularly dispose of all garbage in a neat manner, encasing all garbage in appropriate garbage bags, and to follow all rules and regulations imposed by any governmental authority with respect to the disposal of garbage or refuse.

13. INDEMNIFICAITON: Tenant agrees to indemnify and hold Landlord harmless from any and all claims, actions, damages, liabilities and expenses for any loss of life, personal injury or damage to property arising from any act or omission of the Tenant, his/her family, employees, occupants, servants, guests, invitees, or pets.

14. ABANDONMENT: The parties agree that any of the following acts will constitute common-law abandonment, and entitle the Landlord to take immediate possession or take steps to commence an eviction action:

a. Absence from the dwelling unit for seven (7) days without notification in writing to the landlord.
b. Termination of any utility service.
c. The establishment of another residence.

15. PHONE: Tenant agrees to keep Landlord informed of his/her phone number at all times.

16. DEFAULT IN RENT: In the event any rent is not paid when due, Landlord may terminate this lease after three days' written notice and take action for possession as provided by State law.

17. DEFAULT OTHER THAN RENT: If the Tenant shall default in fulfilling any of the terms, conditions or covenants of this lease agreement, other than the covenant for the payment of rent, the Landlord may terminate this lease be delivering a written notice to the Tenant specifying the breach and stating that the rental agreement will terminate 30 days after receipt of the notice if the breach is not remedied in 14 days. If substantially the same act(s) or omissions(s) occur within six (6) months, the Landlord may terminate the lease upon fourteen (14) days' notice specifying the breach and the day of termination. If this lease is month-to-month, nothing herein contained shall prevent the Landlord from terminating the tenancy at any time upon written notice being given to the Tenant at least thirty (30) days before the rental due date by which the Tenant must vacate the premises

18. PETS: The following applies to this lease:
    No pets under any circumstances even for a visit._____
    Dog(s) allowed: Deposit to be_____
    Cat(s) allowed: Deposit to be _____
    Other: _____

19. NOTICES: All notice to the Tenant shall be mailed or delivered to the Tenant at the address of the premises. All notices to the Landlord shall be made only to the following address or at such other address the Landlord may furnish to the Tenant.

20. INSURANCE: Tenant acknowledges that there is no security system at above-named property. LANDLORD STRONGLY RECOMMENDS THAT TENANT OBTAIN INSURANCE TO PROTECT SELF AND PROPERTY FROM LOSS that may occur from theft, vandalism, fire, water, water leaks or seepage from any source, rainstorms, smoke, explosions, sonic booms or other any other unforeseen damages that may occur. Landlord shall not be liable for any damage or losses to persons or property caused by acts or omissions of other tenants or other persons; tenant accepts all risks of loss or damage and agrees to hold Landlord harmless therefrom.

21. JOINT LIABILITY: In the event that this instrument is executed on behalf of the Tenant by more than one person, the liability of all persons so signing shall be joint and several.

22. SMOKE DETECTORS: Tenant has inspected the smoke detector(s) and agrees that they are operating properly. Tenant will ensure that detector(s) are tested monthly and batteries are changed as necessary.

23. OTHER CONDITIONS: No waterbeds allowed. Tenant responsible for snow removal of driveway and sidewalks. Tenant responsible for lawn care.

IN WITNESS WHEREOF, the Landlord and the Tenant(s) have executed this rental agreement on the date above first written. By signing this Agreement, the Tenant states that he/she has read this lease and understands the same. This is a legal and binding contract. Please read carefully before signing.

LANDLORD_____

TENANT(S)_____

_____

Address_____

City_____State_____ Zip_____

Make-Ready Checklist

Task
Date finished
Initials

1. Make sure stove, refrigerator, and dishwasher are clean.

   _____

2. Make sure kitchen cabinets are clean and cabinet doors open
   and close properly. _____

3. Clean and caulk tub/shower, clean medicine cabinet, clean and
   secure toilet and seat. _____

4. Make sure all windows open and close, have locks, and are
   clean. _____

5. Replace broken window blinds and ensure that blinds work
   properly. _____

6. Check furnace filter and change if necessary. _____

7. Make sure garage is clean._____

8. Make sure all doors open and close properly and storm doors
   have closers and chains. _____

9. Make sure there are no broken screens or broken glass on storm
   windows and doors. _____

10. Mow yard and remove junk. _____

11. Make sure all electrical outlets work. _____

12. Replace all burned-out light bulbs. _____

13. Make sure smoke and carbon monoxide detectors are working
    properly. _____

14. Make sure there is one carbon monoxide detector on each
    finished floor. _____

15. Make sure there is one smoke detector in each bedroom, one
    in basement, and one between living room and kitchen.

    _____

16. Check all closets to make sure they are clean and have closet
    poles. _____

17. Check all ceiling fans to make sure they work and are clean.

   _____   _____

18. Make sure there are no leaks under kitchen and bathroom sinks
    and faucets work properly.   _____

19. Check/wipe all walls to make sure they are clean; touch up with
    paint as necessary.   _____

20. Check for mold in basement and under kitchen and bathroom
    sinks and clean with mold spray as needed.   _____

21. Make sure entire house has been cleaned. _____

22. Make sure gutters are clean.   _____

23. Replace any missing corners on siding.   _____

24. Make sure all drains work properly.   _____

25. Make sure all interior and exterior handrails are secured.

   _____

26. Make sure carpet is clean._____

Notes_____

_____

_____

_____

_____

_____

_____

Date completed_____ Signature _____

An Open Letter To Tenants Who Don't
Pay The Rent On Time

What would you do if you worked hard all week long and on payday your boss told you that you were not going to get paid and ... that you would have to wait and wait and wait for your money and... that he did not know when (or if) you would ever get paid?

How long would you work without getting paid? How would you feel? And what would you do about it? Would you just say, "Okay, I understand. Just pay me whenever you can?" Or would you...

Call your boss on the phone? What if he refused to return your calls? Would you send letters? What if your letters were ignored? Then what would you do? Would you go to his or her office? Would you argue? Would you report your boss to a government agency whose job is to protect working people like you? Would you hire a lawyer and pay big bucks that you will never see again? Would you agree to pay court costs and the legal fees that begin to pile up the moment you tell you lawyer to sue? The bottom line is you would not be very happy as your bills would pile up and then you would have to borrow money from relatives, friends, etc., to pay your bills, buy groceries, put gas in your car, and on and on. You likely would have to make choices as to what bills you would pay first, right? For sure you would buy groceries, gas to get to work, pay your utilities, etc., and other bills, and maybe if anything was left over you would pay part of the rent, and I wonder why.

Unfortunately, as a property owner I don't have many choices with the bank as my mortgage payment must be paid on time each and every month; otherwise, I am charged a late-payment penalty and my credit score is affected. The bank doesn't care if you pay your rent on time or not, but I do. If you don't, I'll get into financial difficulties myself. I have to make choices of which bills I pay first, and the answer is always my mortgage before anything else, and in your case it should be your rent.

So in conclusion, I expect to receive the rent on time each and every month, just as you expect to get your paycheck on time each and every time. My guess is that you would not be very happy if you did not get your paycheck on time, so hopefully the next time you are thinking about picking up the phone, or I have to call you and you tell me that you cannot pay your rent on time this month because (fill in the blank), it will not make me very happy either, so I hope you understand.

Someone gave me this list of reasons why the rent is late. Hopefully, none of these will apply to your situation.

I'm sorry my rent is late, but...

_____ A. The check I've been waiting for did not come in the mail.

_____ B. I was in the hospital/jail and I couldn't get to you.

_____ C. I missed a week of work because I had to take care of my sick mother / son / daughter.

_____ D. I had to have some teeth pulled and the dentist won't start work until I give him some money.

_____ E. I was in an automobile accident and I won't have any money until my attorney works things out with the other guy's insurance.

_____ F. I had my billfold stolen when this guy jumped me on my way to the bank / post office / my office.

_____ G. Someone broke into my place and took my money. No, I didn't file a police report. Should I?

_____ H. I had to have my car fixed so I could get to work, so I could pay you.

_____ I. My mother / sister / uncle hasn't mailed me my money yet.

_____ J. I couldn't find your address, and I put the wrong address on the envelope.

_____ K. I got laid off from my job and I won't get unemployment for a couple of weeks.

___ L. I was not able to get a money order and I know you didn't want me to send cash.

___ M. You didn't come by when I had the money.

___ N. My husband / wife / boyfriend / girlfriend / roommate left and I didn't have all the money.

___ O. They garnished my check and I don't understand it, because the guy told me it would be okay to just pay so much per month and I only missed a couple of payments.

___ P. I told my friend to bring it or send it to you while I was out of town.

___ Q. I haven't received my tax refund yet.

___ R. I got a new job, and I have to work three weeks before I get my first check.

___ S. I didn't pay the rent because my ___ is not fixed. No, I'm sorry I didn't tell you there was a problem before now. I didn't think about it until now.

___ T. My car is broken and I didn't have a ride to your office.

___ U. I had to help my brother / sister / friend who had a serious problem.

___ V. I didn't have, or I forgot to put, a stamp on the envelope.

___ W. The check is in the mail. Didn't you get it?

___ X. I ran out of checks.

Please briefly explain if your reason is not listed above.

_____
_____
_____
_____
_____
_____

You will never get penalized for paying your rent early; however, you will pay a late payment penalty of $25 if the rent is not paid in full by midnight on the third day after the rent is due, plus an additional $5 per day until the rent is paid in full.

2020 Real Estate Business Plan for Mr. Smart Investor

Especially Prepared for Jim Slick, Vice President of We Want Your Business Bank

BUSINESS GOALS

Mission
Our mission is to create income by purchasing undervalued properties to remodel and sell or retain as a long-term investment.

Mr. Smart Investor has over 7 years of experience as an investor and is a Mortgage Broker with Last Chance Mortgage. He currently has a rental portfolio of ten single homes, five duplexes and one fiveplex.

Profit will be generated by:
(1) Performing cosmetic improvements to single-family homes and selling them to generate 40–50% profit.
(2) Maintaining long-term rentals that generate a minimum of 10% cash on cash return.

Short-Term Goals
We will create and uphold a reputation in our community for honesty in our business dealings, and we will aim to achieve win-win results. We will focus on acquiring distressed properties that can be fixed and either sell them or use them as rentals.

During 2020we will purchase five properties to flip and five properties to rent. This will be the beginning of our long-term investment strategy to accumulate income-producing properties.

Actual number of properties purchased in 2018:
flipped: 3   sold: 2   rentals: 3

Long-Term Goals
Our objective in 2020 and each year thereafter until 2025 will be to purchase an average of five properties per year to fix and sell and five properties per year to increase our rental portfolio.

Pursuing this strategy over a five-year period will add 30 properties to our portfolio (single-family dwellings and duplexes) to go along with the 25 units currently in our portfolio (mix of single-family dwellings and multi units, each returning an average of $3,000 positive annual cash flow for a total income of $75,000 per year and annual asset appreciation of 3%.

Also during this five-year period, it is our objective that more than 30 properties will be sold for an average of $15,000 profit each, for a total of more than $450,000 cash income.

Ownership
Want To Be Wealthy LLC
We intend to be highly leveraged. All renovations will be done by licensed contractors.

DEVELOPING KNOWLEDGE OF THE MARKETPLACE

Target Neighborhoods
We will operate in the Midtown, Benson, and Northeast and Southeast part of the Omaha Metro area. These areas were chosen because properties can be purchased in the price range of $50,000 to $60,000 and because of our significant knowledge of the area.

Selecting Properties
We have developed a strategy involving purchases in the $50,000 to $60,000 price range. This price represents the lower end of what properties are selling for in the area, at least 20 to 40% less than average.
1. $30,000 between our purchase price and typical sales price is necessary to achieve our profit margin of approximately $15,000.
2. For our rental portfolio a purchase price of at least 20–40% price differential from market value is necessary for each purchase.

In order to appeal to homeowners and renters, these properties should be 3-bedrooms for resale and a minimum of 2-bedrooms for rentals. Properties should be located close to schools and shopping and should include amenities that will attract young families and first-time buyers.

Locating Flexible/Distressed Sellers

Our target market will be sellers who are highly motivated and may
be having financial difficulties, or those whose properties have been
on the market for at least 3–4 months.

Properties that initially will meet our criteria include:
1. Foreclosures
2. Properties in disrepair
3. Property management problems
4. Estate sales
5. Absentee ownership
6. Tenant problems
7. Retirement or relocation

It is anticipated that these sellers will be willing to negotiate to meet
our minimum criteria for purchases.

Developing a Network

To be successful with our strategy, we will establish strong
partnership with other agents, banks, and others.

BUSINESS OPERATIONS

Target Customer

Age group of 25–44 years.

1. Resale Properties

Our target buyer is a young, dual-income family. These buyers will
have adequate to good credit but may lack significant cash reserves to
use as a down payment or closing costs. Purchase price in the
$100,000 to $120,000 price range.

Our approach to these buyers will be to utilize creative solutions to
their cash shortage by utilizing programs such as FHA, VA and
others.

2. Rentals

For our rental portfolio our target market for tenants will include
students, young couples, single parents, and dual-income families.

The target rent will be $650 to $900 per month. These tenants would also serve as perfect candidates to purchase the property in the future.

Performing Market Analysis
The source we will use to determine the value of a property will be market analysis available through Multiple Listing Service and our own experience over the past seven years.

Financial Analysis
Each property to be purchased will be analyzed to determine the value of the property, appropriate purchase price, detailed estimated cost of potential renovation, acquisition costs, and potential sale price as well as anticipated profit.

Financial Arrangements
We have established relationships with the following banks:
> We Want Your Business Badly, Yes We Can, First Preference, Last Resort Banks

so we will know in advance of our ability to purchase properties that meet our criteria. As we will only purchase undervalued properties, after the renovations are completed we will seek permanent financing based on appraisal.

Renovation Process
We intend to purchase properties that are sold well below market value and will require minimal cosmetic updates and improvements. We anticipate that every property will require at least some cosmetic improvements to increase its value. It is our intent for these properties to be sold within a period of 90 to 120 days encompassing acquisition, remodeling, and purchase by buyer.

To perform these renovations as quickly and efficiently as possible we have assembled an experienced crew that we have used extensively over the past seven years. Additionally, we have sufficient experience and knowledge to determine the estimated costs and time frame required to complete a project. We anticipate that each project should be completed within 45 days from start to finish.

Based on our experience, the following improvements will significantly increase the value of each property:
1. Update kitchen: Install new cabinets if necessary, ceramic tile floor, new countertops, dishwasher and other appliances.

2. Replace carpet, refinish wood floors, install new blinds, etc.
3. Update bathroom fixtures including vanities, etc.
4. Paint interior/exterior as necessary.
5. Perform landscaping to improve exterior appearance.
6. Perform general overall polishing of property. We will keep in mind that our target sale price is in the $100,000 to $120,000 range.

Each property will be evaluated on its own merits, but the renovation costs are expected to range between $10,000 and $20,000. Properties that are purchased at $30,000 to $40,000 below market value will provide sufficient differential to achieve our desired return within 90–120 days from acquisition to sale.

Our renovation process model assumes that the six key tasks stated above represent the entire work to be completed. This assumption will be validated prior to purchase by means of a thorough inspection process. Our inspections will be done by licensed contractors, so there will no surprises regarding the renovation costs.

On occasion, however, a property may be available that may require a much higher remodeling price that would be justified by an opportunity to make a lot of money. These properties may require structural improvements or other major remodeling. These could be properties that are in terrible disrepair.

Another exception to our typical purchase criteria may be a small property that is surrounded by much larger and more expensive homes in a very desirable neighborhood. These scenarios do not meet our investment strategy but may be considered depending on the money needed to complete the project.

Selling Properties
After each property has been renovated it will be listed for sale. As our target consists of 25- to 44-year-olds who may only have enough of a down payment for an FHA mortgage, we expect to offer assistance with closing costs.

Rental Portfolio
Careful attention will be given during the purchase process to find potential rental properties that would meet the criteria for our long-

term investment portfolio. In order for these properties to meet our standards they must pass the following performance measures:

1. We must be able to buy and fix the property with minimal cash outlay.
2. The property must be located in a desirable area (family-friendly neighborhood) to ensure better than average appreciation and better tenants, and it must be purchased at a price below market value.
3. The income and expense streams must be favorable to net a positive cash flow of at least $3,000 per year from each property.

Timeline
In summary, following the timeline identified throughout this document, we expect to purchase an average of one property per month

Managing our Properties
We are a very successful enterprise with over seven years of investment experience. We have an excellent system in place to continue to monitor our portfolio. We know every month how each property is performing. This is accomplished by our monthly profit and loss statement.

We are confident that our experience and success over the years merit strong consideration to obtain approval for a working line of credit in the amount of $100,000. Thank you very much for your consideration, and we look forward to establishing a mutually beneficial relationship.

GLOSSARY

Accumulated depreciation The total amount of depreciation expense that has been claimed by a property owner.

Acquisition cost The price and all fees required to obtain a property.

Acquisition loan Money borrowed to purchase a property.

Active investor An investor who manages his or her own properties rather than hiring a property management company to do it.

Adjusted cost basis The cost of any improvements made to a property.

Adjusted tax basis The original cost or other basis of a property, reduced by depreciation deductions and increased by capital expenditures.

Annual debt service (ADS) The total amount of principal and interest that must be paid each year to satisfy the obligations of a loan contract.

Assessed value A property's value for property tax purposes.

Averaging method Method of calculating next year's vacancy rate for a rental property by averaging previous years' vacancy rates.

Balloon loan A loan that has level monthly payments that will amortize it over a stated term (such as 30 years) but requires a lump sum payment of the entire principal balance at the end of a shorter term (for example, 10 years).

Balloon payment An installment payment that is much larger than the other scheduled payments. It is usually the last payment of a balloon loan.

Bird dog A person who finds properties for potential investors and receives a referral fee if the investor buys the property.

Bridge loan Mortgage financing between the termination of one loan and the beginning of another loan.

Building permit Permission granted by a local government or agency to build a specific structure at a specific site.

Break-even ratio (BER) This ratio measures the amount of money going out of an investment property against the amount of money coming in. The BER must be less than 100% for an investment to be viable. Lenders typically require a BER of 85% or less.

Buy and hold Investment strategy in which the investor purchases a residential property with the intention of holding it for several years and renting it to tenants.

Capital Money used to create income, either as an investment in a business or an income property.

Capital expenditure The cost of an improvement made to extend the useful life of a property or to raise its value, such as adding a room. The cost of repairing a property is not a capital expenditure. Capital expenditures are appreciated over their useful life, but repairs are subtracted from income for the current year.

Capital improvement Any structure or component erected as a permanent improvement to real property that increases the property's value and/or extends its useful life.

Capitalization (Cap) rate The ratio of the net operating income of a property to the proposed asking price. This figure is used to estimate the potential return on a real estate investment.

Carrying charges Expenses necessary for holding property, such as taxes and interest on idle property or property under construction.

Cash flow before taxes (CFBT): Net operating income from an investment property, minus debt service and capital expenditures, plus loan proceeds (if any) and interest earned (if any). CFBT represents the annual cash flow available before income tax deductions are considered.

Cash flow after taxes (CFAT) Cash generated from a property after taxes have been taken into account. This figure is calculated by subtracting the tax liability from cash flow before taxes.

Cash on cash return (COC) Ratio used to evaluate the long-term performance of a real estate investment. To obtain the COC, divide the property's annual cash flow (usually the first year before taxes) by the amount of the initial capital investment (down payment, loan fees, and acquisition costs).

Cash out Cash given to the borrower from the proceeds of a loan.

Cash-out refinance A refinance transaction in which the new loan amount exceeds the total of the principal balance of the existing first mortgage and any secondary mortgages or liens, together with closing costs and points for the new loan. This excess is usually given to the borrower in cash.

Collateral Property pledged as security for a debt.

Common area maintenance (CAM) Charges paid by the tenant of a commercial property for the upkeep of areas designated for use and benefit of all tenants. CAM charges are common in shopping centers, where tenants are charged for parking lot maintenance, snow removal, and utilities.

Contractor A person who contracts to provide specific goods or services.

Creative financing Any financing arrangement other than a traditional mortgage from a third-party lending institution.

Credit line A loan that allows revolving use of the credit; that is, after funds have been borrowed and repaid they may be borrowed again without applying for a new loan.

Debt coverage ratio (also known as debt service coverage ratio) (DCR) A ratio used in underwriting loans for income-producing property. To calculate DCR, divide the property's net operating income by its total annual debt service. Lenders typically require a DCR of 1.2 or more.

Deferred maintenance Physical depreciation of a property due to lack of normal upkeep.

Depreciation A method of allocating the cost of a tangible asset over its useful life. Businesses depreciate long-term assets for both tax and accounting purposes.

Double net lease (NN) Lease in which the tenant agrees to pay a basic monthly rent as well as property taxes and property insurance, and the property owner is responsible for paying all other operating expenses.

Down payment An initial amount paid on a property at the time of purchase.

Due diligence The act of carefully reviewing, checking, and verifying all of the facts and issues involved in a transaction before proceeding.

Federal Fair Housing Law A federal law that forbids discrimination on the basis of race, color, sex, religion, or national origin in the selling or renting of property.

Flipping Buying a property, improving it, and reselling it for a profit.

Gross operating income (GOI) The scheduled income for a rental property, less vacancy and credit loss, plus income from other sources such as coin-operated laundry equipment, vending machines, and garage rentals.

Gross rent multiplier (GRM) The purchase price of a property divided by its annual rental income before expenses such as property taxes, insurance, utilities, and maintenance.

Gross scheduled income The total annual income that would be produced if every unit in a rental property was rented and rent was collected from every tenant.

Highest and best use The use that is most likely to produce the greatest net return to the land and/or building over a given period.

Holdover tenant A tenant who remains in possession of leased property after the expiration of the lease term.

Housing code Local government ordinance that sets minimum standards of safety and sanitation for existing residential buildings.

Improvements Additions to raw land (such as buildings, streets, and sewers) that increase the value of the property.

Interim financing A loan, including a construction loan, that is used when the property owner is unable or unwilling to arrange permanent financing.

Internal rate of return (IRR) Rate of return on investment capital each year it remains in the investment. To compute IRR, divide the annual cash flow (return on investment) by the purchase price of the property.

Lease A contract in which, in exchange for a rent payment, the owner of a real property transfers the rights of possession to a tenant for a specified period of time (the term of the lease).

Lease option A lease combined with an option agreement that gives the tenant the right to purchase the property under specified conditions.

Lease purchase A lease combined with a purchase agreement that obligates the tenant to purchase the property under specified conditions.

Lessee (Tenant) A person to whom property is rented under a lease.

Lessor (Landlord) One who rents property to another under a lease.

Letter of intent Written expression of desire to enter into a contract without actually doing so.

Lien A claim on a property of another as security for money owed. Liens may include legal judgments, mechanics' liens, mortgages, and unpaid taxes.

Like-kind property Property having the same nature as another property.

Limited partnership Business arrangement in which at least one partner is passive and limits liability to the amount invested and at least one partner has liability beyond the monetary investment.

Line of credit An agreement by a lender to extend credit up to a certain amount for a certain time without the need for the borrower to file another application.

Loan to value Ratio of the loan amount to the appraised value of a property. A higher LTV means greater leverage for the investor and higher financial risk for the lender. A lower LTV means less leverage for the investor and lower financial risk for the lender.

Net cash flow Income produced by an investment property after subtracting expenses such as principal, interest, taxes, and insurance.

Net operating income (NOI) The total income an investment property generates after expenses (not including debt service).

No cash out refinance Refinance in which the amount of the new mortgage covers the remaining balance of the first loan, closing costs, any liens and cash no more than 1% of the principal on the new loan.

Non-disclosure non-compete (NDNC) Term used in commercial and multi-unit property listings. Sellers can require potential buyers to sign a NDNC prior to showing them the property's financials or scheduling an on-site visit.

Operating expense (OE) The total cost associated with operating a rental property, not including debt service, income taxes, or depreciation.

Operating expense ratio (OER) The ratio of a property's total operating expenses to its gross operating income (GOI). OER is useful for comparing the expenses of similar properties.

Option The right to purchase or lease a property upon specified terms within a specified period of time.

Ordinances Municipal rules governing the use of land.

Owner financing (also known as seller financing) A financing method in which a buyer borrows from and makes payments to the seller instead of a bank. Sometimes the buyer takes over the seller's payments. Owner financing can be done when a buyer cannot qualify for a bank loan for the full purchase price.

Passive investor A real estate investor who pays a property management company to handle day-to-day maintenance, repairs, rent collection, and other responsibilities.

Pro forma A presentation of data, such as a balance of income statement, in which certain amounts are hypothetical. For example, a pro forma balance sheet might show a debt issue that has been proposed but has not been consummated.

Raw land See Unimproved property

Real estate investment Non-owner-occupied real property.

Real estate investor A person who buys real estate for investment purposes rather than for their primary residence.

Refinance Process in which a borrower pays off one loan with the proceeds from another.

Regression The idea that the value of a better-quality property is adversely affected by the proximity of a lesser-quality property.

Regulation Z Federal regulation requiring creditors to provide full disclosure of the terms of a loan.

REO Property that has been reclaimed by a bank or government agency after the foreclosed property failed to sell at a real estate auction.

Residual Value or income remaining after deducting an amount necessary to meet fixed obligations.

Return on investment (ROI) with appreciation This figure takes into account the four benefits of investing in real estate: income, principal reduction, appreciation, and depreciation. It shows how the potential investment compares against other properties that are under consideration.

Return on investment (ROI) without appreciation This figure takes into account three of the four benefits of investing in real estate: income, principal reduction, and depreciation. It shows how the potential investment compares against other properties that are under consideration.

Section 1031 Section of the Internal Revenue Code dealing with tax-free exchanges of like-kind property.

Section 8 Privately owned rental dwelling units participating in the low-income rental assistance program created by 1974 amendments to Section 8 of the 1937 Housing Act.

Security deposit Cash payment required by landlord to be held during the term of the lease to offset damages incurred due to actions of the tenant.

Seller financing. See Owner financing

Single net or "N" lease Lease in which the tenant pays the basic monthly rent plus property taxes, and the property owner pays operating expenses (common area maintenance, or CAM) and property insurance.

Taxable income or loss Net operating income from an investment property, minus interest, depreciation, and loan costs, plus interest earned on property bank accounts.

Time is of the essence A phrase that, when inserted in a contract, requires that all references to specific dates and times of day noted in the contract be interpreted exactly as stated.

Triple net lease Lease in which the tenant pays a basic monthly rent as well as property taxes, property insurance, and maintenance expenses.

Unimproved property Land that has received no development, construction, or site preparation (also known as raw land).

Unrealized gain Excess of current market value over cost for an asset that is not sold.

Unrecorded deed Instrument that transfers title from one party (grantor) to another party (grantee) without providing public notice of the change in ownership.

Vacancy and credit loss Income that is not generated by a rental property due to vacant units (vacancy) or non-payment of rent (credit loss).

Wholesale Purchasing a property with the intention of reselling it quickly at a higher price.

Wraparound mortgage Loan arrangement in which an existing loan is retained and an additional loan is made that equals or exceeds the existing loan.

Yield Measurement of the rate of earnings of an investment.